BENEFIT-COST ANALYSIS OF GOVERNMENT PROGRAMS

EDWARD M. GRAMLICH

Department of Economics and
Institute of Public Policy Studies
The University of Michigan

PRENTICE-HALL, INC., Englewood Cliffs, New Jersey 07632

Library of Congress Cataloging in Publication Data

GRAMLICH, EDWARD M

   Benefit-cost analysis of government programs.

   Includes bibliographical references and index.
   1. Expenditures, Public—Cost effectiveness.
I. Title.
HJ7451.G72   351.007′8   80-21353
ISBN   0-13-074757-2

Editorial production/supervision and
      interior design by Sonia Meyer
Cover design by Infield/D'Astolfo Associates
Manufacturing buyer: Gordon Osbourne

Printed in the United States of America
10 9 8 7 6 5 4 3 2

Prentice-Hall International, Inc., *London*
Prentice-Hall of Australia Pty. Limited, *Sydney*
Prentice-Hall of Canada, Ltd., *Toronto*
Prentice-Hall of India Private Limited, *New Delhi*
Prentice-Hall of Japan, Inc., *Tokyo*
Prentice-Hall of Southeast Asia Pte. Ltd., *Singapore*
Whitehall Books Limited, *Wellington, New Zealand*

To my always supportive parents

Jacob E. Gramlich
Harriet W. Gramlich

Contents

Preface   xiii

1 Introduction   1

BENEFIT-COST ANALYSIS AND THE GOVERNMENT / 4
MISCONCEPTIONS ABOUT BENEFIT-COST ANALYSIS / 5
TYPES OF EVALUATIONS / 6
A BRIEF HISTORY OF BENEFIT-COST ANALYSIS / 7
NOTES / 10

2 The Objectives of Government Intervention in a Market Economy   12

THE FUNCTIONS OF GOVERNMENT / 13
ECONOMIC EFFICIENCY / 17

      Public Goods 17; Externalities 19;
      Natural Monopolies 20; Paying for the Public Sector 22

DISTRIBUTIVE EQUITY / 24
SUMMARY / 26   NOTES / 27
APPENDIX: CONSUMER SURPLUS / 29
PROBLEMS / 32

3 **The Activities of Government** 35

THE FEDERAL GOVERNMENT / 36
STATE GOVERNMENTS / 38
LOCAL GOVERNMENTS / 39
THE PROGRAMS TO EVALUATE / 40

4 **Benefit-Cost Analysis
and Governmental
Decision Making** 41

THE FUNDAMENTAL PRINCIPLE OF EVALUATION / 43
THE EASY CASE: COMPLETE INFORMATION AND
    NO CONSTRAINTS / 45
INADEQUATE INFORMATION / 45
PHYSICAL CONSTRAINTS / 47
POLITICAL CONSTRAINTS / 48
EVALUATION, BUDGETING, AND POLITICS / 49
SUMMARY / 50   NOTES / 51
PROBLEMS / 52

5 **Valuation of Resources Used
or Benefits Created
When They Occur** 53

MARKET PRICES EXIST AND ACCURATELY REPRESENT
    SOCIAL VALUES / 54
MARKET PRICES EXIST BUT DO NOT REPRESENT
    SOCIAL VALUES / 58

    Unemployed Labor 61;
    Scarce Foreign Exchange 67

MARKETS DO NOT EXIST / 68

    Loss of Life 69; Time Saving 72;
    Environmental and Recreational Benefits 74

UNCERTAINTY / 75
SUMMARY / 77   NOTES / 78
APPENDIX: SECONDARY MARKETS / 83
PROBLEMS / 86

**6 Valuation of Resources Used
or Benefits Created
at Different Times** 88

THE RELATIONSHIP BETWEEN PRESENT VALUES AND
    DISCOUNT RATES / 90
THE PRESENT VALUE OR THE INTERNAL
    RATE OF RETURN / 92
HOW TO DEAL WITH INFLATION / 94
THE APPROPRIATE DISCOUNT RATE / 95

    The Before-Tax Rate of Return on
    Private Investment *95;*
    The Weighted-Average Rate of Return *98;*
    The Social Discount Rate *101*

AN APPROACH FOR DISCOUNTING / 107
SUMMARY / 108   NOTES / 109
PROBLEMS / 114

**7 Distributional Considerations:
The Gains and Losses of
Different Groups** 116

DIFFERENTIAL WEIGHTS / 118
ESTIMATING THE WEIGHTS / 120

    Displaying the Gains and Losses *120;*
    Inferring the Weights *121;*
    Bracketing the Weights *121;*
    Finding the Internal Weights *122;*
    Specifying the Properties of the Weights *122;*
    Cost Effectiveness *123*

A COST-EFFECTIVENESS STUDY OF ALTERNATIVE INCOME
    REDISTRIBUTION PROGRAMS / 123

    The Standards for Redistribution *124;*
    The Programs *126;* The Results *131*

SUMMARY / 133   NOTES / 134
PROBLEMS / 136

8 Physical Investments and the Environment   138

THE PROJECT WITHOUT ENVIRONMENTAL COSTS / 139
INCLUDING ENVIRONMENTAL COSTS / 142
THE TELLICO DAM / 146

Benefits and Costs of the Tellico Dam   *149*

SUMMARY / 154   NOTES / 155
PROBLEMS / 157

9 Human Investment Programs   158

THE BENEFITS AND COSTS OF HUMAN
    INVESTMENT PROGRAMS / 159
AN ACTUAL HUMAN INVESTMENT EVALUATION / 162
THE METHODOLOGY FOR HUMAN
    INVESTMENT EVALUATIONS / 165
INTERPRETING THE RESULTS / 167
THE IMPLEMENTATION PROBLEM / 169
MEASUREMENT PROBLEMS / 169
SELECTION PROBLEMS / 170
WHAT TO DO? / 171
THE SCALE OF THE EVALUATION / 172
SUMMARY / 175   NOTES / 176
PROBLEMS / 177

10 Intergovernmental Grants   180

THE RATIONALE FOR INTERGOVERNMENTAL GRANTS / 181
THE IMPACT OF DIFFERENT TYPES OF
    GRANTS ON SPENDING / 186
EVALUATING GRANTS / 189
FEDERAL ROAD BUILDING / 190
FOOD STAMPS / 192
SPECIAL REVENUE SHARING AND PUBLIC
    SERVICE EMPLOYMENT / 194
SUMMARY / 195   NOTES / 196
PROBLEMS / 199

11 Government Regulatory Activities   201

A THEORY OF REGULATION / 202
IS THE MARKET SOLUTION OPTIMAL? / 208
SUBTOPICS IN REGULATION / 211
A SPECIFIC CASE STUDY:
   THE OSHA NOISE STANDARD / 214
SUMMARY / 217   NOTES / 218
PROBLEMS / 220

12 Social Experimentation   221

DIFFERENT TYPES OF SOCIAL EXPERIMENTS / 222
DIFFERENT TYPES OF EXPERIMENTAL DESIGNS / 224
THE NEGATIVE-INCOME-TAX EXPERIMENTS / 226
EDUCATIONAL PERFORMANCE CONTRACTING / 234
THE ETHICS OF SOCIAL EXPERIMENTATION / 238
SUMMARY / 240   NOTES / 240

13 The Evaluator's Check List   243

THE TYPE OF EVALUATION / 244
THE PERSPECTIVE / 244
THE POLICIES ASSUMED / 244
HOW DO WE MEASURE BENEFITS AND COSTS? / 245
TO WHAT EXTENT SHOULD MARKETS BE RELIED ON
   TO VALUE BENEFITS AND COSTS? / 246
HOW SHOULD ADVICE BE GIVEN? / 247

Answers to Problems   248

Index   267

Preface

A few years ago the director of our public policy school asked me to teach a course in benefit-cost analysis. This course had for some time been a required course in the two-year public policy curriculum at Michigan, and was viewed as central to the program. In addition to providing many applications of principles learned in other courses—microeconomics, public finance, and statistics, to name a few—it was good discipline for public policy students. In learning how to think about the benefits and costs of a public investment project—the typical topic of benefit-cost analysis—they would learn to use the same framework for analyzing any other policy measure, whether a spending program or a regulation.

There is by no means a dearth of reading material on benefit-cost analysis. The rudiments of benefit-cost analysis were established in the writings of some 19th century economists, the government began thinking about benefit-cost questions as early as 1930, and for the past twenty years there has been a great deal of both theoretical and applied material. But it was still hard to find readings for the public policy school course. Many of the readings available, both textbooks and journal articles, assumed advanced training in economics. Almost all applied the logic of benefit-cost to a very narrow range of government programs, physical investments in dams or roads. They did not treat at all the broad array of programs in modern day government budgets such as income redistribution programs, programs with environmental implications, human investment programs, intergovernmental grants, or regulatory activities. Therefore the aim of this book is to meet these two objectives:

1. Translate the debates of technical economics in a way that they can be understood by students without advanced training in economics

2. Apply the logic of benefit-cost to some of the newer and more rapidly expanding public policy activities.

The first four chapters form an introduction to the principles of benefit-cost analysis. Chapter 1 gives some basic introductory comments, and Chapter 2 reviews some of the rationales for government intervention in a market economy—stressing activities that promote economic efficiency or distributional equity. Chapter 3 then examines actual budgets at the federal, state, and local level, to see how much is spent on various types of activities and to identify the growth areas. Chapter 4 turns to evaluation and its role in governmental decision making—which of the various benefit-cost indicators is the most meaningful, and how benefit-cost information should be used in the presence of physical or political constraints on budgets.

The standard economics literature on benefit-cost analysis is summarized in Chapters 5 to 7, the heart of the book. These chapters conduct an evaluation for a prototype government physical investment program. Chapter 5 investigates the valuation of resources used in government projects: what to do when markets are not working properly or when resources are underemployed, and how to value commodities for which no market exists. Chapter 6 considers problems of discounting that arise when benefits and costs are realized over time. Chapter 7 considers how and whether the results of evaluation should be adjusted to account for gains and losses realized by various groups in the society.

In Chapters 8 to 11 the logic of benefit-cost analysis is applied to four different types of governmental programs: physical investment programs in Chapter 8, human investment programs in Chapter 9, intergovernmental grant programs in Chapter 10, and regulatory programs in Chapter 11. Each of these types of analysis uses the basic logic of benefit-cost analysis, but each raises unique issues.

Chapter 12 is somewhat more methodological, examining a new technique for evaluating programs—social experimentation. It reviews the weaknesses in alternative statistical designs for making evaluative inferences and discusses the comparative strengths and weaknesses of social experimentation. It then reviews two widely publicized social experiments in the area of income maintenance and education.

Chapter 13 is a brief summary of the book. The chapter reviews a list of issues that must be resolved before an evaluation can be completed.

I am indebted to many people for help on this book. Several colleagues—Harvey Brazer, Roy Bahl, Paul Courant, Ronald Ehrenberg, Robert Haveman, George Johnson, Richard Porter, Hal Varian, and Michael Wolkoff—have read and made extensive comments on earlier drafts. Several current and past students—Susan Albert, Jeannette Austin, James Kleinbaum, Stephen Morrison, and Deborah Swift—have also read and commented on drafts, checked and rechecked problems, and found references. In a more indirect sense, I owe much to the Institute of Public Policy Studies at the University of Michigan, for giving me the opportunity to teach the course on which the book is based, for providing interesting and challenging faculty colleagues, and for supplying alert and demanding students. I could not ask for a more stimulating work environment. I benefited as well from the chance to try out some of these ideas on an international audience—graduate students in the Department of Economics at Stockholm University.

I am also indebted to Mary Lou Piehl and Judith Jackson, who typed and retyped most of the manuscript, and to my family for putting up with my idiosyncracies, which undoubtedly became more pronounced while I was working on this manuscript.

1

Introduction

London, 19 September, 1772

Dear Sir,

In the affair of so much importance to you, wherein you ask my advice, I cannot, for want of sufficient premises, advise you what to determine, but if you please I will tell you how. When those difficult cases occur, they are difficult, chiefly because while we have them under consideration, all the reasons pro and con are not present to the mind at the same time; but sometimes one set present themselves, and at other times another, the first being out of sight. Hence the various purposes or inclinations that alternately prevail, and the uncertainty that perplexes us. To get over this, my way is to divide half a sheet of paper by a line into two columns; *writing over the one Pro, and over the other Con.* Then, during three or four days consideration, I put down under the different heads short hints of the different motives, that at different times occur to me, for or against the measure. When I have thus got them all together in one view, *I endeavor to estimate their respective weights;* and where I find two, one on each side, that seem equal, I strike them both out. If I find a reason pro equal to some two reasons con, I strike out the three. If I judge some two reasons con, equal to some three reasons pro, I strike out the five;

1

and thus proceeding I find at length where the balance lies; and if, after a day or two of further consideration, nothing new that is of importance occurs on either side, I come to a determination accordingly. And, though the weight of reasons cannot be taken with the precision of algebraic quantities, yet when each is thus considered, separately and comparatively, and the whole lies before me, *I think I can judge better, and am less liable to make a rash step,* and in fact I have found great advantage from this kind of equation, in what may be called moral or prudential algebra.

Wishing sincerely that you may determine for the best, I am ever, my dear friend, yours most affectionately.

B. Franklin

Apparently, Benjamin Franklin was one early user of benefit-cost analysis. In this letter he demonstrates all the essentials: when confronted with a difficult decision, he enumerated pros (benefits) and cons (costs), attempted to place a weight (value) on each, and tried to figure out which course of action was most beneficial.

Many other examples of crude benefit-cost analyses can be drawn from everyday life. Pasted on the refrigerator of a neighbor's house was the following information:

ANN ARBOR	LOS ANGELES
House +4	Climate +3
Schools +3	Job +1
	Salary +2
	Beach +1
	Mountains + 1
	Pollution − 1

The neighbor was at the time weighing an attractive job offer from a Los Angeles university. As almost everybody does in such circumstances, he carefully weighed the pros and cons of staying in his present position (Ann Arbor) or switching. The posted score resulted in a dead standoff, although as a matter of historical fact he eventually turned down the Los Angeles offer and stayed in Ann Arbor (tie goes in favor of the runner?). As with Benjamin Franklin, the neighbor was comparing two alternatives, the status quo versus a move, and had arrayed the benefits of the move (advantages of Los Angeles) against the costs (advantages of the status quo, or advantages foregone by moving). Each benefit and cost was weighted numerically and the overall benefits were compared to the overall costs. The logic is precisely the same as that employed in the much more elaborate evaluations of government programs that are to be covered in this book.

These examples illustrate how widespread the practice of benefit-cost analysis actually is. It may be couched in fancy terms, such as the Johnson Administration's Planning, Programming, and Budgeting System (PPBS). It may be worshipped as yet another herald of the Age of Technology, or feared and rejected because it tries to put dollar amounts on underlying values. But ultimately it is nothing more than a logical attempt to weigh the pros and cons of a decision. And ultimately, something like it must necessarily be employed in any rational decision.

This book is an attempt to introduce students to the mysteries of benefit-cost analysis of government programs. There is a long tradition of work in the field by economists, work that has gotten into a number of complexities regarding the valuation of resources used in the production of a government project, comparing benefits and costs realized at different times, and so forth. But these subtleties are dealt with only in connection with the evaluation of a relatively narrow class of government projects, usually a bridge or a dam. A first goal of the book is to explain these subtleties in terms that can be understood by a student without advanced training in economics. A second goal of the book is then to extend the logic of benefit-cost analysis to other types of government activities—activities that are much more commonly encountered in modern federal, state, and local governments. These activities consist of such things as programs that affect the environment, educate the population, redistribute income, regulate the private economy, or work through grants to lower levels of government. Finally, the book is meant not only for consumers of benefit-cost evaluations but also for producers of it. It is hoped that a clear explanation of the logic and how it is applied in various cases will give enough advice to permit them to do their own evaluations.

A few caveats are in order. The activities of government (summarized in Chapter 3) are so widely varied these days that any attempt to apply a set of logical rules to them will end up covering quite disparate subject matter—from the fate of the snail darter when the Tellico Dam is built, to the response of consumers to food stamp payments, to the relative efficiency of ear plugs in reducing noise levels in the workplace. There is nothing that can be done about this diversity: indeed, that is one thing that makes the study of government so fascinating. But it should be recognized, whether as a benefit or a cost of the field, that the topics and examples will vary widely. It should also be recognized, this time clearly as a cost, that it is impossible for any medium-length book to cover all the activities of government.

Second, courses in benefit-cost analysis or evaluation are now being taught as part of a curriculum in many different social sciences—economics, political science, and sociology, to name a few. This book is written by an economist and emphasizes the economics side of program evaluation. However, although written from an economic perspective, the book is directed at students or practitioners without advanced training in economics. Most of the subtleties involved in applying the logic of benefit-cost analysis require only the basic training of an introductory economics course to understand and resolve. The material is rather wide-ranging and does draw on aspects of intermediate microeconomic theory, intermediate macroeconomic theory, and elementary statistics and econometrics, but the book does not assume this knowledge unless it is absolutely necessary and attempts to explain the relevant points. Of course, a student who has taken and mastered any or all of these subjects will be better off. But it is still true that a student with a minimal background in economics should, with work, be able to master most of the material in the book.

BENEFIT-COST ANALYSIS AND THE GOVERNMENT

The basic aim of any benefit-cost analysis of a government program is to figure out if the benefits of a program outweigh its costs. This process is similar to the logic that any decision maker, in the public or private sector, goes through in trying to make any decision. Despite this similarity, the simple insertion of the adjective ''government'' before the noun ''program'' adds much complexity and interest to the question of evaluation. There are three reasons for this.

The first is that the government is not an entity separate from taxpayers, but really the collective expression of the will of taxpayers. The benefits and costs of a government project are then to be defined not as an increase or decrease in government revenues but as a gain or loss in welfare of all members of society. Moreover, the government has a responsibility to look beyond the simple monetary gains and losses of some activities and consider whether projects lead to nonmonetary changes in atmospheric pollution, health and safety risks, or even wastes of people's time. Changes in any of these accounts should be considered as much a benefit or cost of a project as a monetary gain or loss, and should be included in the overall tally.

A second reason why a government evaluation activity raises more complicated issues is in the pricing of resources used or the benefits created for a project. To maximize profits, a private entrepreneur makes decisions on the basis of market prices alone. But a public-sector decision maker has the added responsibility of asking whether these prices give a correct measure of social benefits or costs before using them, and may have to adjust them to account for certain omitted considerations. As our discussion will show, the question of how to do this can become very complicated.

A third reason is that the government has other policy measures at its disposal. There is a very basic quandary in the field of evaluation, which we will see throughout the book, as to what the government should assume about these other policies. Say that agreed-upon objectives of government policy are to reduce unemployment, stabilize the price level, improve the rate of economic growth, and equalize the distribution of incomes. If a government project has an effect on one or more of these objectives, should this effect be ignored or included in the evaluation of the overall benefits and costs of the project? We could argue that since the government has already taken measures to deal with these national objectives, presumably in an optimal manner, any impact of the project to be evaluated will or could be offset by these other policies and should be ignored in the evaluation. Or we could argue that it is difficult for other macroeconomic policies to deal with these other matters, because of the intractability of the problem or because of political-institutional constraints on policy. Then positive or negative changes in unemployment, inflation, growth, or income distribution might be considered valid benefits or costs of the project and be worked into the evaluation.

Because of these differences between governmental and private benefit-cost analysis, the techniques discussed here allow the evaluator to determine not only whether the activity should be undertaken at all, but also whether it should be located in the public sector. For some activities there is no important difference between public and private valuations of benefits and costs. Even if these activities pass a benefit-cost test, and hence should be undertaken by *somebody,* there is no point in having the government conduct the activities. Private decision makers can presumably be relied on to make the judgments, and the private sector to conduct the activities. Other activities may not pass the benefit-cost test when evaluated at private valuations of benefits and costs, and hence will not be carried out by the private sector. If they do pass the social benefit-cost test, they are activities that should be carried out by government.[1]

MISCONCEPTIONS ABOUT BENEFIT-COST ANALYSIS

Three misconceptions about benefit-cost analysis are quite common, and it is well to try to clear them up at the beginning. The first is that benefit-cost analysis is a mechanical substitute for common sense. Nothing could be further from the truth. Benefit-cost analysis is really a framework for organizing thoughts, for listing all pros and cons, and for placing a value on each consideration. In any situation encountered in this book and in the real world, there will be some considerations that cannot easily be enumerated or valued and where the benefit-cost analysis becomes somewhat more conjectural. Yet the sensible way to deal with such omitted considerations is not to abandon all efforts to measure and value benefits and costs, but rather to use benefit-cost analysis to quantify what can be quantified, to array and rank nonquantifiable factors, and then to make a decision. Viewed in this light, even if benefit-cost analysis alone does not make any decisions, it can serve a valuable purpose in focusing decisions on the critical elements.[2]

The second misconception regards the difference between a net improvement and a panacea. Too often government programs are overadvertised— program X can cure poverty—and too often they are evaluated in the popular press on these grounds—poverty still exists, so program X must have failed. In this age of cynicism about public policy, it probably will not surprise anybody when we say that government program panaceas are hard to come by. Rare is the program that can even be shown to work well, let alone by itself cure a problem that may have been developing for decades. But whether or not panaceas exist, this surely is not the proper standard by which to evaluate government programs. As in the earlier Benjamin Franklin example, a policy measure should be adopted if its properly defined benefits outweigh its properly defined costs, and not otherwise. Its properly defined benefits may be small relative to the scope of the problem, but the program is helping in its own way if it does satisfy this narrow benefit-cost criterion, and society can hardly afford to forgo programs that pass such a test.

A final misconception relates to the difference between positive social science and normative social science. Positive social science refers to attempts to describe the way the world is; normative social science refers to attempts to describe the way the world should be. This book is dealing with benefit-cost analysis from a normative standpoint, that is, with how public-sector decisions should ideally be made. Those with real-world knowledge of how government actually works can find any number of cases where benefit-cost analysis is not now used or is buried by an avalanche of political considerations, or where public decision making is less than ideal.[3] But that does not mean that benefit-cost analysis should not be used, and it does not make it wrong or illogical to teach benefit-cost principles. Sometimes, as will be shown, these principles can be used within political constraints—to find the best or least costly solution within these constraints. Sometimes the fruits of benefit-cost research will modify polit- ical constraints over time—yesterday's sacred cow may not be today's. In any event, there will always be some value in having aspiring public policymakers learn how to think through the benefits and costs of various measures, and at least know what they believe to be the right procedure, even if they may be prevented from carrying it out by intervening forces.

TYPES OF EVALUATIONS

There is one respect in which benefit-cost analysis as discussed in this book may be somewhat confining. The standard analysis inquires into the benefits and costs being created by an existing or proposed government program. The program is assumed to be given and independent of the analysis—a black box. One might imagine going beyond these guidelines and asking not only whether the black box works—whether its benefits outweigh its costs—but whether it could be made to work better. This extension lies behind what has now become a standard classification of evaluation studies into

     1. Summative evaluations.
     2. Formative evaluations.

Summative evaluations, which ask whether the black box works or not, are the ones dealt with for the most part in this book. Typically, but not always, such studies will be undertaken before a project is started, to see if it should be started. Formative evaluations use essentially the same tools, but they use them to a different end. They ask whether the program, or black box, could be made to work better. Usually, these analyses are done during the operation of a program, to see how the program can be improved. In effect, formative evaluations might be thought of as benefit-cost analyses on individual components of the black box.[4]

Within the set of summative evaluations—those that take the black box as given—it is also possible to ask two different types of benefit-cost questions. The first is the complete benefit-cost question: whether the value of all benefits exceeds that of all costs. But often it will be impossible to answer such a question because, say, values cannot be placed on all the benefits of a program. We might, for example, be dealing with government programs that reduce loss of life or improve highway beauty. Sometimes techniques can be found for quantifying such gains, but sometimes they cannot. If they cannot but if we can think of two or more alternative programs that accomplish these goals, we can still meaningfully apply evaluation principles to public sector decision making. We can turn the evaluation question around and ask the second type of question: for two alternative programs that accomplish a particular goal, which is cheaper? Here we are performing a comparative, or "cost-effectiveness" evaluation. Since we cannot measure benefits, we can never be sure whether either program will satisfy the usual benefit-cost test. But we can be sure that we are minimizing the cost of accomplishing this end, or maximizing the net benefits from the activity.

A BRIEF HISTORY OF BENEFIT-COST ANALYSIS

Benefit-cost analysis has been around a long time. Apart from Benjamin Franklin and all those earlier policymakers who may have used it, it formally appeared first in the writings of Jules Dupuit, a nineteenth-century French economist. The concepts defining social improvements were refined by an Italian social scientist, Vilfredo Pareto, and later, in 1940, by the British economists, Nicholas Kaldor and Sir John Hicks.[5] At about this time, evaluation was creeping into official government activities. The U.S. Flood Control Act of 1939 first enunciated the now familiar standard that "the benefits to whomsoever they may accrue [be] in excess of the estimated costs," but gave no specific guidance on how to define benefits and costs. Other examples of early use of a rudimentary form of benefit-cost analysis are found in the program budgeting systems of the Tennessee Valley Authority and the Department of Agriculture.[6]

In the early 1950s there was another flowering of official benefit-cost activity. In an attempt to reconcile interdepartmental differences in evaluation techniques, the 1950 report of the Inter-Agency Committee on Water Resources, commonly known as the Green Book, tried to bring economic analysis to bear on evaluation decisions. By 1952, the Budget Bureau had adopted its own set of criteria for appraisal of river development techniques.[7]

   Benefit-cost analysis changed from a subject of relatively arcane academic interest to one of lively political interest in the Great Society days of President Johnson. At the time, the federal budget was growing rapidly: in the defense area because of the early buildup of expenditures for Vietnam and in the civilian area because of the rash of new domestic programs for health, education, manpower, and so forth. A common characteristic of almost all of these new programs was the ''thin end of the wedge'' phenomenon; budget expenditures might be small at first, but later, when the program became national in scope, they would be large. Some technique for budgetary planning, for weighing the benefits and costs of expanding different programs and for setting priorities, was needed; and the Budget Bureau grabbed the one most readily available, the program budgeting system developed a few years earlier in Robert McNamara's Department of Defense.

   The Planning Programming Budgeting System (PPBS), as it came to be called, was formally adopted by the federal government in 1965. It featured five main elements:

   1. A careful specification of basic program objectives in *each* major area of governmental activity.

   2. An attempt to analyze the *outputs* of each governmental program.

   3. An attempt to measure the *costs* of the program, not for one year but over the next several years.

   4. An attempt to compare alternative activities.

   5. An attempt to establish common analytic techniques throughout the government.[8]

These five points remain the pillars of benefit-cost analysis. Alternatives are to be compared; benefits and costs are to be specified and measured, for the future as well as the present; and the entire approach is to be applied with common techniques throughout the government.

   Although a noble beginning, attempts at implementing PPBS were not long sustained by the government. The reasons were much the same as the underlying limitations of benefit-cost analysis. On the one hand, precise implementation of benefit-cost analysis, including a definition and measurement of all the social benefits and costs of governmental intervention, is and will remain for the foreseeable future, impossible. As we see in the book, when competing governmental activities are trying to achieve the same objective, there is a hope of using benefit-cost logic to find the preferred alternative. When they are trying to achieve entirely different objectives or intrinsically unmeasurable objectives, there is much less hope. Combining bureaucratic realities with the fact that government bureaucrats, by training or inclination, are probably not the ideal candidates to evaluate their own programs or are too busy with day-to-day crises to do so, the PPBS effort soon seemed to be a lot of idle paperwork and was effectively abandoned.

But the legacy of PPBS did not die out. Governmental bureaucracies one by one created planning and analysis staffs, typically hiring younger and better-trained social scientists in the process, and gradually developed the tradition of asking benefit-cost questions. What is program X designed to do? Can the objectives be fulfilled more easily in an alternative manner? What are the short- and long-run budget costs of program X? A whole new series of questions sprang up, within and without the Executive Department, and the general quality of the decision-making process increased markedly.[9] Many of these developments are now spreading to the state and local sector and should ultimately be responsible for improved decision making at that level. On the other side, the mid-1960s' need to evaluate programs had, by the early 1970s, spawned a series of actual evaluations or benefit-cost analyses of various programs. These were published in the professional journals, stimulated discussion, sponsored rejoinders, led to the creation of courses, and so forth.[10] The field of evaluation was created almost overnight. As with everything else, it has its strong points and its weaknesses, but its disciplines and conventions should be mastered by aspiring policy analysts.

There have also been some more directly political developments related to efforts at implementing PPBS. When the Nixon Administration took over the government in 1969, it was confronted with both a growing inflation problem and a budget wedge that was beginning to thicken. Its goal, adhered to with more or less intensity during the entire 8-year Republican reign, was to limit the growth of federal expenditures. From time to time it found a ready ally in the few evaluations that were conducted—evaluations that more often gave a negative verdict about a program than a positive one. As a result, it seems fair to say that the whole field of evaluation and benefit-cost analysis is now viewed more favorably by budget conservatives than by liberals, by Republicans than by Democrats. Although there is inescapable political logic in this association, there need not be substantive logic. Both liberals and conservatives should favor superior programs to inferior ones, and both should agree on the factors in any benefit-cost analysis that can be quantified and those that cannot be quantified. There may be and probably is a vast difference in the subjective weights or valuations placed on some of these unmeasurable factors, but both sides should be able to use profitably the factual mediation that can be provided by benefit-cost analysis properly done. To recall the point made above, benefit-cost analysis will not make decisions, but it can be of great help in focusing them on the proper issues.

Finally, it is of interest to Budget Bureau historians to note that in 1977, exactly 12 years after the formal adoption of PPBS, the renamed Office of Management and Budget (OMB) has formally adopted a new system that attempts to incorporate benefit-cost logic into budgetary decisions. The system is known as Zero-Based Budgeting (ZBB), and it is patterned after a scheme that President Carter employed while Governor of Georgia. The documentation on ZBB is not as extensive as that for PPBS, but the system sounds much the same.

Federal agencies are to prepare statements of major program objectives and descriptions of alternative ways of accomplishing them. They are then to rank their activities from a minimum level (that level below which the activity can no longer be conducted) up through various incremental levels. In principle, OMB can select from these agency's rankings—lopping off the lowest-priority activities of various agencies. As with PPBS, in the first few years this effort to rationalize budgetary decision making seems to have generated more paperwork than true budgetary savings, although again there may be less obvious and measurable benefits that become more important over time.[11]

NOTES

[1]This position does not appear to be shared by Cotton M. Lindsay and Don Norman, "Reopening the Question of Government Spending," in Thomas E. Borcherding, ed., *Budgets and Bureaucrats: The Sources of Government Growth,* Duke University Press, Durham, N.C., 1977, p. 264. Lindsay and Norman appear to be using a concept of benefit-cost analysis that does not distinguish between market valuations and social valuations of benefits and costs.

[2]Essentially this position is argued in a nice justification of benefit-cost analysis by Alan Williams, "Cost-Benefit Analysis, Bastard Science? And/or Insidious Poison in the Body Politick?" *Journal of Public Economics,* August 1972, p. 199.

[3]See, for example, John T. Dunlop, "Policy Decisions and Research in Economics and Industrial Relations," *Industrial and Labor Relations Review,* April, 1977; and Sar A. Levitan and Gregory Wurzburg, *Evaluating Federal Social Programs: An Uncertain Art,* the W. E. Upjohn Institute for Employment Research, 1979. A counterargument is given by Ronald G. Ehrenberg, Daniel S. Hamermesh, and George E. Johnson, "Policy Decisions and Research in Economics and Industrial Relations: An Exchange of Views," *Industrial and Labor Relations Review,* October 1977.

[4]This difference is described in more detail by Carol H. Weiss, *Evaluation Research: Methods of Assessing Program Effectiveness* (Englewood Cliffs, N.J.: Prentice-Hall, 1972), chap. 2. It parallels a similar taxonomy proposed by Glen G. Cain and Robinson G. Hollister, "The Methodology of Evaluating Social Action Programs," in Peter H. Rossi and Walter Williams, eds., *Evaluating Social Programs* (New York: Seminar Press, 1974).

[5]See Jules Dupuit, "On the Measurement of the Utility of Public Works," *International Economic Papers,* 1952 (translated from French, 1844); Nicholas Kaldor, "Welfare Propositions of Economists and Interpersonal Comparisons of Utility," *Economic Journal,* September 1939; and Sir John R. Hicks, "The Valuation of the Social Income," *Economica,* May 1940.

[6]See the discussion by Peter O. Steiner, "Public Expenditure Budgeting," in Alan S. Blinder *et al., The Economics of Public Finance* (Washington, D.C.: Brookings Institution, 1974), p. 331. A number of other references are given there.

[7]Ibid., p. 332.

[8]See Charles L. Schultze, ''Why Benefit-Cost Analysis?'' in Harley H. Hinrichs and Graeme M. Taylor, *Program Budgeting and Benefit-Cost Analysis* (Santa Monica, Calif.: Goodyear, 1969); and Robert H. Haveman, *The Economics of the Public Sector,* 2nd ed. (New York: Wiley–Hamilton, 1976), p. 171.

[9]At least according to Alice M. Rivlin, *Systematic Thinking for Social Action* (Washington, D.C.: Brookings Institution, 1971), chaps. 2, 5.

[10]One illustration of the burgeoning literature is the fact that Sage Publications (Beverly Hills, Calif.) now puts out an *Evaluation Studies Review Annual,* featuring the best of the evaluation studies in that year; 1979 marked the publication of vol. 4 of this series.

[11]An early prediction that puts ZBB in a somewhat unfavorable light can be found in Robert W. Hartman, ''Budget Prospects and Process,'' in Joseph A. Pechman, ed., *Setting National Priorities: The 1978 Budget* (Washington, D.C.: Brookings Institution, 1977), pp. 379ff.

2

The Objectives
of Government Intervention
in a Market Economy

By 1977, total government spending at all levels in the United States had reached $620 billion, one-third of the gross national product. At the federal level, this spending included everything from national defense to public assistance to subsidies for the postal service. At the local level it included items ranging from education to trash collection to public hospitals. Obviously, any attempt to catalogue such a wide array of activities will not be perfect and may lead to awkward mixed cases. Yet we must do some simplifying to give some order to our attempt to analyze the workings of various programs. This chapter identifies the normative objectives of government intervention—the range of things the government might be trying to accomplish and why it is necessary for the public sector rather than the private sector to accomplish them. A descriptive analysis of the ways in which the government tries to achieve these objectives is given in Chapter 3.

THE FUNCTIONS OF GOVERNMENT

Some years ago Richard Musgrave developed what is still a useful way to classify the bewildering array of government programs: dividing government programs into those undertaken for allocation reasons, for distribution reasons, and for stabilization reasons.[1] Allocation programs include measures to affect relative prices and/or the allocation of resources in an economy, motivated by considerations of economic efficiency. Distribution programs consist of efforts to alter the distribution of incomes in society, motivated by considerations of distributive equity. Stabilization measures are designed to achieve a series of objectives: they refer to governmental efforts to regulate the pace of economic activity, motivated partly by a desire to stabilize employment at a high level, partly by a desire to stabilize prices, and partly by a desire to ensure that overall output levels are growing at the right pace. Since the third set of objectives can be accomplished by manipulating overall tax and spending levels in line with the teachings of macroeconomics, they do not arise in a very central way in this book; these macroeconomic ideas are brought in only indirectly when we try to value the labor of unemployed workers or weigh benefits and costs realized at different times. But the first two objectives of government do involve specific government expenditure programs and will be discussed extensively throughout the book.

The way in which the various objectives fit together can be seen by reviewing briefly the role of prices in a market economy.[2] In Figure 2.1, assume that

FIGURE 2.1   Economically Efficient Allocation of Resources

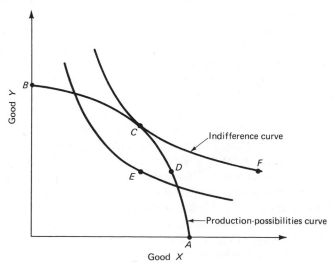

two goods, X and Y, are produced by this economy. (If it bothers you to make such a drastic simplification, consider Y to be "all other" goods besides X.) The production-possibilities curve, labeled BA on the diagram, gives the locus of points showing how much of X and Y can be *produced*. The economy can swing all the way to the X axis at point A, where no Y is produced, or all the way to the Y axis (point B), where no X is produced.

Now say that the economy moves from point C to point D. As it does, it gives up CE of good Y and gains ED of good X. As Y is given up, the total saving in resources equals $(CE)\,(\mathrm{MC}_Y)$, the change in Y times the marginal cost (in terms of resources) of producing Y. If it takes 10 people to produce every unit of Y, the labor saved in reducing the production of Y is $(10)(CE$ people). Since the production-possibilities curve shows how much can be produced by the economy, we can assume that these resources are totally devoted to expanding the production of X, so that $(CE)\,(\mathrm{MC}_Y) = (ED)(\mathrm{MC}_X)$, where MC_X is the marginal cost of X. Since we know from high school geometry that the slope of the production-possibilities curve over this interval is $-CE/ED$, we have

(1)
$$\frac{\mathrm{MC}_X}{\mathrm{MC}_Y} = \frac{CE}{ED} = -\text{slope of production-possibilities curve}$$

We note from Figure 2.1 that as the economy moves toward the right along the production-possibilities curve, the slope becomes more negative and $\mathrm{MC}_X/\mathrm{MC}_Y$ rises. This happens because as the economy moves toward the right, those resources better specialized for the production of Y are drawn into the production of X, hence both raising the marginal cost of producing X (because the resources are not as ideal) and lowering the marginal cost of producing Y (because the only resources remaining in the Y industry will be those that are superbly specialized for the production of Y).

The production-possibilities curve has dealt with the production capabilities in the economy. We now turn to the question of consumer tastes, as measured along what is known as an indifference curve. The production-possibilities curve takes the level of resources as given and looks at how much production of X and Y takes place; the indifference curve takes the level of consumer satisfaction as given and looks at how much consumption of X and Y would be necessary to yield this constant level of satisfaction. If we compare two indifference curves, one going through point E and one through point C, the one through C obviously represents a higher level of satisfaction because consumers consume the same X but more Y. The optimal point for this economy will be the one on the highest indifference curve that is still feasible. Since we have already measured feasible levels of production by the production-possibilities curve, the feasible set of production opportunities is given by all those points on or inside the production-possibilities curve. The optimal point then is the one on the indifference curve going through C, tangent to the production-possibilities curve. Any indifference curve that intersects the production-possibilities curve, such as the curve that passes through point E, represents a lower level of satisfaction.

We know, again from high school geometry, that at the point of tangency the slope of the production-possibilities curve equals the slope of the indifference curve. It remains to determine this slope, and this can be done in the same manner as before. If consumers were to move from point C to point F, they would sacrifice $(CE)(\text{MU}_Y)$ units of utility, where MU_Y is the marginal utility of Y to consumers over this interval. Following our previous numerical example, say that each unit of Y generated 20 "utiles." Then a reduction in consumption of CE units of Y would lower utility by $20CE$ utiles. To make consumers equally well off, they must be given back these units of utility, or

$$(CE)(\text{MU}_Y) = (EF)(\text{MU}_X)$$

so that

(2) $$\frac{\text{MU}_X}{\text{MU}_Y} = \frac{CE}{EF} = -\text{slope of indifference curve}$$

At the precise point of tangency, then, the two slopes are equal and the condition for optimality is

(3) $$\frac{\text{MU}_X}{\text{MU}_Y} = \frac{\text{MC}_X}{\text{MC}_Y}$$

This condition is in terms of two goods or markets, X and Y. We will often have occasion in the book to use just one good or market, assuming that all other markets are already at their optimum point. It can be seen from eq. (3) that if production in Y has taken place up to the point where $\text{MU}_Y = \text{MC}_Y$, production in X should also proceed until $\text{MU}_X = \text{MC}_X$: that is, the marginal benefit or utility of producing the last unit of output exactly equals the marginal resources cost. We call this optimal point "economically efficient," and describe movements toward it as gains in economic efficiency.

Now that we know where the economy wants to go to achieve an efficient allocation of resources, we should consider how it gets there. How do consumers know that they should buy a good until $\text{MU}_X = \text{MC}_X$, and how do producers know that they should produce until the same condition is fulfilled? The answer involves the price level. Prices serve both as a resource allocation signal and a market equilibrating device in a market economy. If there are excess demands for good X, its price is driven up until these excess demands are eliminated—and vice versa if there are excess supplies. Consumers consume the good until their marginal utility of their last unit of consumption is equal to this market price, and perfectly competitive suppliers will supply until their marginal costs are also equal to this price. This condition ensures that in a perfectly competitive equilibrium,

(4) $$\mathrm{MU}_X = P_X = \mathrm{MC}_X$$

where P_X is both the price that equates demand and supply and the value of the last unit of consumption to *both* consumers and producers. In valuing the benefits and costs of a project later in the book, it may appear that economists have a built-in bias that favors the price system. This is why: The competitive price of a good is that value which simultaneously assures that all production is purchased, and indeed is valued equally by consumers and producers. There are arguments for ignoring or adjusting prices, as will be discussed at some length, but there is at least a presumption in this logic that prices should be used as measures of value unless these other arguments are made.

Having made this pitch for a market system as a means of allocating resources and market prices as a way of valuing them, there are some cases in which the necessary assumptions are not fulfilled and where governmental intervention could be desirable. A first is market imperfections, the standard examples being either monopolistic sellers or monopsonistic buyers. If there were a monopolistic seller, he is spared the rigors of competition and thus can charge a price above marginal cost. Consumers still equate marginal utility to this price, and thus we have a situation where $\mathrm{MU}_X = P_X > \mathrm{MC}_X$: the efficiency condition is not satisfied. And if there were some other peculiarities in the industry, interactions of consumption or declining costs of production (concepts that will be explained below), $\mathrm{MU}_X \neq \mathrm{MC}_X$ and there would be an economically inefficient solution. Society is not on the highest attainable indifference level but on a curve that intersects the production-possibilities curve. The task of the allocation or efficiency branch of government is to deal with cases such as these, where for one reason or another MU_X does not equal MC_X, the social indifference curve crosses the production-possibilities curve, and resources can be *reallocated* to improve economic efficiency.

The second function of government involves the distribution of income. Until now we have considered only the efficiency goal of trying to allocate resources so that consumer satisfaction, as measured by the indifference curve reflecting market demands for goods, is maximized. But any indifference curve is based on an underlying distribution of income which gives rich people with many dollars to spend more weight than poor people without many dollars. The second goal of government activity then questions the equity of this particular expression of consumer tastes: Does the underlying distribution of income or spending power on which it is based conform to any standards of interpersonal equity?

For all its importance, the equity notion is much more difficult to define and deal with analytically. A competitive market will only distribute incomes according to the productive abilities, or marginal products, of workers. Those who are unfortunate enough to have a low marginal product, whether by virtue of a physical or mental impairment or simply lack of education or opportunity, may not earn enough to live a satisfying life. The obvious remedy is to give them more income support or employment opportunities, in effect changing the overall tastes of society. In Figure 2.1, we might think of this as altering the tastes of society to move to a point where more of the services produced by poor people are consumed. Whereas the efficiency problem can be thought of as a movement toward the optimal point with consumer tastes taken as given, the distribution problem involves a direct alteration of the indifference curve to yield higher incomes for disadvantaged groups.

The third function of government involves macroeconomic considerations. Because of alterations and cycles in spending demands, there are periods when the productive resources of the nation are not fully utilized. If spending demands suddenly drop, there will exist periods of excess unemployment; if demands should suddenly increase, there will exist periods of excess demand, demand that does not generate output gains but does cause inflation, thereby eroding the value of the dollar and making it more risky and costly to carry out day-to-day monetary transactions. By altering either its own spending or tax levels or the money supply, the government can stabilize these overall spending demands to conform with the economy's productive power and to avoid periods of excessively high unemployment or excessively rapid inflation.[3] But since this manipulation of overall spending and taxing power can be done without altering spending on any individual government program, benefit-cost analyses of individual projects will for the most part not involve macroeconomic questions. Stabilization issues arise continually in a book on macroeconomics but will do so only rarely in this book.

Another aspect of macroeconomic policy involves economic growth: how rapidly the production-possibilities curve shifts out over time. It is obviously good to have a growing production-possibilities frontier, one that enables society to enjoy growing levels of satisfaction, but there is a cost in terms of the current consumption reductions necessary to bring about this growth. These issues become central as we try to value benefits and costs of public projects that are received or paid out at different times, discussed in Chapter 6.

ECONOMIC EFFICIENCY

In this section we consider these deviations from economic efficiency that might be taken care of through government spending activities. We do not explicitly consider problems of establishing workable competition, for it is assumed that those deviations from a competitive equilibrium can best be dealt with through some form of antitrust policy. For now we focus on inefficiencies that would exist even if all markets were perfectly competitive.

Public Goods

One inefficiency is known as the public goods problem. Consider Figure 2.2(a), dealing with the demand for a private good. There we assume that the good is supplied along the competitive supply curve S and that there are two consumers, with demand curves D_A and D_B. Since the purchases of these

FIGURE 2.2   Public and Private Goods

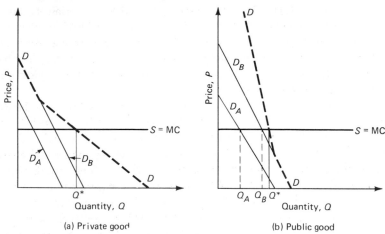

(a) Private good

(b) Public good

consumers are additive, the market demand curve can be derived by summing the individuals' demands horizontally at each price. That yields the dashed line and the market equilibrium Q^*, where B buys the amount read from his demand curve and A the amount read from hers. Note that for each consumer $MU = P$, and since $P = MC$ from the supply curve, the solution is economically efficient.

Now consider a class of goods known as public goods [Figure 2.2(b)]. Both the supply curve and each individual's demand curve are the same as before, but the good is such that if one person consumes it, the other does automatically. Examples might be a national defense system (if A defends herself against a Russian missile attack, she also defends her neighbor B), a police security system, city sidewalks and streets. In each case it is technically infeasible (or very costly) to exclude others from consuming the good when one person does, and the consumption of all consumers in the market thereby becomes the same. In the private market, exclusion is possible and all consumers consume different amounts at the same price; now we have turned things around so that all consumers are forced, by the physical properties of the good, to consume the same amount, but they might pay different prices.

To find the efficient equilibrium it is necessary to derive a market demand curve from the individual demands. The demand curve shows how much a consumer will pay for each consumption unit, so it is reasonable to take that as a measure of the self-expressed marginal benefit of each unit of consumption. If all consumers consume the same amount, the aggregate marginal benefit is the sum of the individual benefits at each unit of Q, or the *vertical* sum of individual demands. That is drawn as the dashed demand curve in Figure 2.2(b) and yields the public good equilibrium of Q^*.

The next question is why the physical infeasibility of exclusion of other consumers implies that the good is a public good. The reason is very simple. In Figure 2.2(b) we can see that if B were left to his own devices, he would buy Q_B units. At that level, the aggregate social valuation (from the vertically summed demand curve) exceeds the marginal cost and the solution is inefficient—too few public goods are consumed. Were A left to her devices, the solution would be even more inefficient. The only efficient solution is to have A and B decide jointly on a level of consumption $Q*$ greater than either Q_A or Q_B. They would presumably need to make that decision in some sort of a political way, hence putting the activity out of the domain of the private sector and into that of the public sector.[4]

To integrate this analysis with the rest of the book, we might ask how a benefit-cost evaluator would deal with this situation. As described in Chapter 4 the best evaluation technique is to compare the costs with the benefits from expanding output 1 more unit. This is exactly the same as comparing marginal benefits (from the D curve) and marginal costs (from the S curve) at every Q. It can be seen from Figure 2.2 that net benefits of expansion of output (marginal benefits minus marginal costs) will be positive at the margin until $Q = Q*$, and after that they will be negative. If the evaluator could measure benefits and costs this precisely, finding the point where net benefits at the margin are zero would be an exact indicator of the socially optimal point.

Externalities

A second phenomenon that could justify government intervention in even a freely competitive market economy is known as an externality. As the name suggests, an externality designates a benefit or a cost of a market transaction that is neither paid for nor received by those making the transaction, and therefore is not incorporated into the market demand or supply curve. If, for example, a manufacturing plant emits smoke that pollutes a town and causes its citizens to get lung cancer, there is a social cost to the operations of the firm that will not be felt by the firm and will not influence its price or quantity supplied. On the other side, if a firm were to sell a product that made uninvolved outsiders better off, such as emission-free engines, the firm would not capture all of the benefits of its production in its selling price.

Figure 2.3 displays examples of externalities on both the benefit and the cost side. Part (a) gives the case of the emission-free engines, where the social benefits from the good are not entirely included in the consumer's demand curve and the firm's selling price. The free-market equilibrium for this firm is (Q_0, P_0), but the point of optimal economic efficiency is where the demand curve that includes the benefits to innocent bystanders intersects the supply curve, $(Q*, P*)$. Some policy measure, whether a subsidy to demanders or suppliers, is necessary to ensure the appropriate expansion of engine production.[5] An evaluator trying to find the optimal output of engines would again compute net benefits at the margin for various levels of Q. This computation will give

FIGURE 2.3   Externalities

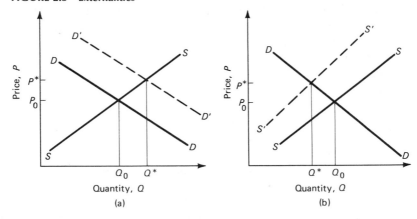

(a)   (b)

marginal net benefits equal to zero just at Q^*, indicating that expansion of Q is justified to that point but not beyond. Obviously, if the evaluator for some reason did not include the external benefits of the activity in the evaluation, the marginal benefits of the activity would be understated and the evaluation would indicate an incorrect value of Q.

The logic is precisely the same in the case of external costs, given in Figure 2.3(b). If these costs were not ''internal to,'' or charged to, the supplier, as in the case of the smoke example, the free market would yield the solution (Q_0, P_0). This time the market leads to overexpansion of the industry, the optimal point for which is (Q^*, P^*). Some way must be found to ensure that the supplier pays the full social cost (internal plus external), perhaps through a pollution tax. An evaluation of the activity would again only yield the correct solution if the external costs as well as the internal costs were included in marginal costs.

The discussion has proceeded as if public goods and externalities were distinguishable phenomena, but in fact that may not always be the case. The reason is that in some sense public goods might be considered an extreme case of externalities: the externalities from A's consumption of national defense are so strong that B is effectively forced to consume exactly the same amount. In both cases the social benefits are found by aggregating the individual benefits, and in both cases the market solution and the evaluation will be inaccurate if some of these benefits are not counted. Indeed, we will see later that in both cases the way in which these benefits are valued will generally cause much more difficult analytical problems than that of merely classifying the activity as a public good or an externality.

Natural Monopolies

A third type of deviation involves what are known as natural monopolies, instances where the fixed costs of providing a good are very large relative to the marginal cost, so that the average cost is declining over the relevant consumption range. Illustrations would be a bridge or toll road, a public utility, or a subway. The large fixed cost implies that a government subsidy will generally be needed for construction of the facility and that the industry cannot support enough suppliers to make it competitive—hence the term natural monopoly.

An example is shown in Figure 2.4. Assume that the marginal cost of supplying the service (say crossings of a bridge) is given by the MC curve. MC could be rising or falling slightly over this range, as long as it is low relative to the fixed cost of constructing the bridge; we will make it constant at P_1 for the sake of simplicity. The average total cost is the sum of average fixed costs and the average variable cost. The latter is given simply by the marginal cost when the marginal cost is constant, as in this case. The former, average fixed costs, are large but declining as Q increases, because the constant fixed cost of construction is averaged over a greater number of units. The result is the ATC curve shown, above MC but declining as Q increases.

The efficiency condition is always that MU = MC, or if consumers move along their demand curve, that P = MC. That happens at (Q_1, P_1). But at this output level the price is less than the average total cost. The supplier is not covering fixed costs and will not make a profit. Were the supplier free to charge a profit-maximizing price, it would be well above MC—high enough to cover fixed costs and earn monopoly profits as well. Hence because average total costs are declining over the range, there is an inconsistency in the law of perfect competition: the perfectly competitive solution will not yield prices high enough to encourage any firm to supply the service, and the large fixed cost provides an incentive to monopolize the industry. Some form of intervention by the government is necessary to bring about an economically efficient solution.

There are several possibilities. A common one in practice, although it is not quite efficient economically, is to allow a private supplier to construct and

FIGURE 2.4   Natural Monopoly

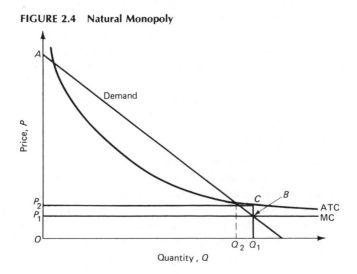

own the facility and to charge a price equal to the ATC, high enough to cover both its fixed costs of construction and its variable costs. The supplier would obviously prefer to charge a higher monopolistic price, but can be prevented from doing so by a public rate commission or similar agency. This solution is preferable to having the good supplied by an unregulated monopolist because the price is closer to marginal cost, but it is not the optimal solution because price is still above marginal cost. A better solution would be to have the government build the facility and provide it free of charge to the supplier, then regulating the price to the marginal cost level P_1. Another alternative is to have the government run and operate the facility and charge the economically efficient price, $P_1 = MC$.

The evaluation question then becomes whether or not to build the facility. We know that *if* the facility is built, it is optimal to charge P_1, but we do not know whether to build it. The evaluator can answer that question with the same sort of benefit-cost logic used before—comparing the total benefits to society with the bridge to the total costs of building the bridge. In the case shown, let us say that bridge crossings are priced efficiently at P_1, so that crossings equal Q_1. We remember that the demand curve shows how much consumers would be willing to pay for each crossing. The sum of these demand values, or the area under the demand curve, is then the total value placed by consumers on having the bridge if the price per crossing were zero. Since the price per crossing is P_1, the total utility gain is given by the trapezoid $OABQ_1$, the excess of this gain over toll revenue is the triangle P_1AB. This triangle, the difference between marginal utility and price on all units up to Q_1, represents how much consumers are better off by virtue of having the bridge and is usually called *consumer surplus,* a very important concept in evaluating those government programs that aim to provide goods more cheaply to consumers. (The appendix to this chapter illustrates the concept from another perspective, dealing also with some more esoteric issues in its measurement.[6]) The bridge is a net benefit to society then if its consumer surplus exceeds its fixed cost of construction, given by the rectangle P_1P_2CB (average fixed costs times the number of crossings). If $P_1AB >$ P_1P_2CB, society benefits by having the bridge; if not, it does not and should not build it. Clearly, the bridge should be built in the case shown in the diagram, but if the demand curve swiveled so that point A were at point P_2, the bridge should not be built.

Paying for the Public Sector

A final point refers not to private market deviations that require government intervention to bring about economically efficient solutions, but to indirect or hidden costs of government intervention. Often, when the government intervenes, it purchases a good or a facility. With public goods, the usual solution is for the government simply to buy a facility and provide its services free of charge to taxpayers; with a natural monopoly the efficient solution is to build the facility and charge users only marginal, not average, costs. But taxes have to be paid to the government to allow it to carry out these activities. Here we examine these taxes to see if there are any hidden costs that should be included in the overall costs of the policy measure. In general, there are.

Say that the government is building a bridge to provide crossings at P_1. We know from the foregoing discussion that such an action makes sense, but we still have to impose taxes to pay the fixed costs of construction. We decide to pay for the bridge by a tax on some activity, say that of earning income (the widely feared income tax). We could just as well have taxed general consumption through a sales tax, investment through a profits tax, or property holdings through a property tax—the analytics are the same in each case.

The income tax to build the bridge is shown in Figure 2.5. Instead of having prices and quantities on the axes, we have wage rates (W) and hours of work (L) and show the demand and supply for labor. The supply of labor SS in effect gives workers' marginal valuation of their leisure time. If W is low, they will choose to consume more leisure time and work very few hours. But as W rises, hours of work do also. The demand curve gives employers' demand for this type of labor and is downward-sloping with respect to the wage rate. The competitive equilibrium is (L_1, W_1).

Now, say that society votes to build the bridge of Figure 2.4 and to finance it with a new income tax on wage income. Tax revenues must equal $P_1 P_2 CB$ in Figure 2.4. Assume that a proportional 20 percent income tax exactly provides the revenue to build the bridge. Since workers' marginal valuation of leisure time is presumably unchanged by this income tax, the supply of labor curve is shifted up to SS'—at each unit of L, higher by just 20 percent so that workers make

FIGURE 2.5   Income Tax to Finance the Bridge

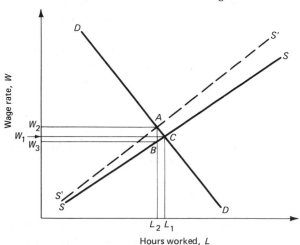

Hours worked, L

exactly the same after-tax wage and are just as well off as before. The new equilibrium is at a before-tax wage rate of W_2 and a quantity of hours of L_2, with $W_3 W_2 AB$ paid to the government in the form of income taxes to build the bridge.

What is the true social cost of building the bridge? We can determine this by summing the losses of workers and firms due to the imposition of the tax. Firms used to be able to buy labor for W_1, but now the wage rate has risen to W_2—their loss is the loss in their consumer surplus, $W_1 W_2 AC$. The profits of firms would decline by just this amount. Workers, on the other hand, used to supply labor for W_1, substantially more than their valuation of the leisure given up on all hours up to L_1. Now with the tax they only earn W_3, suffering a loss in producer surplus (the supply curve analogue of consumer surplus) of $W_3 W_1 CB$. The sum of these two trapezoids is the shape $W_3 W_2 ACB$. Of this amount, the rectangle $W_3 W_2 AB$ is paid to the government in the form of taxes and is not a loss. But the triangle BAC, which is sometimes known as the deadweight loss, is a true social loss from the tax. That loss occurs because the tax introduces a wedge between employers' marginal valuation of the hours of work from a production standpoint and that of the workers from a leisure-time standpoint; at the margin, the marginal benefit of the last hour worked does not equal but exceeds the marginal cost. In principle, then, the appropriate benefit-cost analysis for building the bridge should be to compare the consumer surplus of Figure 2.4 to $W_3 W_2 ACB$, the sum of the tax revenues to cover fixed bridge-building costs and the deadweight loss of raising this revenue.[7]

Since there is an efficiency cost in simply providing the tax revenue to build the bridge, it makes sense to investigate the circumstances under which deadweight losses can be minimized. Consider the situation where the supply of labor in Figure 2.5 is given not by SS but by the line CL_1. Under this assumption, workers will supply L_1 hours regardless of how much they earn. Since their labor supply is inelastic, they obviously will not shift their supply curve, and the labor market equilibrium will be unaffected by the tax. In this case there is no deadweight loss—a wedge is introduced but it does not change the amount of labor provided from the previous optimum—and the budget cost represents the entire social cost. Generalizing from this example, we can see that, other things equal, the social cost of providing the tax revenues to support some activity are smaller the more inelastic are supply and demand curves in the taxed activity.[8] From an efficiency or allocation standpoint, the best tax is one that taxes an activity that would have gone forth anyway and thus is paid out of the surplus of either the producer or the consumer, without changing the market's allocation of resources.

DISTRIBUTIVE EQUITY

The concern of the allocation branch has been exclusively with economic efficiency, but now we will broaden our focus to deal with the income distribution as well. As was said before, distribution is an objective of government because the competitive free market only ensures that all workers get paid their marginal product in production, not necessarily a living wage. On the other hand, certain people have such a high marginal product—or, to be sure, own or control so much monopoly power—that they get paid an amount that society views as "too much." The income distribution function of government involves an effort to tax some income and spending power away from the rich and transfer it to the poor.

There are two senses in which income can be redistributed: a short-run sense and a long-run sense. Referring to Figure 2.6, say that the solid line gives the distribution of earnings generated by a market economy. There are some people in poverty status to the left of some arbitrary "poverty" line, and some others in high-income status to the right of some arbitrary "high-income" line. Society then decides that it would be just for those at the top to help out those at the bottom.

One way in which this could be done would be by a direct tax and transfer system. All those in poverty would be the beneficiaries and those with high incomes would be the payers. The distribution of incomes (as opposed to earnings) would be shifted according to the small-dashed line, with the very low income people now bunched up around the poverty line and the very high income people bunched up around the high-income line. To use a statistical term, the variance of the income distribution would be reduced by the transfer program.

The advantage of this form of transfer is that it is the most direct. Anybody in the low range would be eligible for payments and anybody in the high range would make payments. Payments could be directed to whomever was judged to be the neediest relatively easily. But there are also some disadvantages. One is that the recipients are getting a form of "welfare" payment, with the social stigma that goes along with it. A second is that there could be a form of deadweight loss implicit in this transfer. The positive taxpayers will feel this deadweight loss in the manner diagrammed in Figure 2.5. For the transfer recipients

FIGURE 2.6 Distribution of Earnings and Income

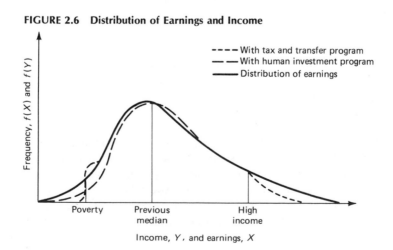

Income, Y, and earnings, X

also, there could be a deadweight loss if the transfer encouraged them to devote part of their newfound improvement in circumstances toward increasing their consumption of leisure time (i.e., working less). Arthur Okun referred to both of these deadweight losses as the ''leaky bucket'' problem; society may try to transfer water from one group to another group, but the effort may be thwarted or may not proceed on as big a scale if the bucket used to transfer the water leaks.[9]

A second type of redistribution focuses on the long run. To use politicians' language, rather than giving the poor a handout (transfer payment), society should extend a helping hand. Efforts to aid poor people should feature education, training, or employment support, programs that will enable the poor to help themselves. Whereas the handout programs try to reduce the variance in the rewards society confers, these helping-hand programs, known as human investment programs, try to give the poor a fair chance at getting those rewards.

The advantage of this approach is obvious. If it is successful in raising the incomes of the poor, they will feel better about their new earning power, society will sacrifice little (subject to the restrictions in Chapter 9), and the deadweight loss will be replaced with a production gain, to the extent that one segment of the work force is now more productive. A successful program will raise both the income of low-income groups and the overall mean income in society. The disadvantage is that the approach may not be successful and/or it may just enable the lowest-income people to replace those just above them in the pecking order—changing the identity of the poor but not their numbers, and not raising the overall level of income in society. Moreover, it is unlikely to be successful with *all* the poor—the handicapped, those who are forced to remain at home for family reasons, and so on. Even if it is successful, the success may only be realized over a long period, say a generation, because it is difficult for any human investment program to improve the status of today's older poor. The likely shift in the income distribution with a successful program—one that raises incomes of low income groups without lowering anybody's income—is shown with the dashed line.

SUMMARY

This chapter has reviewed the three objectives of government intervention in a market economy. Problems in resource allocation involve expenditure programs on particular goods or in particular areas—public goods, externalities, and natural monopolies—so as to bring marginal social benefits in line with marginal social costs and improve economic efficiency. Problems in income distribution involve overriding the market distribution of income to yield an actual distribution that conforms better to social standards of fairness. As was seen, this could be done either in a comprehensive short-run sense through a tax and transfer program that could generate efficiency losses; or in a long-run sense through education and training programs, which are less comprehensive but could involve efficiency gains. The final set of objectives, not dealt with in any detail here, refers to macroeconomic stabilization goals to minimize unemployment and inflation and to provide for economic growth.

NOTES

[1]Musgrave's book *The Theory of Public Finance* (New York: McGraw-Hill) came out in 1959. Its latest incarnation is Richard A. Musgrave and Peggy B. Musgrave, *Public Finance in Theory and Practice* (New York: McGraw-Hill, 1973). See particularly chap. 1.

[2]The following demonstration is standard for those who have had an undergraduate microeconomics course. Those so well-endowed can go directly to page 17.

[3]Any casual reader of the newspapers knows that the government cannot do this perfectly. Stabilization policy is taking its lumps these days. The reason unemployment and inflation can coexist, and the relevance for benefit-cost analysis, will be examined in Chapter 5.

[4]A more technical point must be clarified to justify these operations. To add individual demand curves, we must make the assumption that all individual demands are weighted equally in forming the social indifference curve. As a related point, it is possible to use the vertical addition logic to derive the appropriate tax shares for this quantity of public goods. At the equilibrium solution Q^*, if A paid her marginal utility (given by the value of D_A at Q^*) and B paid his (value of D_B), the sum would just equal the marginal cost. The tax shares would be assigned according to benefit shares, or by the willingness-to-pay principle, and society would be said to be in Lindahl equilibrium. See Erik Lindahl, "Just Taxation: A Positive Solution," in Richard A. Musgrave and Alan Peacock, eds., *Classics in the Theory of Public Finances* (New York: Macmillan, 1958); and two articles by Paul A. Samuelson, "The Pure Theory of Public Expenditure," *Review of Economics and Statistics*, November 1954, and "Diagrammatic Exposition of a Theory of Public Expenditure," *Review of Economics and Statistics*, November 1955. In operational terms it appears to be very difficult to implement benefit taxation for pure public goods because of difficulties in getting people to reveal their preferences: one would have the incentive to understate gains so as to reduce tax shares, and thus there would be a tendency for society as a whole to understate its demand.

[5]Using either part (a) or part (b), it can be seen that in equilibrium it does not matter whether a demand or supply adjustment is chosen. In part (a), either the supply curve should be reduced or the demand curve increased by the vertical distance between the SS curve and the DD curve at Q^*. Whichever form is chosen, the subsidy will be that distance times Q^*, and the market output will be at Q^*. Hence there is no obvious economic difference between the two.

[6]This very old concept originated with the work of Jules Dupuit, "On the Measurement of Utility of Public Works," *International Economic Papers*, 1952 (translated from the

French, 1844). Some date the beginning of project evaluation as we now know it to Dupuit's work.

[7]At this point it should also be mentioned that if there are extra administrative costs involved in raising the revenue or building the bridge, they too should be included in costs.

[8]Readers can convince themselves of this proposition by swiveling the supply curve in a counterclockwise position, measuring the area of the deadwight-loss triangle. As the supply curve becomes more vertical, the intersection of the shifted supply curve and the demand curve occurs closer and closer to L_1, and the area of the triangle declines. Henry George, a mayoral candidate in New York City in 1886, realized this point long ago and made it the centerpiece of his single-tax movement. See his *Progress and Poverty* (New York: Appleton, 1882).

[9]Arthur M. Okun, *Equality and Efficiency: The Big Tradeoff* (Washington, D.C.: Brookings Institution, 1975) chap. 4.

APPENDIX / CHAPTER 2

CONSUMER SURPLUS

As is shown by the examples in the chapter, one of the most fundamental concepts in measuring the benefits or costs of a policy that alters prices is that of consumer surplus. This appendix is devoted to explaining the concept in more detail, showing how it can be measured, and then dealing with a more esoteric issue—the difference between the ''compensated'' and ''uncompensated'' notions of consumer surplus.

The chapter made the point that the demand curve was an expression of consumers' marginal utility for a good, and took consumer surplus as the distance between the demand curve and the price consumers actually pay for a good. Another way to make the same point is to assume that the good is sold by a ''price-discriminating'' monopolist. Instead of just charging one price for a good, this monopolist is so powerful that he can charge different consumers different prices. He then tries to extract every last unit of utility from consumers, leaving them no better off than they would be without the good. In doing this, he charges P_1 for the first Q_1 units on Figure 2A.1, P_2 for the units between Q_1 and Q_2, and so on, down to the equilibrium price of P^* for the Q^* unit. Were he to charge one price to all consumers, it would be P^* and he would gain revenues of OP^*EQ^*. But if he can discriminate in this way he can gain revenues equal to the shaded area in the diagram. In the limiting case (as the Q intervals get smaller and smaller), his price discrimination revenues approach $ODEQ^*$. Since the monopolist has extracted enough revenue that consumers are no better off from having consumed the good, this area must be the total benefit derived from consumption of the good by all consumers. And in the usual case where a price of P^* is charged, consumer surplus then also equals the difference between the revenues of discriminating sellers and nondiscriminating sellers, or P^*DE, just as was explained earlier. To measure this consumer surplus, one needs to know the equilibrium position and the slope of the demand curve.

There is, however, a subtlety that has often confused economists. In Figure 2A.1, the demand curve slopes downward to the right for two reasons:

1. As the price of the good falls, consumers will buy more of this good and less of other goods, even at a constant level of utility—the so-called substitution effect.

2. As the price of the good falls, consumers will not have to spend as much of their income to purchase their initial quantity of the good. Their real income and utility

FIGURE 2A.1   Demand Curve and Consumer Surplus

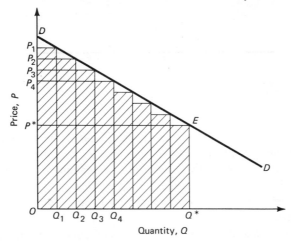

levels are increased, and they may spend some of this newfound income on buying more of the good—the income effect.

It turns out that when there is an income effect (reason 2), there are *three* different notions of consumer surplus. Those are shown in Figure 2A.2 for the case of a public project that lowers a good's price from P_0 to P_1, and are described as follows:

FIGURE 2A.2   Normal, Compensating, and Equivalent Variations Demand Curves

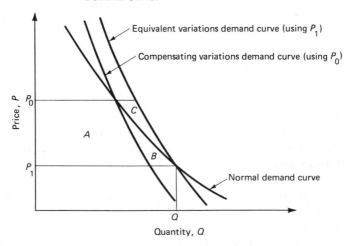

1. The normal and observed demand curve, which slopes downward because it includes *both* income and substitution effects.[1]

2. The "compensating variation" demand curve, which includes only the substitution effect. It uses the base-period price level P_0, and assumes that as prices fall, the consumer is taxed to keep her on her initial utility level and to neutralize the income effect.

3. The "equivalent variation" demand curve, which also includes only the substitution effect but measures compensation on the basis of the final period price level, P_1.[2]

Note that both the compensating and equivalent variation demand curves are steeper than the Marshallian curve, because both eliminate income effects. But there are two ways to eliminate this income effect, either by holding utility constant either at that achieved under base prices P_0 or that achieved under final prices P_1. Since base prices were higher, utility is lower and the compensating variation curve is placed to the left of the equivalent variations curve.

The operational problem in all of this is in deciding which demand curve to use in measuring consumer surplus and benefits and costs. When income effects are absent, there is no problem, for then all three curves are identical, and using the observed normal demand curve is the same as using the others. When income effects are present but small, it can be shown that the errors involved in using the observed normal demand curve are tiny, so that there again the normal demand curve serves as a good approximation.[3] But when income effects are large, one must be careful: there it all depends on the price levels used to compensate consumers. If they are base-period price levels, the compensating variations notion of consumer surplus must be used (area A). If they are final-period price levels, the equivalent variations notion should be used (areas A + B + C). As can be seen, the normal demand curve notion (areas $A + B$) can either over- or understate these areas.[4]

In either case, an intuitive rationale for using either the compensating or equivalent variations notion is given by the following illustration. Say that we were trying to measure the benefits of some magical process that created goods out of thin air. The first good was produced and sold for the maximum amount a consumer is willing to pay for it, say $10. In making this payment, the consumer experiences no utility gain—she must part with the $10. The second is then sold for $9, with the payment made in the same way. Each unit is then valued at the price that leaves the consumer indifferent between buying and not buying, with the consumer's utility held constant throughout by the fact that she has had to make the payments. By the same token, as a government project lowers the price of some good, each unit of consumption made possible by the lower price must be valued as if the consumer did not gain utility on the previous units, or by moving along either the compensating or equivalent variations demand curve.

APPENDIX NOTES

[1]The normal demand curve is sometimes called the Marshallian demand curve, after Alfred Marshall (1842–1924), a British economist who invented demand and supply analysis (see his *Principles of Economics,* Macmillan & Co., 1890).

[2]These definitions correspond to those of John R. Hicks, *A Revision of Demand Theory* (London: Oxford University Press, 1956), and Paul A. Samuelson, *Foundations of Economic Analysis* (Cambridge, Mass.: Harvard University Press, 1947), especially Chapter 5.

[3]See, for example, Robert D. Willig, "Consumer's Surplus without Apology," *American Economic Review,* September, 1976.

[4]Note that if we had switched positions between the base period and final period price, the compensating variations curve would be measured on the basis of lower prices, higher utility, and it would be to the right of the equivalent variations curve. A text that shows how to get these same results from indifference curve diagrams is Peter Bohm, *Social Efficiency: A Concise Introduction to Welfare Economics* (New York: Macmillan, 1974), app. 2, pp. 143–145; those at a more advanced level should consult Hal R. Varian, *Microeconomic Analysis* (New York: Norton, 1978), p. 211.

PROBLEMS

2.1 Assume that we have a facility, defined as a natural monopoly, for which the demand curves of three consumers (A, B, and C) are given by

$$Q_A = 20 - P$$
$$Q_B = 25 - P$$
$$Q_C = 15 - .5P$$

If the economy is made up of just these three consumers, compute the market demand curve for prices $5, $10, $15, and $20. Then compute the arc elasticity of demand between each price, using the formula for the arc elasticity of $\eta = \Delta Q/\overline{Q} \div \Delta P/\overline{P}$, where $\overline{Q}$ and $\overline{P}$ are averages of the price and quantity before and after the change. Then compute the aggregate consumer surplus at each price. Finally, compute the average fixed cost that would make society indifferent between building and not building the facility if the marginal cost of using the facility is each of the four prices.

2.2 a. Now say that the facility is a pure public good with the same individual demand curves for the same three-person economy as in Problem 2.1. If the marginal utility of each consumer never goes below zero, find the public goods demand curve (or marginal utility of various quantity levels) for quantities of 5, 10, 15, and 20 units. Find the consumer surplus at each quantity level.

b. Say we ascertain that the price of this public good to the community is 35. How many units should the community buy to maximize overall welfare? Who would pay how much if taxes were set equal to marginal utilities? Compute individual consumer surpluses at this set of tax prices.

c. Now let individual C learn that taxes are set equal to marginal utilities. He therefore tells the town meeting that his marginal utility for the public good is zero. If the price remains at 35, find how much the community would buy now, and the consumer surpluses of A, B, and C. What difficulty in finding an optimal voting rule does this problem illustrate?

2.3 Say that we have a market where the demand curve is given by $Q = 60 - P$ and the supply curve by $Q = .5P$. An excise tax is assessed on the commodity with a tax rate of .5. Compute the old equilibrium, the new equilibrium, the amount of revenue raised by the tax, the deadweight loss of the tax, and the loss of consumer and producer surplus.

2.4 In Problem 2.3, assume that external costs are given by the function $Q = P$. Hence the original supply curve is $P = 2Q$, the true social cost curve is $P = 3Q$, and the supply curve with tax is $P = 4Q$. Find the three different equilibrium price and quantity solutions and the deadweight loss (relative to the optimum) of the original equilibrium and the recomputed loss of the with-tax equilibrium.

2.5 Say that we have a society with 10 people having the following record of wage rates, hours worked, and income in a year:

PERSON	HOURLY WAGE RATE (DOLLARS)	HOURS WORKED (THOUSANDS)	ANNUAL INCOME (THOUSANDS OF DOLLARS)
A	2	1	2
B	3	2	6
C	4	1	4
D	5	2	10
E	6	1	6
F	2	2	4
G	3	1	3
H	4	2	8
I	5	1	5
J	6	2	12

Compute the initial mean income level for the society and the variance of income around this mean. For those who have not had statistics, the formula for the variance is

$$V = .1 \left[\sum_{i=1}^{10} (Y_i - \bar{Y})^2 \right],$$ where Y_i is the ith family's income level and $\bar{Y}$ is the mean income level.

Then say that society tried to equalize incomes by a tax and transfer program that gave all families an amount equal to $2.5 - .5Y_i$ if their initial income was less than 5, and taxed away $.2(Y_i - 5)$ if their income was greater than 5. Compute the new mean and variance. Say verbally what would happen to both if hours worked depended on taxed and transfer rates. Finally, say that society tried to equalize incomes by taxing families with incomes greater than 5 the same amount, but using the money to train low-wage workers, raising their wage by $.4(4 - W_i)$ for all workers with an initial wage less than 4 and thereby eligible for the program. Recompute the mean and variance of income, and say verbally what happens as the training program is made less productive (.4 falls to zero) or more productive.

2.6 Suppose that the market demand for a product is known to be $Q = 37.5 - .5P$ and the supply curve is $P = 25 + .5Q$. Now say that the government decides to lower the price of the good to help consumers, so it gives a subsidy of 25 per unit. Find

a. The presubsidy price and quantity equilibrium.

b. The postsubsidy price and quantity equilibrum.

c. The change in consumer surplus as a result of the subsidy.

d. The change in producer surplus.

e. The net cost to society, assuming that the presubsidy curves properly reflected social benefits and costs.

3

The Activities
of Government

The focus of Chapter 2 was normative: it tried to show why there is a need for government intervention in a market economy. This chapter is descriptive and focuses on actual data. The simple object is to examine federal, state, and local government spending in the United States to see what programs are in fact being carried out, what share of revenues are being devoted to various activities, and how these expenditures have changed over the years.

For these purposes expenditures will be divided into four broad categories:

1. Allocation functions.
2. Distribution functions.
3. Grants to other governments.
4. Housekeeping functions.

The first two categories are the same as were used in Chapter 2. As was true there, allocation expenditures refer to all attempts to alter the allocation of resources—national defense expenditures, the classic example of a pure public good at the national level; police and fire protection, examples of public goods at the local level; and physical investment activities such as the construction of dams, roads, sewage treatment plants, and so forth.

Distribution expenditures refer to all attempts to change the income distribution in society. They can be carried out in either of the ways mentioned in Chapter 2. The first, straight transfer programs, directly try to equalize the income distribution either in the form of cash assistance—social security, public assistance, and unemployment insurance—or "in-kind" transfers, such as food stamps, medicaid, and public housing, which try to support the consumption of certain activities. (We see in Chapter 10 that they may not be successful and, if they are, there may be some further efficiency losses.) The other form of distribution expenditures, human investment programs, consist mainly of education at the local level, although here is one case where tight categorization of expenditures is impossible: there is also an allocation motive, externalities, for most local public education expenditures.

The third category, intergovernmental grants, reflects the growing tendency of both the federal and state governments to carry out programs at one remove. Rather than raising their own direct expenditures to deal with a problem, these governments simply transfer money to a lower level of government to have it do so. Hence the Interstate Highway Program of 1956 featured categorical federal grants to state governments to have the states build highways. Similarly, much of the Great Society legislation of President Johnson was accomplished through categorical grants to state and local governments. When grants are categorical, they can be subdivided into the same allocation and distribution categories used for direct expenditures. In some cases, however, grants are noncategorical—they can be used for any purpose that the local government desires, including tax reduction. The outstanding example of this type of program is President Nixon's federal general revenue-sharing program.

A final category of spending refers to the more mundane housekeeping functions of various levels of government. These governments must operate a tax collection agency, engage in some regulatory activities, pay pensions to their employees, and pay interest on their debt. All such activities are considered to be part of the general housekeeping operation and are not assigned to any specific category.

THE FEDERAL GOVERNMENT

A look at the activities of the federal government and how they have changed over time is given in Table 3.1. Total expenditures equaled $385.2 billion in 1976, about 23 percent of the economy's total output. The largest single item in both 1960 and 1976 was expenditures for national defense, part of the allocation

TABLE 3.1 Activities of the Federal Government, 1960 and 1976[a] (billions of current dollars)

	1960	PERCENT OF TOTAL	1976	PERCENT OF TOTAL
Total expenditures	93.4	100.0	385.2	100.0
Allocation branch	62.4	66.8	150.7	39.1
National defense	53.8	57.6	122.1	31.7
Physical investment programs	8.6	9.2	28.6	7.4
Distribution branch	15.5	16.6	131.5	34.1
Cash assistance	15.0	16.0	105.2	27.3
In-kind assistance	0.3	0.3	22.6	5.9
Human investment	0.2	0.2	3.7	1.0
Grants to state and local governments	6.1	6.5	59.8	15.5
Allocation	3.0	3.2	15.6	4.0
Distribution	3.1	3.3	37.2	9.7
Cash assistance	2.3	2.5	12.7	3.3
In-kind assistance	0.4	0.4	18.4	4.8
Human investment	0.4	0.4	6.1	1.6
Noncategorical assistance	—	—	7.0	1.8
Housekeeping functions	9.4	10.1	43.3	11.2

[a] Items may not add to totals because of rounding error.

Source: Office of Business Economics, *Survey of Current Business,* July issues, Table 3.14. Classification done by author.

branch. By 1976 the second most important item had become cash assistance, mainly social security payments for the elderly but also including a fairly large outlay for unemployment insurance. Grants of all kinds took an appreciable share of the budget, as did housekeeping expenditures.

It is interesting to see how these expenditures have changed over time. Overall expenditures were more than four times as large as in 1960, but this growth was mainly due to higher prices and the greater demand for public expenditures coming from higher family incomes: the share of total output of the economy devoted to government has only slightly increased. More interesting yet is the change in the composition of federal expenditures. In 1960, 58 percent of the federal budget was devoted to national defense and related activities (space, foreign aid, and veterans' benefits); by 1976 this share had fallen to 32 percent. On the other hand, the share of direct cash assistance had risen from 16 to 27 percent, and that of all kinds of grants from 7 to 16 percent. More and more we observe a federal government not running allocation programs directly (with the important exception of national defense), but either giving cash payments to people or grants to state and local governments. This is one strong reason for extending the logic of evaluation to these "check-writing" programs.

The next level of governments in the U.S. hierarchy is at the state level. The states are intermediate on the scale, maintaining some functions (road building, parks, state universities) not carried on at the federal level, but also having a grant-giving and supervisory role over local governments. Data on their activities are shown in Table 3.2. In 1976 the total expenditures of the 50 state governments amounted to $147.6 billion, about 40 percent of the federal expenditures for the same year. About $100 billion of this total represented expenditures out of "own" revenues; the remainder was financed by grants from the federal government. Over the 16-year period, state expenditures have more than quintupled, however, implying that the state government share of total economy-wide spending is rising more rapidly than for any other level of government.

As with federal spending, the share of state budgets in allocation-type physical investment programs has declined over the period, from 39 percent in 1970 to 21 percent by 1976. The slack has been made up by a rising share of expenditures devoted to distribution programs of all sorts, with human investment spending for higher education now taking the largest share. The share of grants to local governments has remained stable, as has the share devoted to housekeeping expenditures. Although less true than at the federal level, it remains true for states that the simple act of check writing is growing more important over time, and accordingly it makes sense to extend the scope of the evaluation logic to these other areas.

TABLE 3.2 Activities of State Governments, 1960 and 1976[a] (billions of current dollars)

	1960	PERCENT OF TOTAL	1976	PERCENT OF TOTAL
Total expenditures	26.2	100.0	147.6	100.0
Allocation branch	10.2	38.9	31.4	21.3
Distribution branch	5.1	19.5	48.9	33.1
Cash assistance	2.2	8.4	12.0	8.1
In-kind assistance	—	—	10.0	6.8
Human investment	2.9	11.1	26.9	18.2
Grants to local governments	9.4	35.9	56.5	38.3
Allocation	1.4	5.3	4.9	3.3
Distribution	7.0	26.7	43.4	29.4
Cash assistance	1.4	5.3	7.8	5.3
Human investment	5.6	21.4	35.6	24.1
Noncategorical assistance	1.0	3.8	8.2	5.6
Housekeeping functions	1.8	6.9	10.8	7.3

[a]Items may not add to totals because of rounding error.

Source: Office of Business Economics, *Survey of Current Business,* May 1978, Table 3, p. 18. Classification done by author.

TABLE 3.3   Activities of Local Governments,
1960 and 1976[a] (billions of current dollars)

	1960	PERCENT OF TOTAL	1976	PERCENT OF TOTAL
Total expenditures	33.0	100.0	155.1	100.0
Allocation branch	11.4	34.5	47.5	30.6
Distribution branch	17.5	53.0	86.4	55.7
Cash assistance	2.3	7.0	12.5	8.1
Human investment	15.2	46.1	73.9	47.6
Housekeeping functions	4.2	12.7	21.2	13.7

[a]Items may not add to totals because of rounding error.

Source: Office of Business Economics, *Survey of Current Business*, May 1978, Table 4, p. 20. Classification done by author.

LOCAL GOVERNMENTS

By far the most difficult governments to comprehend and analyze are local governments. There is one federal government in the United States, 50 state governments, and approximately 75,000 local governments. These localities consist of city, village, and county governments, independent school districts, water districts, transit authorities, parking authorities, and on and on. It is not uncommon for certain citizens to be served by as many as 10 independent local authorities at once. Although all localities have a measure of fiscal autonomy, either the state, regional conventions, or their own charter will often vastly circumscribe their taxing and spending behavior.

The aggregated spending levels of these 75,000 local governments are shown in Table 3.3. In 1976 spending amounted to $155.1 billion, just slightly more than state government spending. Again about $100 billion was financed by own revenues. Expenditures have almost quintupled over the 16-year period, putting localities midway between the more rapidly expanding state governments and the more slowly expanding federal government in growth.

The major activity of local governments has always been the operation of public schools—human investment expenditures have totaled from 46 to 48 percent of total expenditures since 1960. There is a relatively small cash distribution program, largely financed by grants from higher levels of government, and also about one-third of the budget devoted to allocation-type physical expenditures on streets, parks, and public safety. The share of expenditures devoted to housekeeping is larger than at the other levels of government, perhaps because the local property tax is more costly to administer than are state and federal income and sales taxes.

These factual details are introduced to rationalize the organization of the book. At the local level, allocation-type physical investment projects that until now have been the focus of most evaluation literature are still important, and they are treated here. But at least at the federal and state levels, a large and growing portion of budgetary activity takes the form of check writing—either direct income distribution programs or programs of grants to local governments. Thus it becomes particularly important for aspiring evaluators to know how to extend the logic of the evaluation of physical investment projects to these other areas, a task we turn to later in the book.

4

Benefit-Cost Analysis and Governmental Decision Making

Until now we have examined certain respects in which a free market may fail to yield an allocation of resources that is judged to be economically efficient or a distribution of income that is judged to be equitable. It is conceivable that certain types of government programs—direct expenditures, transfer payments, or even regulation of the behavior of private enterprise—will "improve the situation." Deciding whether or not this is so, or whether or not the government programs are on balance beneficial, is precisely what evaluation is all about. In this chapter we switch the focus to the question of how, on a methodological plane, government decision makers can make this judgment. We try to answer this question in a world with perfect evaluation information and no political constraints on budgetary activities, and then see how the methodological lessons change when we relax both assumptions.

The issue would be relatively straightforward but for a complex and difficult interrelationship between the efficiency and equity aspects of any policy change. Let us say that there is some defect in the market allocation of resources that requires government intervention to improve economic efficiency. Were this intervention to be evaluated solely on efficiency grounds, it might be possible to make clear, unambiguous decisions: the benefits of this change to some consumers exceed the costs of resources used to other consumers, or the loss in factor incomes of suppliers, and the change is beneficial. But involved in this operation, as with any such operation in complex and interrelated modern societies, is the fact that some people—consumers—gain from the transaction while others—other consumers or producers—lose. In deciding that the overall change is beneficial on balance, then, decision makers cannot avoid making a judgment that the gains to one group (winners) have a greater social value than the losses to another group (losers). Given the modern democratic and philosophical reluctance to make such interpersonal utility comparisons, the decision maker has in some sense no right to make such judgments and no right to decide that the policy is beneficial on balance.

Economists concerned with these issues—known as welfare economists—have pondered this apparently insoluble enigma for almost a century without coming up with any terribly persuasive guide to action. The original logical criterion for *proving* that a policy change, or any other change for that matter, is beneficial comes from the writings of Vilfredo Pareto (1848–1923), an Italian economist and sociologist who pioneered in developing the concept of economic efficiency. The Paretian standard is that situation A is preferred to situation B if at least one person is better off and no one is worse off in A. Since nobody is worse off, the policymaker is not required to make interpersonal judgments. The only problem is: How can one ever find any policy change that makes nobody worse off?

The Paretian principle has more practical applicability than might at first be apparent because it could allow for a system of side payments from winners to losers, thus reducing the individual gains while eliminating the losses. There is at least one example of side payments in current U.S. federal government policy. It has long been recognized that a reduction in tariffs on imported goods will make most consumers better off—reducing the prices of imported goods—while hurting domestic producers of competing goods, such as textiles, autos, and color television sets. Since 1974, the Trade Readjustment Assistance Act has contained a provision for just such side payments: if an industry can establish that it has been harmed due to rapid increases in imports, its unemployed workers are eligible for Trade Readjustment Assistance payments, which are designed to do little more than compensate workers for being harmed. Although fiscal conservatives often rail at these "handouts," perhaps assuming them to be a modern liberal idea, in fact the philosophical rationale can be taken directly from the writings of Pareto in the nineteenth century.

Just as it is impossible to find a program that does not harm anybody, realistically speaking it is also impossible to imagine a system of side payments that will not leave some people worse off on balance (even the Trade Readjustment payments will not compensate workers forever, will not replace their now-outmoded skills, will not go to all displaced workers, and will require some taxes paid by people who do not benefit from increased world trade). Hence in practice governments and evaluators have been forced to adopt a less stringent principle, this time developed from the work of two British economists, Nicholas Kaldor and John Hicks, as a guide for policy changes. The Kaldor–Hicks principle is that situation A is preferred to situation B if the gainers *could* compensate the losers and still be better off.[1] Notice that the Kaldor–Hicks principle does not require that the gainers actually *do* compensate the losers and so does not deal with the distributive consequences of policy changes. One can imagine cases in which undesirable social outcomes would result: low-income consumers could find their sales tax payments being used to dam a river and provide increased flood protection for wealthy farmers. But if a society consistently followed the Kaldor–Hicks criteria, and if it had other mechanisms for dealing with income distribution (including side payments, which after all are not outlawed by Kaldor–Hicks), that society would probably be making as sensible policy decisions as can be imagined in this messy world.[2]

In the fashion of government decision makers, we have to act in this chapter, and we will act by showing how programs can be evaluated under the Kaldor–Hicks criterion. This is not to ignore the distribution of gains and losses (these issues will be dealt with extensively in Chapter 7) but simply to postpone them until we are ready. The chapter will first show how evaluation decisions ought to be made under the admittedly imperfect Kaldor–Hicks criterion. It will then show how even these rules have to be modified when policymakers lack the information to apply the Kaldor–Hicks rule or when they face political or institutional constraints on their actions. In the latter two cases, our stance will be to try to find the level or type of government program that brings about the maximum gain in social welfare under the constraint of inadequate information or the political impossibility of certain courses of action.

THE FUNDAMENTAL PRINCIPLE OF EVALUATION

The Kaldor–Hicks criterion can be restated as what Edith Stokey and Richard Zeckhauser call the "fundamental principle" of evaluation: "In any choice situation, select the (policy) alternative that produces the greatest net benefit."[3]

The hypothetical examples given in Table 4.1 show how this principle can be used in a variety of situations. For every project we have listed the gains to the winners, the losses to suppliers, taxpayer costs (assumed to measure net real resource costs and not simply to be transfers to some other group), the net benefits to society under the Kaldor–Hicks rule, and the commonly calculated benefit-cost ratio. Each of these examples can be thought of as cases where the government builds something (a road or a dam), consumers benefit in lower

TABLE 4.1   Benefits and Costs of Different Projects

PROJECT	GAINS TO CONSUMERS	LOSSES TO SUPPLIERS	COSTS TO TAXPAYERS	NET BENEFITS	BENEFIT-COST[a] RATIO
A	200	50	100	50	1.50
B	200	50	200	−50	.75
C	450	50	300	100	1.33
D	100	10	100	−10	.90
E	650	0	500	150	1.30

[a] Using taxpayer costs as the denominator.

prices (for transported goods or electric power), alternative suppliers lose (railroads or producers of coal), and taxpayers also lose.

The standard ways of scoring the projects are given in the two right-hand columns of Table 4.1. The "net benefits" column obviously adopts our distributionally neutral stance because it simply sums the gains and losses to all groups in society; consumers may gain $200 million from lower prices in project A but suppliers lose $50 million and taxpayers lose $100 million, so there is a net gain of $50 million. This net gain *could* be used to satisfy the Paretian criterion if consumers reimbursed suppliers and taxpayers and just kept $50 million; then we would know that nobody is worse off and some are better off. But if the compensation is not paid, we cannot be certain that the program is beneficial on balance because it could be that, dollar for dollar, taxpayers and suppliers are either more deserving or have greater use for the money than do consumers of goods. But as we said earlier, real-world policy discussions will fall short of this Paretian ideal, and decisions must be made. If there are alternative policies or social arrangements for dealing with the distribution of income, it is reasonable to make the decision on the basis of the Kaldor–Hicks criterion, which simply adds up all gains and losses in the manner shown.

The last column in Table 4.1 gives a famous ratio, the benefit-cost ratio. Its numerator is gains to consumers less losses to suppliers, and its denominator is taxpayer costs. The logic of computing the ratio in this way is that government decision makers want to put their budget dollars to best use, so they find the average net benefit for each tax, or budget, dollar for a project. In project A, for example, the cost to taxpayers is $100 million and the net benefit to the rest of society is $150 million—the benefit-cost ratio computed in this way is then $150/100 = 1.5$.[4] Whenever a program shows positive net benefits—gains outweigh losses—its benefit-cost ratio will also be greater than 1; whenever net benefits are negative, the benefit-cost ratio will be less than 1. It would seem that either measure could be used to identify a worthwhile project—positive net benefits or a benefit-cost ratio greater than 1—and in general this is true. When there are political constraints on the size of the government budget, however, the benefit-cost ratio can give a misleading signal, so in general it must be viewed as being less reliable than simply computing net social benefits, as the fundamental principle would have us do.

The approach taken in the chapter is to assume that we have a budgetary planning officer, and that the agencies have submitted the information shown in Table 4.1. This planning officer must determine what projects will be proposed to Congress for funding this year. We begin by looking at a situation where the officer has all the relevant information under the Kaldor–Hicks rule, and then progressively complicate things by taking away information and/or imposing physical or political constraints on budgetary actions. The examples are all hopelessly oversimplified and perhaps even naive; they are used only to illustrate the basic points.

THE EASY CASE: COMPLETE INFORMATION AND NO CONSTRAINTS

The first case we take up is the easiest. Say that the information given in Table 4.1 is reliable and that the only task is to make a budgetary decision. Whether the officer is using the positive net benefit rule or the unitary benefit-cost ratio rule, projects A, C, and E are the worthwhile ones, and the officer recommends a budget of size $900 (the sum of the taxpayers' cost of A, C, and E). This yields net benefits of $300 million or total benefits of $1.2 billion. Note that the budget officer has simultaneously decided on the optimal level of government spending ($900 million) and its allocation among various programs ($100 million for project A, $300 million for C, and $500 million for E).

INADEQUATE INFORMATION

Unfortunately, budget planners rarely have such complete information. Far and away the most perplexing difficulty is that the benefits of many programs cannot be valued and compared very precisely. Some of the projects under consideration may be for research on the prevention of cancer, with benefits in terms of lives saved. Others may clean up a river and facilitate its recreational use. Still others may be training programs for welfare recipients, enabling them to get a chance for a decent job. Throughout the book we will be reviewing techniques for valuing benefits that have made headway in dealing with programs such as these, but ultimately there will always be some nonquantifiable aspects. How might the decision maker proceed when there are such gaps in information?

If all the projects listed in Table 4.1 do quite different things, decision makers may indeed not find any rigorous guidelines. But let us simplify the problem some to make it more manageable. Assume that two of the projects in the list do substantially the same thing—that both projects A and B are designed to enable the aged to travel around town more readily. Project A might involve simply giving aged persons vouchers that could be used as currency on existing buses; project B might involve running a special bus system for the aged. In either case the aged gain increased consumer surplus due to their now less expensive transportation; in either case existing taxicab companies lose some producer surplus worth $50 million. We decide that it is simply impossible to value the total social benefits of the aged being able to transport themselves and of the harm to taxi drivers. Hence we cannot measure the sum of gains to consumers and losses to alternative suppliers in dollar terms. But we do know that those two unknown sums are equal. We can hold the program benefits constant and make comparisons between the programs that do the same thing. We can find the *cheapest* way to enable the aged to get around town—in effect maximizing the net benefits of the program even if we are not valuing them. On this basis we can select project A as the better alternative and reject project B. This technique of finding the cheapest way of doing something has become known as "cost-effectiveness" analysis in the Defense Department (where the benefits of a program can almost never be quantified).

Two things can be noted about the cost-effectiveness technique. First, we do not know that the program yields positive net benefits. If, for example, project A cost taxpayers $200 million and project B $300 million, A would still be preferred, even though, unknown to decision makers, it would no longer yield positive net benefits. The second thing to be noted is that the technique can be turned around. We have compared the costs of different programs that accomplish the same purpose: we could just as well have held constant program costs and have seen which of two approaches yielded the greatest amount of nonquantified net benefits. If decision makers were to use this inverse approach, they might decide to spend $100 million and no more on transportation for the aged (using the initial cost estimates of Table 4.1). Under approach A this sum would be sufficient to provide transportation for all the aged in the country; under approach B, only half of the aged. Project A is still preferred. Again we have not actually placed a value on the benefits of providing transportation for the aged, but we have come as close as we could to implementing the fundamental principle given the inadequate information at our disposal.

A second type of information gap refers to a favorite topic of economists, the distinction between a marginal concept and an average concept. To illustrate how this distinction could cause difficulties, let us assume now that projects C and D are really components of the same program. Say that both involve the training of unemployed teenagers for jobs, which both benefits the teenagers and causes some loss in wages or employment possibilities to adults (alternative suppliers) once the teenagers become more productive. Project C involves running full-day programs to teach skills such as welding or computer programming, and project D involves extending these programs to provide after-work instruction to other teenagers. Possessed with complete information, we can see that project C satisfies the fundamental principle whereas project D does not. But for some reason the evaluators hired by the Labor Department do not realize this; in their analysis of the program they do not distinguish between the workers in program C and those in program D. Except for that, they do the evaluation correctly, however, and come up with total budget costs of $300 million + $100 million = $400 million and net benefits of $100 million − $10 million = $90 million. They pronounce a favorable verdict for *both* programs, although in reality C is worthwhile and D is not. The difficulty here can be thought of as a failure to distinguish marginal from average net benefits: the program has net benefits on average, but the marginal extension to the after-work projects does not. Conducting disaggregated evaluations of both components would have shown this.

This difficulty is a rather basic one in evaluation studies. In trying to say whether an extension of program C is beneficial or not, the natural impulse is to look just at C and evaluate whether or not it is worthwhile. But an assumption is being made here that the net benefits of the extension will be the same as those of the original project, and that assumption may not always hold. In studies of private capital investment projects, it is standard to worry about the diminishing returns to the investment as the early profit opportunities are used up, and it should be just as standard to worry about the same problems with evaluations of government programs.

PHYSICAL CONSTRAINTS

A second set of amendments to the procedure for applying the fundamental principle involves physical constraints. Often projects, such as those listed in Table 4.1, simply cannot be selected independently of the other selections, but decisions must be made simultaneously. Next, we review a few of the most obvious examples of benefit-cost decision making with programs that are physically interdependent.

One such case is that of the travel voucher example used above. That was posed as a problem in measuring benefits, but it could also have been posed as a problem in physical interdependencies. The reason is that A and B are competing projects—if the government does one, it need not or cannot do the other. In this case, then, the benefit-cost test is based only partly on whether A or B have positive net benefits. Of the set of competing programs that pass the net benefits test, the government should select only the one with the highest net benefits. Since the programs are competing, the selected program should not only be better than the status quo, but also better than all other alternatives. We are still not looking for a panacea, but we are looking for the best available program.

This was an example of competing, or substitute, programs. But programs can also be complementary. Perhaps the benefits of the training program C can be realized only if students have taken the preparatory program D. In this case the two programs must be evaluated as a package: we cannot have one without the other. Even though by itself D does not pass the net benefits test, as a component of an overall package with C it does, because the overall package passes the net benefits test.

The amendments are much the same when budgetary decision makers are operating under political constraints, but the environment is different. Again, these constraints may stand in the way of a strict application of the fundamental principle but still do not prevent decision makers from doing the best they can under the circumstances. As with inadequacies of information, instead of using an unconstrained maximization rule, the decision maker is now forced to find the constrained maximization point.

A first constraint might be one imposed by outside "political considerations" on the size of government.[5] Let us say, for example, that programs A, C, and E satisfy the benefit-cost test but that the implied level of government spending of $900 million exceeds the rigid constraint the President has set down on total spending. In view of these political constraints, the President decides that an austere budget is politically necessary and forces the budget office to recommend a total no larger than $400 million. No longer are decision makers free to decide on both the level and the composition of the overall budget, but they are still free to set individual totals within this overall constraint. The way to do it, determined by maximizing net benefits *subject to the constraint that overall spending be $400 million,* is by proposing projects A and C. Net benefits total $150 million with this budget, greater than with any other combination of programs which are themselves beneficial. The project accounting for the largest total of net benefits, E, cannot be utilized simply because it costs too much money (even though its own benefit-cost ratio is nearly as high as that of all the others). Note further that if the President's constraint total rises to $800 million, the preferred composition shifts: now decision makers propose just C and E but not A, hence not even recommending the project with the highest benefit-cost ratio. This is a good illustration of how the benefit-cost ratio can give misleading signals.[6] Depending on his convictions and will to keep his job, the budget officer should perhaps point out to the President that these artificial constraints are ruling out effective programs that would yield Kaldor–Hicks benefits, but if it is necessary to maximize within a constraint, that can and should be done.

From time to time this constraint may work on the other side. Government contractors are well aware of the fact that as the end of the fiscal year nears, agencies begin to spend increased amounts, fearing the fact that unexpended appropriations will be used by Congress as evidence that their budget should be cut in the next year. Were the information in Table 4.1 to apply to this Department of Bigger Spending, the Secretary might recommend that for political reasons it is necessary to spend $1 billion this year. In that event, the Department would propose a budget of A, C, D, and E—again realizing, but no doubt not pointing out, that program D does not yield net benefits at the margin.

Another constraint on budgetary decisions, all too commonly observed in practice, is the existence of sacred cows. A budget office operating as if there were no constraints would propose a budget of $900 million, made up of A, C, and E. The budget message goes to Congress, whence it becomes known that Congress will not tolerate the closing down of project D. Were the budget size flexible, the optimizing procedure would be simply to add D to the budget and spend $1 billion—programs A, C, and E do not presumably lose their net benefits simply because Congress insists on carrying out program D. But it may be that Congress "earmarks" money for this sacred cow *and* preserves the initial overall total of $900 million. Then the preferred course would be to drop program A and have total net benefits of $240 million, $60 million less than in the unconstrained case because you lose project A and are also forced to swallow project D.

This information could also be used to construct an example of the ancient practice of logrolling. Let us say that the chairman of the Senate Finance Committee hails from a state where project D, a dam, will be built. He is dead set against cutting off this project, and tells the budget office that if they do so, he will delay hearings on training program A. The budget office has a choice: propose a $1 billion budget that includes both D and A and yields total net benefits of $290 million; or propose a budget without either D or A, yielding net benefits of $250 million. It naturally follows the former course, perhaps secure in the knowledge that even though taxpayers do lose from project D, they would have lost more had the budget office not rolled logs with the good senator.

EVALUATION, BUDGETING, AND POLITICS

The preceding examples show the obvious connection between evaluation and budgeting. One is an explicit tool for the other. But as the sections on gaps in information and political constraints make clear, the connection gets looser and looser as the situation gets further and further from our simplified ideal. In real-world situations, budgets are decided on the basis of much more straightforward rules of thumb—for example, last year's total plus 5 percent—than they are on the basis of underlying benefit and cost considerations. It is nevertheless still helpful, both to evaluation and to budgeting, to know how the two would fit together in the ideal world we have been discussing here. The goal of all good evaluations is to provide information useful to budgetary decision makers— benefit-cost information if possible, or cost effectiveness information if that is the best that is available. The goal of good budgeting should be to try to move society toward a better allocation of resources. In the short run there may be constraints of one sort or another or information gaps that prevent immediate movement. But over time it matters greatly whether spending on program X is last year's total plus 5 percent or last year's total plus 1 percent. Something must guide these marginal choices, and evaluation considerations are the proper thing, or at least the thing that enables society to come closest to an equitable and efficient allocation of resources.

The examples of evaluation decision making in a world with political constraints also suggests the connection between evaluation and political considerations. As with budgeting, the street has two directions. Politics refers to the entire set of procedures by which representative democratic governments work. Often economists throw up their hands at "political constraints," but just as often these constraints serve a valuable purpose. There may be no other way to ensure that intensities of preference are expressed in a representative democracy or that certain morally offensive actions are ruled out. In the case we dealt with here, a strong lobby for the aged may be the only device available to ensure that society worries about their transportation needs. We have seen that benefit-cost analysis of the Kaldor–Hicks type has a fundamental weakness when it comes to balancing the benefits and costs received by winners and losers, and the political process might be a good way to limit unwarranted extensions of this supposed objective analysis. But for strong "interest groups," the nation would never have had pathbreaking legislation in the areas of civil rights or environmental protection.

At the same time, pure politics can easily degenerate into a rough-and-tumble fight on the basis of political muscle or potential campaign contributions. Evaluation information, even of the Kaldor–Hicks type, can be very helpful in providing perspective on various policy questions—does the nation as a whole gain or lose from this action? In this chapter we showed further how the logic of evaluation could be used to find a preferred solution consistent with a set of constraints, and it could even be used in shaping these supposed constraints. In the short run, a project such as our D may be a sacred cow, but a series of negative evaluations will gradually cut into this sacredness, and in time the former sacred cow may no longer exist.

Beyond that, evaluators should recognize that there are many ways to do evaluations, ranging from a go/no go summative evaluation of a program to cost-effectiveness evaluations that take the benefits for granted (and thus do not roil up client groups) and simply try to minimize costs. If it is impossible to attack a program frontally (with direct questions, such as, Does it provide net benefits?), it may still be possible to find a cheaper alternative.

SUMMARY

In this chapter we first showed what evaluations we could never even hope to do—proving that a policy is good in the Paretian sense where nobody is harmed—and those we could—showing that a policy would generate net benefits in the Kaldor–Hicks sense that total real income increased. We examined how the Kaldor–Hicks principle might be applied in a world of perfect information and no constraints, and then how the principle could still be approached in a world featuring inadequate information, various political constraints on behavior, or both. The explicit examples used to make the points are highly oversimplified, but the lessons are still relevant. Both evaluators and budgeters should try to come as close as they can to the net benefits principle, recognizing the information gaps and constraints that exist. Of course, there is not enough information to follow the ideal procedure, but one can adapt the procedure so that it fits the information available. There are obvious political constraints on budget activities, but one can still maximize within these constraints, and one can also try to influence them. Moreover, in some cases political constraints may be necessary to enforce overall moral rules, and it may be inoffensive, and even desirable, to work within them.

NOTES

[1]The Kaldor criterion is that gainers be able to compensate losers and still be better off (see his "Welfare Propositions of Economics and Interpersonal Comparisons of Utility," *Economic Journal,* September 1939). The Hicks criterion is that the losers should not be able profitably to bribe the gainers not to change. (See his "The Valuation of the Social Income," *Economica,* May 1940). Tibor Scitovsky suggested that both criteria be used (see his "A Note on Welfare Propositions in Economics," *Review of Economic Studies,* November 1941).

[2]One could protect against some of the more undesirable outcomes by adopting an amendment proposed by I. M. D. Little in *A Critique of Welfare Economics,* 2nd ed. (Oxford: Clarendon Press, 1957). Little's amendment is that in addition to passing the Kaldor–Hicks test, a project must cause "a good redistribution of wealth." Such a proviso sounds reasonable, but it could still rule out some projects that are desirable on efficiency grounds even though they do not improve on wealth distribution. In principle, those undesirable consequences could be offset by greater redistribution policies. We are back to the logic of the Kaldor–Hicks standard.

A modern equity concept that is beginning to get some attention is that of a "fair" allocation of consumer goods, defined as a state where person A does not envy the consumption bundle of person B were he willing to produce as much as person B. [See Hal R. Varian, *Microeconomic Analysis* (New York: Norton, 1978) pp. 225–228.] It is not clear how this concept can be made operational for the benefit-cost literature, but presumably a test could be defined that reduces envy in this sense.

[3]This time the quote is exact, from Edith Stokey and Richard Zeckhauser, *A Primer for Policy Analysis* (New York: Norton, 1978), p. 137.

[4]Those who are mathematically astute will realize that the benefit-cost ratio depends on what is in the numerator and denominator. If, for example, all costs (suppliers as well as taxpayers) are in the denominator, the benefit-cost ratio for project A is 200/150 = 1.33. There is not a strong reason for preferring one way of computing the ratio over another.

Indeed, we will see that this is a problem with the ratio. But usually the ratio is computed in the way shown in Table 4.1, to measure net social benefits per dollar of budget cost.

[5]This section is written as if political constraints on the size of the budget are impediments that need to be operated within. An interesting argument that these constraints may be desirable (and in any case are inevitable) is that of Peter O. Steiner, "Public Expenditure Budgeting," in Alan S. Blinder et al., *The Economics of Public Finance* (Washington, D.C.: Brookings Institution, 1974), p. 300.

[6]As was shown above, the reason for the misleading signal is that it is totally arbitrary whether a cost is considered a negative benefit and subtracted from the numerator or added to the denominator. The net benefits concept described in the chapter has no such problem.

PROBLEMS

4.1 The Director of the Army Corps of Engineers has proposals for building six dams. Consultants have estimated the value of benefits (B) and costs (C) to be as follows:

PROJECT	B	C
A	40	20
B	30	10
C	30	20
D	10	20
E	15	10
F	15	20

Compute the net benefits and benefit-cost ratio for each dam. Find the optimal size budget and the dams that should be built within it. Find the dams that should be built when the budget is constrained politically to 40 and 80 respectively. If dams C, D, E, and F are alternatives for the same river basin, which should be built? How well have the net benefit and benefit-cost ratio rules fared in each case?

4.2 Now let us change the rules somewhat. Focus on the C dam, ignoring all the others. The Corps' behavior is unconstrained; that is, it is allowed to build the dam if net benefits are positive but not otherwise. If the Corps is certain that the cost of the dam is 20 but does not know benefits, what would be the social value of an evaluation study that estimates benefits exactly at 30, the true value, when the initial estimate of benefits is

a. 18?

b. 22?

c. 18 with probability ½ and 22 with probability ½?

5

Valuation
of Resources Used
or Benefits Created
When They Occur

In Chapter 4 we showed how budgeting decisions would follow from evaluation information but did not say where the evaluation information would come from. That is the task of this chapter and the next. In this chapter we consider how benefits and costs should be valued when they occur; in Chapter 6 we show how benefits and costs received or paid at different times should be valued. In both cases we simply add up all gains and losses realized, deferring until Chapter 7 the question of how gains and losses realized by different groups, or different income classes, should be valued.

The context here will be the standard one in the evaluation literature where the government provides some physical good or service. The benefits of this good or service are received either by consumers in the form of cheaper or less-time-consuming consumption, or by producers, who pass on the benefits either to consumers or their stockholders. Some costs are borne by alternative suppliers of these services, who may lose customers and monopoly profits. Other costs are borne by taxpayers in procuring the resources used by the government project. But one must be careful in equating the budget costs of the project with the true social costs because sometimes budget costs represent only transfers from one group to another, with no sacrifice of aggregate economic welfare. Budget costs are equal to social costs only when they represent resources actually used up in the production of the services offered by the government, and hence not available for the private consumption of members of society. And further social costs may be entailed if the production of government services generates undesirable environmental or other side effects that reduce the welfare of members of society.

The evaluation question dealt with here—when the identity of the gainers and losers is not considered and when all benefits and costs are in terms of annual flows in the present year—is the relatively straightforward one of comparing the gains of consumers or producers to the losses of alternative suppliers, of those harmed by any environmental side effects, and of taxpayers. The comparison attempts to arrive at an overall social gain or loss for the project, which gain or loss in effect nets out all transfers that help or hurt particular groups. We consider first the basic case where markets exist and their prices can be used as the accurate social valuations of all benefits and costs, and then go on to deal with cases where market prices form less reliable guides for valuing benefits and costs. There are some instances where markets exist but their prices must be adjusted to deal with some known social externality, others where markets do not exist but marketlike behavior can be used to impute values, and still others where markets do not exist and some other method must be used for benefit-cost valuation. In the process, we will deal with issues such as the proper valuation of unemployed resources, foreign exchange, lives saved or risked, and uncertainty about benefits and costs.

MARKET PRICES EXIST AND
ACCURATELY REPRESENT SOCIAL VALUES

The first case to be considered is where private markets exist and their prices can be used in valuing the benefits or costs of a government project. The philosophical argument in favor of this posture is a very powerful and a very democratic one. Rather than having the state set the values of goods and services created or resources used up for a government project, the use of market valuations leaves it up to individual citizens, whose buying and selling behavior establishes these prices in an impersonal and nonpolitical way. Of course, there are times when markets do not work properly—this is the reason it is necessary to have and to evaluate government programs in the first place, and also why certain market valuations may have to be ignored or adjusted. But it is still probably true that for most commodities in a free-enterprise economy, market valuations will form a tolerable estimate of the social costs or gains.

To begin with this case, then, let us take the natural monopoly example of

Chapter 2. Say that the city of Urbania is considering building a subway system that will benefit consumers, hurt alternative suppliers of transportation services, and cost taxpayers. Transportation planners figure that the marginal cost per ride on the completed subway will be $.25, and having taken economics, they realized that the toll should also be set at that price. Currently, the fare charged by a private bus company over the same routes is $.50, of which $.40 is the marginal and average cost and $.10 represents monopoly profits. Transportation planners do not know how many people will ride the subway, but they do know that 100,000 riders now use the bus each year, and that two years ago, when the bus company was forced to price at its marginal cost of $.40, 140,000 riders used it. They therefore reason that every $.05 decrease in fare adds 20,000 riders, such that there will be 200,000 riders per year with a fare of $.25. Initially, we make the problem easy by assuming that convenience, accessibility, and commuting time will be the same on the bus and subway and that there will be no significant externalities on either, assumptions that will be relaxed presently. How much would the subway system be worth?

Consider first the old riders, ones who used the bus even when the fare was $.50. In Chapter 2 we introduced the concept of consumer surplus to measure their benefits. Using this notion, or consumers' "willingness to pay" for the subway, they clearly gain an amount equal to area A plus area C in Figure 5.1, a total benefit of $(100,000)$ $($.25$)$ = $25,000. In addition, there will be new subway riders, and their gain, again measured by their willingness to pay from the demand curve, will equal the added consumer surplus between 100,000 and 200,000 rides, which is the area B plus D plus E, or $(\frac{1}{2})$ $(100,000)$ $($.25$)$ = $12,500. At the same time, owners of the bus company will lose on the old

FIGURE 5.1   Benefits of the Urbania Subway

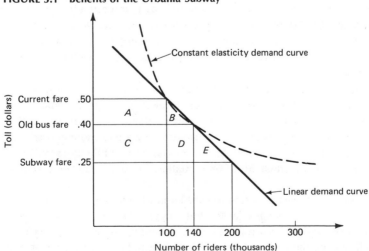

riders: before, these owners earned a profit of area A on the old riders, and presumably all switch to the cheaper subway and the bus company profits drop by (100,000) ($.10) = 10,000. The social gain in this simple example is the total gain in consumer surplus, $25,000 plus $12,500, less the loss of bus company profits of $10,000, for a total benefit of $27,500 per year. If the annual cost of the subway is less than $27,500, its net benefits will be positive and it should be built. If the annual cost is more than $27,500, the subway should not be built.

There are two other ways of arriving at the social benefit of $27,500, both of them economically illuminating. A first is to try to decompose the total gain of consumers into real resource savings and transfers from other members of society. Of the total consumer gain of $37,500, $10,000 represents a transfer from the bus company and should not be included as a project benefit; the balance, $27,500, does represent a real resource saving. This is exactly the benefit of the project.

A second way to arrive at this figure is to focus on just the real resource changes. In this example 100,000 riders are taken more cheaply—the saving in resources here is (100,000) ($.40 − .25) = $15,000. Then another 100,000 rides are taken that were not before—the saving here is the excess of marginal benefits over marginal costs for these rides, or (½) (100,000) (.50 − .25) = $12,500. The sum of these two gains is just the $27,500 in project benefits we arrived at above. Note that in this latter calculation we again ignore the transfer between the bus company and consumers.

Of the various methods, it does not matter how one does the calculation. Probably the best idea is to do the calculation all three ways to see if you get consistent answers. If you do not, something is wrong.

Almost every aspect of this problem is highly oversimplified, and to give more operational guidance we must track down a host of complicating features. To begin with, the example deals with only one market in a full general equilibrium system. If the subway fare is lowered, this may change commuting patterns enough to alter prices and quantities in some other markets, which alterations could yield secondary gains and losses of producer and consumer surplus in those other markets.

It can be shown that these secondary gains and losses come about only if demands or supplies are changed enough to alter prices in secondary markets. If there are no taxes, these secondary market changes will in general result in additional costs. If there are taxes, the situation becomes more unpredictable, but typically a drop in output generates additional costs while an increase in output generates additional gains. All of these matters are treated in the appendix to this chapter.

A second difficulty refers to problems of inferring the sensitivity of the number of rides to changes in the toll. Typically, only a few points on the demand curve will be known from real data, and it may be necessary to extrapolate well outside the range of these points to estimate the number of rides were the subway to be built. These estimates will be the more arbitrary and unreliable the greater the extrapolation. In our example, the two observed points were for a toll of $.50 and $.40, respectively, and rides of 100,000 and 140,000. If the demand curve fitting these points were linear, as shown by the solid line in Figure 5.1, area E correctly measures the remaining consumer surplus to be gained on the new rides. But another common assumption is that the demand curve has a constant *elasticity,* or is expressed in constant percentage changes. Recalling that the elasticity is the percentage change in quantity consumed divided by the percentage change in the toll, and computing these percentage changes from the formula for the arc elasticity,[1] we have

$$\eta = \frac{\Delta \text{ rides}}{.5(\text{old rides + new rides})} \div \frac{\Delta \text{ toll}}{.5(\text{old toll + new toll})}$$

$$= \frac{40,000}{.5(100,000 + 140,000)} \div \frac{.10}{.5(.50 + .40)} = 1.5$$

where η is the arc elasticity of demand with respect to changes in the toll. This elasticity of demand between the two observed points comes out to 1.5—for every 10 percent change in the toll, the number of rides changes by 15 percent. We can then find ridership for the $.25 subway toll by plugging in this formula, now solving for Δ rides using the assumption that $\eta = 1.5$ (remember that new rides = old rides plus Δ rides):

$$\eta = 1.5 = \frac{\Delta \text{ rides}}{.5(\text{old rides + old rides} + \Delta \text{ rides})} \div \frac{\Delta \text{ toll}}{.5(\text{old toll + new toll})}$$

$$1.5 = \frac{\Delta \text{ rides}}{.5(200,000 + \Delta \text{ rides})} \div \frac{.25}{.5(.50 + .25)}$$

Δ rides $= 200,000$, so new rides $= 300,000$.

Under this proportional, or constant elasticity assumption, the change in rides between a toll of $.40 and that of $.25 grows from the 60,000 in Figure 5.1 to 160,000, as shown by the dashed line in Figure 5.1. The area of triangle E then grows from ($\frac{1}{2}$) (60,000) ($.15) = $4500 to approximately ($\frac{1}{2}$) (160,000) ($.15) = $12,000, and this difference of approximately $7500 should be added to the program benefits.[2]

This problem may appear an idle one but in fact can become quite important. As the changes in the toll get larger and larger, the difference in the consumer surplus area computed under the two assumptions does also, and the benefits of the government program could differ by a large and growing amount, a difficulty made all the more serious because there is little reason for choosing one assumption over the other.[3] The only sensible thing to do in a case like this is to compute benefits both ways, using the linear and the constant elasticity assumption, see how great the difference is, and see if that makes a difference in the evaluation results. In our case here, the linear assumption gives the smallest program benefits, $27,500, whereas the constant elasticity assumption gives benefits of $27,500 + $7500 = $35,000. Should the subway's actual cost be less than $27,500, we can be sure that its net benefits are positive; should it cost more than $35,000, we know that net benefits are negative; and should its annual cost lie between $27,500 and $35,000, we honestly cannot tell unless we have more information about the shape of the demand curve.

A final complication involves the difference between consumer and producer goods. Often, a government investment project of this sort will not make benefits directly available to consumers, as does our subway, but to producers. Examples might be an investment in energy supplies or a dam that provides cheaper irrigation of farmland. The relevant notion of a demand curve in this case is not the consumers' final demand for the product, but the producers' derived demand for the factor of production. If the price of this factor is constant, the benefit of this activity is just the price, or market value, of output (as it would be on the cost side if the same resource were used up in the activity). If the price of the factor is lowered, benefits will accrue to firms using these factors of production in the same way that lower consumer prices entail consumer surplus gains for households. These added social benefits for firms will then either be passed along to the ultimate consumers of the firms' output or accrue to the stockholders of the firm. Simply looking at the firm's derived demand curve for the factor is sufficient to include all the benefits in this case: this derived demand should measure the total valuation of the factor, including all sources of profit or gains to ultimate consumers, and regardless of how many stages of production the factor will pass through before it becomes a final consumer good.[4] Since more stages of production are involved in this case, there is perhaps a greater likelihood of induced changes in other markets, particularly if these cheaper factor supplies increase the degree of competition in some market. Moreover, were we not operating under the Kaldor–Hicks distributionally neutral standard, the evaluation would be much more complicated when the output of a government activity is a producer good, because it would then be necessary to compute the split of gains between final consumers and producers.

MARKET PRICES EXIST BUT DO NOT REPRESENT SOCIAL VALUES

We turn now to problems that arise in valuing benefits and costs when, for some social reason, we do not choose to believe market prices. Normally, market prices will determine the social value of either resources created or resources used up by the project, and will be sufficient to determine overall net benefits. But there are some cases for which that is not so. Let us say, for example, that the materials for building our subway are supplied in a monopolistic market where the price paid by the subway authority is substantially more than the true social cost of supplying these materials. Do market prices and the budget costs on which they are based overstate the true social cost of using the resources, and if so, by how much?

Before going through the analysis, we can make an intuitive argument that it all depends on whether or not the increased demand for materials raises their output. If not, then the output of the materials monopolist is constant, profits are constant, and the entire price goes to buy resources and must be counted as a cost of the project. If there is an increase in market output, the materials monopolist presumably makes *more* profits. Part of the price is then simply transferred to the monopolist and then should not count as a resource cost borne by the whole society. As in finding net benefits in the first place, note that we must again distinguish those budget expenditures that reflect resources given up to produce subway materials—which are a true cost because the resources cannot be devoted to some other consumption use—from those expenditures that are simply transferred from one group to another group and do not lower aggregate social consumption possibilities.

The general case can be analyzed with the aid of Figure 5.2. Drawn on the diagram are the demand curve for materials with and without the subway, the marginal cost curve, and, above that, the market supply with monopoly profits included. Before the subway, the market reaches an equilibrium where the quantity of materials sold is Q_1, the price is P_1, and marginal costs are P_0—hence monopoly profits on the marginal unit are given by the distance $P_1 - P_0$.[5] The subway then shifts the demand curve in a parallel fashion, yielding a new equilibrium at a quantity of Q_2, of which private demand is Q_3 and subway demand is $Q_2 - Q_3$. The higher demand drives up the market price to P_2 and marginal cost

FIGURE 5.2   Cost of Resources Used in the Urbania Subway

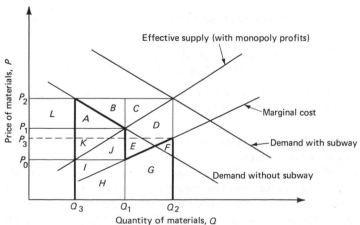

to P_3. The budget expenditures of the subway authority are the market price P_2 times the amount bought, $Q_2 - Q_3$. The evaluation question is whether this amount should be viewed as the resource cost of the project—the cost of resources given up that can now no longer be used to provide for the consumption of members of the society.

We can compute the true social costs in this sense by adding up costs to taxpayers and to private consumers of materials, and then subtracting any gains realized by suppliers of these materials. Budget costs to taxpayers in Figure 5.2 can be represented by the sum of areas A through K. The cost to existing consumers can be represented by the loss of their consumer surplus as the price rises from P_1 to P_2, or area A plus area L.[6] The gain to producers is then the increase in producer's surplus due to the rise in price, areas L plus A plus B, plus the *added* monopoly profits due to differences between prices and costs on the expanded output, areas C, D, and E. The net social cost of the materials supplied is given by adding and subtracting as follows:

	Cost to taxpayers:	$A+B+C+D+E+F+G+H+I+J+K$	
	Cost to consumers:	$A+$	$+L$
Less:	Gain of producers:	$-A-B-C-D-E$	$-L$
	Net social cost:	A $\qquad\qquad$ $+F+G+H+I+J+K$	

Instead of being the budget cost rectangle given by P_2 and $Q_2 - Q_3$, the social cost of materials supplied is the strange geometric shape denoted by the solid bold line on Figure 5.2. This social cost can be thought of as the sum of the cost of providing the government output $(H + G + F)$ and the additional deadweight loss occasioned by the fact that private sales between Q_1 and Q_3 are not taking place $(A + I + J + K)$. The cost can be expressed in more condensed form by defining, for linear demand and supply curves, the following quantities:

Average market price over the interval:	$P = \tfrac{1}{2}(P_1 + P_2)$
Average marginal cost over the interval:	$MC = \tfrac{1}{2}(P_0 + P_3)$
Proportion of quantity purchased representing expansion of total demand:	$q = \dfrac{Q_2 - Q_1}{Q_2 - Q_3}$
Proportion of quantity purchased representing displacement of private demand:	$1-q = \dfrac{Q_1 - Q_3}{Q_2 - Q_3}$

With the aid of these definitions, the true social cost of materials used in the subway can be written as $(Q_2 - Q_3) [(1 - q)P + q MC]$, clearly less than the budget cost of $(Q_2 - Q_3)P_2$. The expression in brackets is sometimes known as the "shadow price" of the materials, their true economic price. The intuition for this expression is that when the added demand of the subway adds to market demand by the fraction q, the social cost is only the marginal cost, averaged over the range Q_1 to Q_2.[7] Taxpayers pay more, but the monopoly profits represent a simple transfer and do not reduce the resources devoted to society's consumption. (Remember: we are here *not* worried about the distributional equity or value of this transfer.) But when the expansion of demand raises the price of materials and displaces existing private demand, there is no transfer—monopolists had these profits anyway—and social costs are essentially budget costs. In the case we are considering, say that the subway cost is $30,000 and half of its annual expenses, $15,000, are to be spent on materials. If virtually all of these expenditures displaced private consumption, the expansion proportion q would be close to zero and per unit social costs would equal P over the range, almost as great as the per unit budget cost of P_2 (apart from the tiny area B). In this case the true social cost of the subway would be just slightly less than $30,000. But at the other extreme, if virtually all of these expenditures added to the private consumption of materials, the expansion proportion q would be close to 1 and the per unit social cost would be approximately MC—less than P_2 because the sizable gain of monopolists is netted out. If MC were half of P_2, the social cost of materials falls from $15,000 to $7500, total costs of the subway are now $22,500 and the former conclusion that benefits of the subway did not equal its social costs is altered. Before, when the total benefits of the subway were valued at $27,500, net benefits were negative and the subway should not have been built. But if there is a monopoly in the materials market, net benefits are positive and the subway should be built.

A more complex issue arises in cases where the difference between the supply and the marginal cost curves are not due to monopolistic imperfections in the materials markets but to government-imposed excise taxes. If the taxes do not reflect social external costs, the analytical principles are the same as before, as is the social cost expression developed above. The only difference is that now most of the "monopoly profits" go to the government and are presumably netted directly against budget costs: taxpayers pay out this portion of their budget costs but they get it right back. If on the other hand, taxes do reflect social external costs, the market supply is the true supply and the per unit budget cost of P_2 is also the proper measure of social costs. In this case there would be no reduction of costs, even for the expansion percentage.

Unemployed Labor

A special circumstance in which these lessons might be applied is in valuing the services of laborers who, before the project, were unemployed. This issue becomes extremely important in practice when it is observed that, on average, about five-sixths of the costs of government programs involve direct or indirect compensation of employees.[8] If the gain in jobs can be counted as a benefit of the program or used to reduce budget costs in the manner described above, a great many more programs will pass the benefit-cost test than would otherwise be the case. Indeed, one often hears members of Congress justifying very marginal programs on the grounds that they would "create jobs." In this section we show how this jobs issue should be dealt with in a benefit-cost framework, bringing in not only a microeconomic analysis of unemployment but also the macroeconomic aspects of the unemployment problem.

A depiction of the microeconomic side of the unemployment problem is given in Figure 5.3. Before the subway is built, demand for a certain skill class of labor is given by the curve indicated, as is supply. But for some reason the labor market does not reach a full-employment equilibrium in this preexisting state. The market-clearing wage would be W_1, yielding a quantity of demand and supply of labor of L_1 persons. But let us assume that there is a minimum wage set at W_2 and operating in this market. This prevents the wage from falling to W_1; indeed, it fixes the wage at W_2, where L_2 workers apply for jobs but only L_3 are employed, leaving initial unemployment in the amount $L_2 - L_3$. Minimum wages are the easiest cause of unemployment to see but far from the only cause in real life. Other such causes might be union contracts or simply some aspects of the behavior of workers: if market wages are low relative to what workers think they should be on the basis of past history or other wages in the economy, workers will spend a lot of their labor market time unemployed and searching for jobs rather than taking this low-paying job. Hence we tend to observe labor markets in which wages are higher than they should be to clear the market, unemployment exists, and changes in unemployment are generated primarily by fluctuations in demand.[9]

In any case, we do observe unemployment in the amount of $L_2 - L_3$ existing in this market, and when we build our subway, we hire $L_4 - L_3$ of these workers, leaving $L_2 - L_4$ of them still unemployed. The budget cost of these

FIGURE 5.3 Social Cost of Unemployed Labor from a Micro-economic Perspective

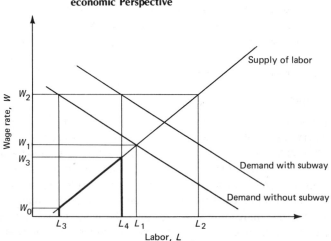

workers is the wage W_2 times their quantity, $L_4 - L_3$. What is the social cost or shadow price?

We might first try to apply the rule developed above. Since there is no increase in the actual wage rate W_2, the displacement percentage is zero and q in the above formula is 1. The social cost of this labor then appears to become $(L_4 - L_3)$MC, or taking MC from the supply curve, $\frac{1}{2}(L_4 - L_3) (W_3 + W_0)$, the bold-lined area in Figure 5.3. But be careful; it may not be that, for several reasons.

The first reason deals with a basic matter of how demand and supply curves are to be interpreted. When a supply curve is drawn with an upward slope, as this one is, there is an underlying assumption that successively higher wage levels are necessary to tempt workers into supplying their labor. So we tend to think of the portion of workers up to L_3 as working before the government boosted employment demand and those in the range $L_4 - L_3$ and as working once the government boosted employment demand, with those in the range $L_2 - L_4$ continuing in unemployment. But when the high wage results from an institutional rigidity such as minimum wages and there is not one monopolistic seller of output but many sellers of labor services, there is no reason why this result must hold. All workers up to L_2 would have worked before the government boosted demand, and all would have worked after the government boosted demand—the wage of W_2 was high enough to tempt these workers in either case. So it may make more sense to say that the jobs represented by the employment increase are allocated *at random* to the entire work force up to L_2, in which case the true social cost of these jobs is the number of workers employed $(L_4 - L_3)$ times the average social cost over the entire range up to L_2, say W_3. In this case the social cost appears to be increased by this randomization assumption, but we could draw other cases for which it would be lowered.[10]

But even apart from this microeconomic reasoning, both political conservatives and liberals would have reason to question our calculation of the true social cost of labor. Conservatives typically do not like to see new spending projects such as this subway, and they would be opposed to any evaluation assumptions which they feel might reduce the social costs of projects to an unwarranted degree. Their specific complaint in this analysis is that the marginal cost of labor is taken from labor's supply curve, as if this supply curve reflected labor's opportunity cost of leisure time. But, they argue, how can you use labor's supply curve in valuing leisure time when labor itself does not use it to drive down the preexisting wage? For whatever the reason, they argue that labor actually moves along a supply curve given in this diagram by the horizontal wage line at W_2, that this is the wage that should be used in valuing labor's services according to labor's own behavior, and that this indicates that the social cost of this labor is *equal to* its budget cost.

Liberals could be just as unhappy about using the supply of labor as an indicator of the marginal cost in the above formula; they might think it *over-*

states the true social cost of using this unemployed labor. Their argument is a simple one based on externalities: it is just bad for people not to have a job in a society where most other people are working. The unemployed lose self-respect, their working skills atrophy, and their work habits degenerate. In this social sense liberals see *no* social value to unemployment, they view the MC term in the formula as zero or even negative—they are willing to pass costly public employment programs just to employ workers—and they would think that the true social cost of hiring these unemployed workers is also zero or negative. As a factual matter, it should be pointed out that a careful analysis of the unemployment problem would presumably temper the argument somewhat, even to liberals. The argument clearly works best for the standard case of an unemployed parent in a two-parent family, where the time spent home or not working does not have any obvious and overwhelming social value. But, in fact, in a typical year of reasonably high employment, only about half of the total number of unemployed workers fall in this category: the remainder are teenagers, who might be going to school or doing something productive while unemployed, or parents in single-parent families, who might have important child-rearing responsibilities. In the latter cases, the argument that the alternative use of time has *no* social value may not be correct, and it may well be appropriate to attach a value to the cost of leisure forgone.[11]

Before even attempting to choose between these arguments, we must introduce two more complicating factors, both of which require some understanding of the macroeconomics of unemployment. The first is that unemployment, like death and taxes, will probably always be with us—a certain amount is necessary to prevent price inflation from accelerating. The second is that above some inevitable unemployment necessary to fight inflation, further unemployment can be avoided through appropriate stabilization of aggregate demand by monetary and fiscal policy. To see how these facts influence our treatment of unemployed labor in an evaluation, we make a short digression into the macroeconomic theory of unemployment.[12]

The standard macroeconomic view of the determination of unemployment suggests that government manipulation of overall spending, by changing its own spending, altering private spending through tax changes, or altering interest rates and private investment, will alter the overall demand for goods and for labor to produce those goods. When the economy is stimulated, the demand for labor increases and unemployment is lowered; when the economy contracts, demand for labor falls and unemployment rises.

From this simple discussion it would always appear wise to stimulate the economy to keep unemployment as low as possible. This is true on the downward side of a business cycle when recession threatens, but not on the upward side, when capacity constraints are impeding the economy's ability to supply this demand. The capacity of the economy to produce is limited by the available supply of capital goods and labor, and as output is stimulated beyond these limits, the economy runs into the situation of "too much money chasing too few goods." Firms cannot respond to the excess demand by producing more, but they can respond by raising prices. Workers cannot respond to the high level of job vacancies by working more, but they can respond by raising wages. Both prices and wages rise, this forces other prices and wages to rise, and inflation is generated. Holding other things constant, as aggregate demand increases and unemployment falls, rates of inflation also increase; as demand decreases and unemployment rises, rates of inflation are reduced.

This inverse relationship between inflation and unemployment was first measured by an Australian economist, A. W. Phillips.[13] In the short run it set up what came to be known as a "cruel choice," a trade-off between unemployment and inflation. Macro policymakers could aim policy so as to keep unemployment high and inflation low, or they could go to the other extreme where unemployment is low and inflation is high, but they could not simultaneously achieve *both* low unemployment and price stability. In this sense the macro policies followed in the United States in the late 1950s generally aimed at reducing inflation rates, even if unemployment was high, whereas those in the late 1960s aimed at reducing unemployment rates even if inflation was high.

The choice may have been cruel, but at least it existed in the basic Phillips curve model. An important theoretical refinement added by Milton Friedman and Edmund Phelps in the late 1960s suggested that even this view was optimistic: no choice at all existed about unemployment, but macro policy must aim toward what is known by conservatives as the "natural rate," or by liberals as the "nonaccelerating inflation rate" of unemployment.[14] The refinement was to make expectations about inflation itself a variable and to use those variable expectations to derive a long-term trade-off curve, which really is not a curve at all but a fixed line identifying something called the natural rate of unemployment.

Both the Phillips argument and the Friedman–Phelps refinement are illustrated in Figure 5.4, which shows the trade-off between inflation and unemployment in both the short and the long run. The solid downward-sloping curve is the short-run Phillips curve, showing the apparent trade-off between inflation ($\Delta P/P$, where P is an index of the overall price level) and unemployment (U). Say that in year 1 the economy has an inflation rate of zero and an unemployment rate of U^*, which will turn out to be the natural or nonaccelerating inflation unemployment rate. In year 2 there is an attempt to reduce unemployment, perhaps by a subway-building public works program, which moves the unemployment rate to U_2, indicated by point 2 on the trade-off curve. This program raises aggregate demand for both goods and labor, making it easier for firms to raise prices and workers to raise wages. The rate of inflation increases to $(\Delta P/P)_2$, higher than the rate in the initial period. The process may take a short or a long time, but eventually workers realize that prices are rising *more* rapidly than before and they insist on inflation protection in their wage contracts. If they

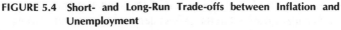

FIGURE 5.4 **Short- and Long-Run Trade-offs between Inflation and Unemployment**

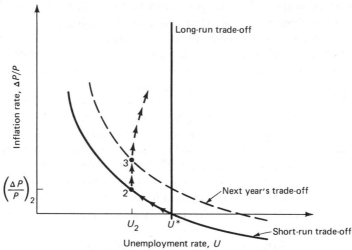

would have settled for a wage increase of 2 percent when prices were expected to be stable, they will insist on 5 percent when prices are expected to rise at a 3 percent rate. The Friedman–Phelps argument is that ultimately this policy change will generate a permanent upward shift in the Phillips trade-off, to the dashed line. Should macro policy try to preserve the low unemployment rate U_2, inflation rates will again be higher than anticipated and the curve will shift again. In the long run a policy of maintaining a low unemployment rate such as U_2 will generate a path shown by the arrows, which in the limit converges to the vertical (nonexisting) trade-off curve shown. Inducing a little bit of inflation is like inducing a little bit of pregnancy.

The relevance of this story for macroeconomic policy is obvious: policymakers can attempt to reduce the variance of U around U^*, but they cannot conduct a permanent policy of maintaining unemployment less than U^*. In this sense U^* is a natural rate of unemployment. (For the United States this natural rate is estimated to be about 6 percent in the late 1970s.[15]) The relevance to evaluation and valuing the services of unemployed resources is more subtle but just as important. If a project aims at reducing unemployment below U^*, this reduction in unemployment must be sustained for it to count as a benefit of the project. It makes no sense to include it if it is simply offset by a hidden increase in unemployment somewhere else to take the inflationary winds out of the system.

On the other side, when unemployment rates are above U^*, reductions in unemployment can surely be sustained, but the evaluation question changes to one of whether this project *caused* the reductions. In this range either monetary or fiscal policy or the long-term flexibility of prices might have reduced unemployment even without the program. Should this happen, the program is not causing the drop in unemployment, and lower unemployment should only be counted as a benefit of the project for the short term period where the project is actually reducing unemployment below what it otherwise would have been.

This elaborate story can be summarized by a set of rules for valuing the services of unemployed labor. The evaluator is permitted to value unemployed labor at less than its market and budget cost if:

1. The reduction in unemployment can be sustained. Inflationary pressures will not be set up which require other cutbacks in spending demand, generating corresponding increases in unemployment somewhere else in the economy.

2. The project is responsible for reducing unemployment. Tax reductions, monetary policy, or price flexibility would not have done so anyway.

3. It can be persuasively argued that the supply curve or some other notion of social externality makes the opportunity cost *below* the market wage W_2 (in Figure 5.3).

When all three of these conditions are satisfied, the drop in unemployment can be considered a lasting social gain, and some wage rate below W_2 in Figure 5.3 can be used. In practice, these conditions *will* occasionally be met—say when the subway is built using unskilled labor that probably would not be employed following a general tax cut, where expansions of demand do not generate inflation and where the unemployment of the parent does not appear to yield a more productive home life for the children. But there will probably be many more cases where the conditions will not all be met—where the subway uses skilled labor and generates inflation-producing job vacancies in the private sector, where the subway boosts the wages of a certain group and generates pressure for catchup increases of other groups, or where time spent unemployed does have alternative value to the worker and his or her family. In such cases the pressures for programs because they create jobs, even if generated by congressional debates (see Chapter 8), must be resisted. Either they do not really create jobs, they are not the only way to create jobs, or the jobs do not have that much social value.

Scarce Foreign Exchange

We just finished talking about a case in which the evaluator might want to value labor services below their market price. Are there any cases where it might be appropriate to value a commodity *above* its market price?

One such case is foreign exchange. Many countries, notably including the United States, have persistent deficits in their international balance of payments. When exchange rates are flexible, as they have been throughout most of the world since 1973, this presents no particular problem: at any moment foreign exchange speculation drives the value of the dollar relative to foreign currencies

FIGURE 5.5   Demand and Supply of Foreign Currency

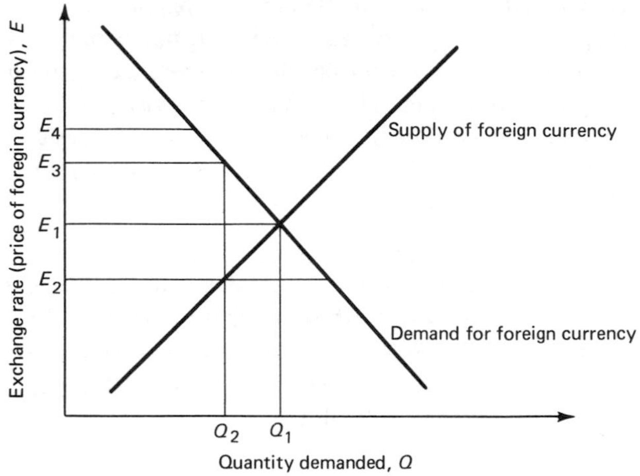

to the exchange rate that speculators figure will continue. This exchange rate then sets the true social price of foreign currency, and as long as all imports are valued at this exchange rate, their true social cost is being reflected.

But when exchange rates are fixed, as they were before 1973 and are now in some countries through government intervention in currency markets, problems can develop. Say that the dollar is overvalued, or that the price of foreign currency in Figure 5.5 is held below the equilibrium exchange rate E_1. At this official exchange rate E_2, there would be excess demand for foreign currency to finance the balance-of-payments deficit. Assume that this excess demand were arbitrarily eliminated by a scheme for rationing available foreign exchange at the level Q_2, with import rights sold so that only those imports with a social value higher than E_3 would be bought. At the margin, the shadow price of foreign currency is then E_3, and imports and exports should be valued at this rate. If, on the other hand, ration tickets were randomly allocated to all importers willing to pay more than E_2, the marginal value of imports becomes the average E value above E_2, or E_4. The reasoning here is exactly the same as in the unemployment case above. Finally, were this excess demand not to be eliminated and the deficit to persist, the relevant shadow price becomes harder to figure. It might be reasonable to assume that ultimately the payments imbalance will have to be corrected, say by an exchange rate of E_1, and that this should be the standard used in valuing imports and exports.[16]

MARKETS DO NOT EXIST

The range of benefits and costs conferred by government activities is by no means confined to those goods and services that are traded in the market. Projects may cause risk of a loss of life or improve safety, they may save or use time, they may pollute the atmosphere or generate noise and congestion. The gains and losses from such occurrences are real, even if they are difficult to measure. To ignore them in an evaluation would bias it seriously. Hence in this section we review some of the techniques that have been developed for measuring such nonmarket benefits and costs. These include household surveys, careful observation of how people respond to similar situations, and measuring changes in property values. Each of these techniques might prove useful in valuing benefits and costs.

Loss of Life

By all odds the most fundamental issue is to deal with changes in the probability of death. This could go up or down with a project—resources devoted to auto safety and road building can lower the probability of death; construction of our subway and the concomitant risk that streets will cave in can raise it. One might feel that evaluators should not even try to value human life as part of the gains and losses of a project, but that makes no more sense than for the ostrich to put its head in the sand. Surely changes in death probabilities cannot be ignored in any evaluation; if they were, no money would be spent on auto safety or cancer research. But society cannot, unfortunately, operate as if the value of saving a life is infinite either, for then an infinite amount of money would be spent on auto safety and cancer research, skyscrapers and tunnels would never be built, and so forth. For better or worse, society must choose some middle ground—human lives are very valuable, but not infinitely valuable—and this middle ground requires that choices must be made. The presumption here is that, macabre as it may seem, these choices should be faced up to and made in as sensible and consistent a manner as is possible.

Essentially two approaches have been used in valuing human lives, the discounted future earnings (DFE) approach and the required compensation (RC) approach. DFE, often used in current evaluations and lawsuits, involves simple addition of all prospective discounted future earnings of the deceased or the person who might become deceased.[17] The assumption appears to be to let the market indicate how valuable the person is.

Except that it is the wrong market. Problems with the DFE approach begin appearing as soon as it is suggested. To begin with, the "market" is only that for the productive services of the person. If the person has a low wage rate but really enjoys life, his or her loss will entail little cost from a DFE standpoint but much more from a broader social welfare standpoint. If the person is already retired, there will be no loss from a DFE standpoint, but again much from a broader social welfare standpoint. If labor market discrimination establishes lower wage rates for women and blacks, the DFE standard will say that their life is also less valuable—a proposition that even the most confirmed sexists and racists might feel uneasy about. There seems little point in taking the DFE approach as a serious guide to social policy.

But there is a market valuation concept that comes closer to establishing what, from a social point of view, might be a reasonable approximation to the value of a human life, the RC standard. According to RC, we should not let the imperfect market for your services value your life, as is done by DFE, but let *you* value it.[18] The difference is precisely the same as the difference between the market price (valuation by others of a good you consume) and the demand curve (your valuation or willingness to pay for the same good). Looking at the market price ignores consumer surplus, and looking at DFE ignores all the added utility you and your family gain from your life. In a practical application, if our subway involved construction risks, these risks would be explained to workers, who have the option to work in the subway or not. To the extent that they were bothered by the risks, they could bid up their asking wage to a level high enough to compensate them for their increased probability of death. The workers are free to use whatever standard they want in insisting on this wage rate. They can insist on a level that compensates them for the value of their potential loss of leisure time, the problems faced by their family, and so forth. This self-assessed value of their leisure time then must be paid by the subway authority to get the subway built and it is automatically built right into the benefit-cost calculation for the subway.[19]

However skeptically one views this market attempt to value human lives, it is clear that the logical basis for the RC standard is far superior to that for the DFE standard. Empirically, it also turns out that the RC standard leads to effective values of human lives much higher than those found by the DFE standard, as we should hope if people enjoy their lives.[20] But it is still true that the market may not always give the right signal, and several problems remain even with the RC standard:

1. Do the workers have good information about the probability of death? If, for some reason, workers do not know that the city streets may cave in when they are laying subway track, they can hardly be expected to bid up their wage and the cost of the project an appropriate amount.

2. Do the workers have alternative job opportunities? If there are no jobs in town but working on the subway, wages will not be bid up appropriately and the riskiness of the jobs will not show up in the benefit-cost calculations for the subway. The most dramatic historical example where this assumption has not been met is coal mining, a very risky occupation that has not been high-paying presumably because the workers had few alternative job opportunities.

3. Do the workers represent the interest of all who want them to keep living? When a person dies, losses accrue to all who either depend on the person or value their interactions with the person. Does the worker really charge for all these possible losses in bidding up his or her wage? Probably not, and if not, the cost of the subway is understated.

4. Are the workers' tastes representative? Let us say that there are 100 daredevils in town who are happy to work in risky jobs with *no* added compensation.

Perhaps (subject to the qualifications above) for the subway we would not change the benefit-cost calculation, because the lives at risk are those of the daredevils. But often, these compensating differentials are used to impute values for lives of other people affected by other programs. Would it follow that because we had daredevils to work in the subway, no benefits are conferred by safer roads? Certainly not.

5. Are the risks voluntary or involuntary? People appear to behave in an asymmetric manner toward risk: they will hang glide for free, but demand an enormous premium to ride an airline with a poor safety record. Apparently people are more willing to forego safety for voluntary than involuntary activities. If this is so, we must be careful that wage premiums properly measure the type of risk actually borne. If workers gain special thrills from working at great heights, the RC approach may yield only the compensation for voluntary risk, which might be below the compensation required by nearby homeowners who want to be compensated for the fact that their houses might be caved in by the subway.[21]

6. Is this RC value general or specific? Continuing with our example, let us say that instead of deciding the fate of X unknown persons who will suffer from lung cancer, we are confronted with the question of whether society should take a costly step, such as providing a kidney machine to save the life of a specifically identified individual, John Jones. The logic of this section suggests that the group that should value the lives is just the group whose lives are at issue. In this case, therefore, John Jones and only John Jones should value his own life. Because of the relative certainty of his death without the kidney machine, John Jones, and by proxy the society that he is a part of, will then value his own life much more highly than would the general RC standard for unknown but similar members of society. What decision rule can be substituted for the RC standard is, of course, a deep mystery raising basic ethical and moral issues that will not be conjectured about here, beyond pointing out that the relevant information cannot be supplied by our RC standard.[22]

To distill from all of this a pragmatic guide for policy action becomes rather difficult, but a few principles can be gleaned. It appears first that the DFE standard is relevant for almost no serious question—at a minimum, society must make an attempt to use the RC standard so as to let the persons involved tell how much their own life is worth. Second, there is a vast difference between the probability of death involving unknown and known individuals—standard evaluation principles might be helpful in the former case but certainly are not in the latter. Further, since taste differences are presumably strong in this area, one must be leery about making inferences across individuals, such as when cancer research is valued in terms of subway worker wage differentials. These wage differentials might be the only available information, but they should be recognized as a poor proxy for the type of information really needed. Finally, even when the RC standard can be used as a standard, the defects of the market should be recognized. A prudent procedure might be for the evaluator to assume that market wage differentials cannot possibly deal with all of the externalities associated with the loss of a life, and to raise costs or benefits an extra amount not justified by the RC standard when human lives are involved.

Time Saving

Another nonmarket item involves the saving of people's time. Very often public projects have as an important benefit the simple saving of time of commuters, weekend travelers, and so forth. Saving of time has been probably the most important benefit of railroads, airports, the interstate highway system, and perhaps even of our subway. How should such time saving be valued?

A natural way to value such time saving, following the logic of the willingness-to-pay approach, is to find people's utility judgments about how much their own time is worth. One area in which people make such judgments is in the labor market, where at least some workers balance their subjective valuation of leisure time against their subjective valuation of the additional material goods they could buy if they worked an extra hour. At this margin, the after-tax wage rate (the wage people actually receive) would give the implicit marginal valuation of leisure time.

For many purposes the after-tax wage may be the best that can be done, but as with wage differentials in the preceding section, there are serious problems. A first problem is that the approach is applicable only if workers have the freedom to vary their hours. All those who are unemployed or cannot work as much as they would like at their wage are not even on their supply curve, and their wage will overestimate their value of leisure time. This is shown by the low demand curve of Figure 5.6. At the existing after-tax wage of W_1, L_1 hours are demanded of the worker. The true value of the worker's time at L_1, read from the supply curve, is W_0, well below the worker's wage of W_1. It might appear that this difficulty would arise only for unemployed workers, but in fact a great many people may not be on their supply curve—all those who cannot get overtime

FIGURE 5.6   Supply of Labor and the Value of Leisure Time

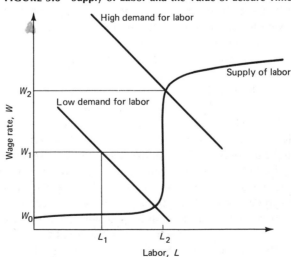

work, cannot find moonlighting work, or are consigned to involuntary part-time status.

A second problem is not so much a conceptual difficulty as an operational one. If the labor supply curve is sharply upward-sloping in the neighborhood of 40 hours a week, as many labor economists think it is, there exists a range where the supposed marginal valuation of leisure time is essentially set by the demand curve. In Figure 5.6, for any demand curve between the low and high values shown, the worker will work approximately L_2 hours a week, but the supposed valuation of leisure time will change between W_0 and W_2, even though neither the underlying taste for leisure or the hours worked have changed. In principle, the evaluator would be correct in calling any wage between W_0 and W_2 the true value of leisure time at the margin around L_2; the wage that actually exists is in some sense only a historical accident set by the demand for the workers' services. Picking some point in this range does not obviously bias up or down the valuation of time saved, but any estimates will be subject to a large margin of error.

A third problem involves the interpretation of the wage rate W. Following the logic of our RC standard for valuing lives, we might expect workers always to demand a higher premium for any kind of unpleasant work. If that is so, any observed wage rate will really represent a package of compensation for risk, unpleasantness, fringe benefits, working conditions, and the time loss. Disentangling the pure time effect from all the others is, to say the least, a Herculean task.

A fourth problem involves the implicit assumption that all hours of leisure time are perfect substitutes. The Urbania subway may save workers' time between 8 and 9 in the morning and 5 and 6 at night. People may feel differently about this time saved than they would feel about an interstate highway that reduces their travel time over long weekends: in the case of a commuting-time reduction, they may have less alternative use for the time than over a long weekend, and their wage at the margin may not be a terribly good proxy for either one.

Although, as before, the market valuation approach does convey some information, there are enough potential problems that it may make sense to come up with a more direct behavioral observation on how people value time saved. One possibility for our subway is by a simple observation of how commuters appear to behave when time is at stake.[23] Suppose that the commuters of Urbania have the option of driving to work or taking the bus. Cost expressions for each mode of transportation can be written as follows:

$$C_B = a_B + bT_B + M_B$$
$$C_A = a_A + bT_A + M_A$$

where C_B and C_A refer to the cost of commuting by bus and automobile, respectively; T_B and T_A refer to time spent; M_B and M_A refer to the monetary costs; and a_B and a_A are intercepts that give the intrinsic psychic costs of each mode of transportation. Notice that the role of the parameter b is to put time loss into dollar cost units: if we knew b, we could measure the respective costs and plug in values to give the benefits of the subway.

The time-value parameter, b, cannot be estimated directly, but it can be inferred by relating the probability of using either mode of transportation to relative costs, as in the expression

$$\log \left(\frac{P_B}{P_A} \right) = c \, \Delta C = c(a_B - a_A + b\Delta T + \Delta M)$$

where ΔC is defined as the cost of bus less that of auto and P_B and P_A refer to the probability of taking bus and auto, respectively.[24] The coefficient of the monetary cost in this regression is c, the impact of costs on usage. The coefficient of time is cb, and with knowledge of c from the money coefficient, the behavioral value of time, b, can be inferred. One use of such a methodology, by the Roskill Commission on the Third London Airport, found the effective cost of commuting time to be about half of the after-tax wage rate. Although the data may not be available to do this in all cases, it is a much more direct way to let people express their willingness to save commuting time than by simply looking at their after-tax wage rate.

Environmental and Recreational Benefits

Similar techniques exist for valuing environmental and recreational benefits. For programs that generate environmental benefits, such as sewage treatment plants or air quality regulations, several methods are commonly used. A direct market test involves using econometric analysis to explain housing values in regressions of the following sort:

$$H = a_0 + a_1 N + a_2 P + a_3 Z$$

where H is the annualized imputed income value of a house, N an index of urban noise and/or congestion, P an air quality index, and Z a set of independent factors. The aggregate benefits from a set of air quality regulations can be computed by altering P by the appropriate amount, using the valuation coefficient a_2 to convert this change in P to a change in average home value, and then multiplying by the number of homes. A similar procedure could be used to compute the benefits from a regulation or other factor (such as an airport) that would alter noise or congestion.[25] The advantages and disadvantages of this technique are much the same as before: market values provide a valuation of the impersonal market of the air you breathe but do not necessarily capture all of your consumer surplus value. Also, in certain cases the market may not possess all the information necessary to make a correct social judgment of the costs of air pollution.

Mentioning asset value changes raises a related problem that often occurs in benefit-cost analysis. Say that some governmental facility such as a subway or a highway alters the value of surrounding farmland. How is this change to be valued or included in the benefit-cost tally?

There is unfortunately no general answer, but there is a good principle to keep in mind. Changes in asset values are a useful way of measuring real changes, such as in air or water quality, but they are *not* themselves gains or losses. Hence, if no other adjustment for air quality change is to be made in the evaluation, the rise in the value of houses in the affected area can be used as a proxy. If some other adjustment is to be made, it would be double counting to include capital value changes. Moreover, if the road or subway causes shifts— some farmland is increased in value while other land declines in value—these capital value changes should again be ignored. The only general guidance is to think through exactly what the asset value changes represent, whether these impacts are included elsewhere, and whether or not the impacts represent real resource savings or gains or are simply transfers from within the district.[26]

Another willingness-to-pay type of technique for valuing recreational benefits or costs of physical investment projects is the travel cost method. As in the time-saving example discussed above, users' willingness to pay is estimated by including time and travel costs together with out-of-pocket costs, a demand curve is estimated, and the consumer surplus is estimated.[27] We defer discussion of this technique until Chapter 8, where we examine some specific applications of it for valuing environmental losses when wilderness areas are destroyed.

A somewhat different technique has been used to measure water quality improvement projects such as sewage treatment plants. Apart from direct lakefront property values, it may be difficult to measure the benefits of all who may value the restoration of a river or lake for swimming and boating. A straightforward technique for finding this missing information is simply to ask a sample of people in the surrounding territory how much they might use the river for swimming or boating, how much they would be willing to pay for such privileges, or how much cleaning up the river would be worth to them.[28] Such a technique avoids some of the problems of interpreting market outcomes, but it is not without its own problems. The information difficulty is no more easily solved with survey data: if people do not possess correct information about the social ills of pollution, they cannot establish the proper market prices, and they will not be able to answer questions correctly. Moreover, a whole new set of potential difficulties is introduced through the use of survey data. The most serious of these is that an answer to a survey is hypothetical. Unlike a market offer, people do not have to act on the basis of their answers, and the answers will undoubtedly not be thought through as carefully as if they directly involved dollar outlays.

UNCERTAINTY

A final problem involves the certainty with which a stream of benefits or costs will be realized. Planners in the Urbania Subway Authority know that the last two major urban subway systems (in San Francisco and Washington D.C.)

overran their budgets by a large amount. Will this happen here? They also realize that ridership projections and consumer surplus estimates are subject to a margin of error. How should they deal with this uncertainty?

The analysis of risk and uncertainty is based on the analysis of Milton Friedman and L. J. Savage in 1948.[29] Referring to Figure 5.7, assume that the solid line gives the utility of a level of household's income over some range. The slope of this line, known as the marginal utility of income (the gain in utility per dollar gain in income), declines as income rises if households satisfy progressively less high priority needs as their income rises. When income is low, most of it is devoted to the necessities of life: food, clothing, shelter, and television sets. As income rises, more and more income can be devoted to luxury goods, such as theater tickets and cross-country skis. Luxury goods are tough to do without, but not as tough as the necessities—hence utility does not increase at the same rate as income, and the slope, or marginal utility, declines.

We will conduct two experiments with this household. The first will be to give the household a certain income, $\overline{Y}$, and observe that its utility is set by $\overline{U}$ from the utility schedule. The second experiment involves a game of random chance. Say that a large share of the household's income comes from the stock market, and there is an equal probability that gains from stock will be high next year—so that family income is $1.5\overline{Y}$—or that the gains from stock will be very low—so that total family income will be $.5\overline{Y}$. The utility of the favorable outcome is given by U_1 and that of the unfavorable outcome by U_2, with their average $E(U)$ being the expected utility of the risky package to the household.[30] The vertical distance, $\overline{U} - E(U)$, gives the cost of stock market uncertainty to

FIGURE 5.7 Marginal Utility of Income and Cost of Uncertainty

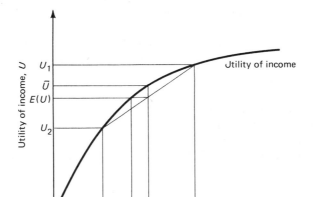

the household. It is positive because the loss due to an unfavorable outcome (some food must be sacrificed) is greater than the gain from a favorable outcome (additional theater tickets can be purchased). An alternative way of making the same point is that the household would willingly part with a certain amount of income $(\overline{Y} - Y_1)$ to gain income security. The household is, in effect, willing to pay up to $(\overline{Y} - Y_1)$ as a stock market insurance premium or to unload its stocks for a loss of up to this amount.

When this analysis is applied to evaluation, the magnitude of individual gains and losses becomes all important. We notice that if there were no decline in the slope of the utility curve, $\overline{U}$ would equal $E(U)$ and there would be no cost of uncertainty. Then the subway authority could just take the expected value of all costs and benefits, do the calculation, and not give uncertainty a thought. This is more likely to be true the smaller the income range being dealt with. If on the cost side the subway only involves a household tax of $10 per year, the range of income variation is small enough that cost overrun uncertainty can be safely ignored.[31] But on the benefit side the magnitude of gains and losses to families may very likely be larger. Homeowners along the routes may realize a large or small capital gain because of the subway, and find that it matters a great deal to their financial well-being. Commuters may be greatly affected by whether the subways are reliable, on time, free of crime, and so forth. Since these potential benefits to certain groups may be rather large, they may well be discounted through declining marginal utility considerations in the manner shown. Since individual variations in benefits are larger than for costs, the subway authority may quite properly use the uncertainty surrounding some of the projections of subway costs and benefits as a reason for adjusting the benefit-cost calculus in a negative direction.

SUMMARY

This lengthy chapter has tried to summarize the most important problems in valuing benefits and costs at the time of occurrence. One consistent message running through the chapter is that it is very difficult to make precise estimates of these benefits and costs. Difficulties abound with almost any procedure, and the evaluator seems to be left rudderless in a sea of complexities.

That would be overplaying it, however. No methodological technique is ever perfect in the social sciences, but that has not prevented striking advances from being made. By the same token, awareness of the many problems that exist in making benefit-cost valuations by no means prevents us from making good evaluations. Indeed, it helps. Being aware of the problems inherent in any technique is an important part of using the technique, of knowing when not to use it, and of knowing what aspects of the results to be leery of. Moreover, the discouraged evaluator should always remember that there is not much in the way of an alternative. It may seem hopeless to try to work through the impossible problems of valuing benefits and costs, but policy decisions must be made. If they are not made on the basis of objective analysis that makes the best possible estimates under the circumstances, they will be made on some other even more arbitrary and inconsistent basis. As long as more information and analysis is better than less, it will pay evaluators and government decisions makers to be as careful and systematic as they can be, difficult problems or not.

On a more operational level, perhaps the key notion in the chapter is a proper understanding of the role of markets and their implicit valuations in evaluation analysis. Market values do give an objective, impersonal guide to valuing benefits and costs, a task that would otherwise be quite difficult. But often markets do not work well or give the appropriate information, and adjustments in their values must be made. The chapter has shown how the existence of monopoly suppliers of output can overstate materials costs in a market, and how the existence of unemployment implies that labor costs can be overstated. It also has shown how market wage differentials can understate the value of a human life or the gains from a cleaner atmosphere, or overstate the value of time saved commuting. There is no general rule on whether one should or should not use market values—the choice must simply be made on a case-by-case basis, where the evaluator keeps clearly in mind what the market is indicating, on the one hand, and what unknown information is needed in the evaluation, on the other.

NOTES

[1]We use the formula for the arc elasticity because if this were not done, the computed elasticity would differ according to whether initial or subsequent quantities were used as the base in computing percentage changes. At the very least, this will not happen with arc elasticities.

[2]The new area of triangle E can only be approximated, because the constant elasticity demand curve is not linear but rather convex to the origin. Hence the area of the new triangle is slightly less than $12,000, as shown in the diagram. Those who know calculus can easily deal with this problem by finding the area described by the demand curve between 100,000 and 300,000 riders through the technique of integration.

[3]Another problem with this notion of consumer surplus is the one noted in Chapter 2. As prices fall and consumers are made better off, they can spend some of this added income on the good itself—hence overstating how much better off they would be at initial income levels as a result of the simple fall in prices.

[4]Peter Bohm analyzes a series of such cases in *Social Efficiency: A Concise Introduction to Welfare Economics* (New York: Macmillan, 1974), pp. 97–101.

[5]To spare the reader a bewildering mass of curves (the diagram is complicated enough already), the difference between the marginal cost and the market supply is not derived in Figure 5.2. That could be done by finding the marginal revenue curves consistent with the two demand curves, going to their intersection with the marginal cost curves (at Q_1 and Q_2, respectively) and then raising the price to P_1 and P_2, respectively.

[6]It may be wondered why we worry here only about the consumer surplus loss of existing consumers but not about any consumer surplus gains the government (or its taxpayers) may receive. The answer is that we do indeed worry about the government's consumer surplus—that is one of the important components of the benefits of the project, the magnitude these costs will be compared to. Many other illustrations of the use of the consumer surplus concept, including its definition when the price is not constant or when markets are interrelated, are given in Edward J. Mishan, *Cost-Benefit Analysis* (New York: Praeger, 1976), chaps. 7–9.

[7]See Richard Layard, Introduction, in Richard Layard, ed., *Cost-Benefit Analysis* (New York: Penguin, 1972) for a further description. Much of the material in this chapter follows Layard's very fine summary.

[8]Compensation of employees is two-thirds of the direct level of government spending, and even this is an underestimate of labor's importance, because much of the spending on materials and construction goes to employees at various steps in the line of supply.

[9]This paragraph is an inadequate attempt to summarize countless numbers of research papers on the question of why so much unemployment exists in the United States. A good paper on why unemployment is high in certain markets, even in times of so-called full employment, is by Robert E. Hall, ''Why Is the Unemployment Rate So High at Full Employment?'' *Brookings Papers on Economic Activity,* 3 (1970). A good paper on cyclical swings in unemployment comes from Martin S. Feldstein, ''The Importance of Temporary Layoffs: An Empirical Analysis,'' *Brookings Papers on Economic Activity,* 3 (1975).

[10]This point may not seem so difficult, but I am embarrassed to admit that I missed it on two separate first drafts of papers dealing with labor markets. The first time was in a paper on minimum wages, where the error was caught by Arthur Okun and corrected. The second time was in a draft for this manuscript, where my savior was Richard Porter. Recognition of the point is implicit in Porter's ''On the Optimal Size of Underpriced Facilities,'' *American Economic Review,* September 1977, pp. 753–760.

[11]Notice that none of these arguments have introduced the presence of unemployment insurance, which now covers about half of the workers who are unemployed. If a worker is eligible for unemployment insurance, his or her effective market supply curve of labor will be shifted up and to the left. This raises the value of MC read from the supply curve but should *not* persuade either the microeconomist, the conservative, or the liberal to use the altered MC in valuing social costs. The microeconomist remains unpersuaded because the MC curve before the unemployment compensation gives the true value of changes in leisure time; the shift only reflects the fact that taxpayers are sharing in the cost of unemployment. The conservative view is that social costs are W_2, just as before. The liberal view is that social costs depend on the underlying value of leisure time to workers or society—something not affected by unemployment insurance, which only transfers losses in labor income between unemployed workers and taxpayers.

[12]The macroeconomics cast of this discussion contrasts with the treatment in Robert H. Haveman, ''Evaluating Public Expenditures under Conditions of Unemployment,'' in Robert H. Haveman and Julius Margolis, *Public Expenditure and Policy Analysis*

(Skokie, Ill.: Rand McNally, 1977). There is no disagreement between my conclusions and those of Haveman: the point of this discussion is to clarify the meaning of workers who would "otherwise" be unemployed. Those who are acquainted with macroeconomics can skip this section without missing anything. For those who are not, more discussion is included than is probably necessary from a strict evaluation standpoint because the matter is so fundamentally important today.

[13]A. W. Phillips, "The Relation between Unemployment and the Rate of Change of Money Wage Rates in the United Kingdom, 1861–1957," *Economica,* November 1958.

[14]Milton Friedman, "The Role of Monetary Policy," *American Economic Review,* March 1968; and Edmund S. Phelps, "Phillips Curves, Expectations of Inflation, and Optimal Unemployment over Time," *Economica,* August 1967.

[15]Since the employment prospects of hundreds of thousands of workers depend on small variations in the estimated natural rate of unemployment, the question of exactly what it is takes on a good deal of importance. Given the obvious imperfections in economists' understanding of the inflation problem, it is rather difficult to make such a precise estimate, but many people have tried and 6 percent is very close to the median estimate. For those interested, a list of citations on this point is given in my "Macro Policy Responses to Price Shocks," *Brookings Papers on Economic Activity,* 1 (1979), pg. 136.

[16]I. M. D. Little and J. A. Mirrlees (*"Manual of Industrial Project Analysis in Developing Countries,"* in *Social Cost Benefit Analysis,* Development Center of the OECD, 1968) call for this valuation even if exchange controls are imposed. The presumption of Figure 5.5 is that the exchange controls put on by the country will be *validated* by pricing imports at E_3. They object to validating artificial impediments in such a way, and suggest that countries should use free international trading prices (E_1) as values for measuring benefits and costs. The issue boils down to one of whether the evaluator should accept or reject the exchange and trade restrictions.

[17]Future earnings are discounted by a factor related to the interest rate to account for the fact that current earnings could be invested to make still more money while future earnings cannot. This issue is the topic of Chapter 6.

[18]My required compensation standard is exactly what Steven E. Rhoads called the willingness-to-pay standard, in "How Much Should We Spend to Save a Life?" *Public Interest,* Spring 1978. I changed the semantic label because unless a person inherits wealth, he or she cannot possibly be willing to pay more than his or her discounted future earnings. Income sets an upper bound to willingness to pay, a bound that normally does not confuse the issue but this time clearly does. Another recent source is a book by M. W. Jones-Lee, *The Value of Life: An Economic Analysis* (London: Martin Robertson & Co., 1976), especially Chapters 4 and 5.

[19]This premium for lifesaving is built into the cost of the subway only for certain classes of transactions. If large holes in the ground increase the risk that a "whole" city will cave in, innocent homeowners may not be able to charge for this externality and it may not be built into costs. In this case, an extra premium should be added.

[20]Robert S. Smith [*The Occupational Safety and Health Act: Its Goals and Its Achievements* (Washington, D.C.: American Enterprise Institute for Public Policy Research, 1976), p. 30] reports that workers need to be compensated by 1.5 percent to accept a probability of death higher by 8/100,000 annually. Making a questionable extrapolation of this estimate over the zero to one range implies that a typical worker would require at least $1.5 million a year to be compensated for risking the statistical certainty of dying that year, 190 times the average wage entering the DFE calculation for the same worker. An earlier study by Sherwin Rosen and Richard Thaler came up with a value of about 20 times the DFE standard, in "The Value of Saving a Life: Evidence from the Labor Market," in

Nester Terleckyj, *Household Production and Consumption* (Cambridge, Mass.: National Bureau of Economic Research, 1975). A theoretical argument along these same lines is made by Theodore C. Bergstrom, ''Is a Man's Life Worth More than His Human Capital?'' University of Michigan Discussion Paper, Ann Arbor, Mich., 1978.

[21]For treatment of this point see, for example, Shaul Ben-David, Allen V. Kneese, and William D. Schulte, ''A Study of the Ethical Foundations of Benefit-Cost Analysis Techniques,'' University of New Mexico Discussion Papers, Albuquerque, N.M., 1979).

[22]The first writer to point out the difference between identified and unidentified, or ''statistical,'' lives was Thomas C. Schelling, ''The Life You Save May Be Your Own,'' in Samuel B. Chase, ed., *Problems in Public Expenditure Analysis* (Washington, D.C.: Brookings Institution, 1968). Schelling's point was even stronger than the one made here, because he argued that the valuation of John Jones's saved life by *other* members of society would also increase when information about the identity of the individual became known. A recent paper that used these ideas to deal with questions of optimal health insurance coverage is one by William Gould and Richard Thaler, ''Public Policy toward Life Saving: Maximize Lives Saved vs. Consumer Sovereignty,'' Mimeo, Cornell University, Ithaca, N.Y., 1979.

[23]An example of this commonly used technique can be found in A. D. J. Flowerdew, ''Choosing a Site for the Third London Airport: The Roskill Commission's Approach,'' in Layard, *Cost-Benefit Analysis*. The specific symbols were taken from Layard's introduction. Other examples will be used in Chapter 8.

[24]The expression must be put in log form because when costs of alternative modes of transportation are equal, ΔC equals zero, the dependent variable should also equal zero, and P_B should equal P_A. The logarithmic form is the most natural way of satisfying all of these objectives.

[25]See David Harrison and Daniel L. Rubinfeld, ''Hedonic Housing Prices and the Willingness to Pay for Clean Air,'' *Journal of Environmental Economics and Management,* March 1978, for a recent study, and A. Myrick Freeman, ''Hedonic Prices, Property Values, and Measuring Environmental Benefits: A Survey of the Issues,'' *The Scandinavian Journal of Economics,* No. 2, 1979 for a summary discussion. The analytics are discussed further by David W. Pearce, in ''Noise Nuisance'' and ''Air Pollution,'' two articles in his edited volume *The Valuation of Social Cost* (London: Allen and Unwin, 1978).

[26]There is an even subtler problem regarding capital values than the one discussed here. Say the government is considering building a dam that will flood some property. The standard way of valuing this land cost is by using the market value of all land and structures taken out of use. However, if private investors *knew* that the government would follow this valuation rule, it would be to their advantage to protect their own property against government dam flooding by overbuilding in valleys. In such a case, the government would be biasing decisions against dams by repeated use of this valuation rule: a better rule would be to consider as costs only the value of the land and structures that would be present without the bulge caused by private investors ''psyching out'' the government evaluators. This point comes up in Lawrence Blume, Daniel Rubinfeld, and Perry Shapiro, ''The Taking of Land: When Should Compensation be Paid?'' University of Michigan Discussion Paper, Ann Arbor, Mich., 1980.

[27]The basic statement of this method is in Marion Clawson, ''Methods of Measuring Demand for a Value of Outdoor Recreation,'' Resources for the Future reprint No. 10, Washington, 1959, and later in Clawson and Jack L. Knetsch, *Economics of Outdoor Recreation,* Resources for the Future, 1966, especially Chapter 5. The intellectual antecedent appears to be some work of Harold Hotelling in the Prewitt Report of 1949 (R. A.

Prewitt, *The Economics of Public Recreation—an Economic Study of the Monetary Evaluation of Recreation in the National Parks,* National Park Service, 1949). A good summary of the issues can be found in John Gibson, "Recreational Land Use," in D. W. Pearce, ed., *The Valuation of Social Cost* (London: Allen and Unwin, 1978).

[28]One application of this technique was aimed at finding the benefits of cleaning up the Charles River. See Frederick W. Gramlich, "The Demand for Clean Water: The Case of the Charles River," *National Tax Journal,* June 1977.

[29]Milton Friedman and L. J. Savage, "The Utility Analysis of Choices Involving Risk," *Journal of Political Economy,* August 1948.

[30]This average comes from weighting each outcome by its probability, or $E(U) = .5U_1 + .5U_2$. Graphically, we merely connect the two points and find the midpoint of the line, as shown.

[31]Essentially, this is the position taken by Kenneth J. Arrow and Robert C. Lind, "Uncertainty and the Value of Public Investment Decisions," *American Economic Review,* June 1970. They show that uncertainty can often be ignored because the government distributes investment risks among a large number of people, and they derive procedures for dealing with uncertainty in the general case.

APPENDIX / CHAPTER 5

SECONDARY MARKETS

Most discussions and applications of benefit-cost analysis have involved finding the gains and losses in one market—that most directly affected by the policy change. But often other markets are affected, too. If the impact of a change in one market is strong enough to cause either a price or a quantity change in some other market, that market must also be analyzed to give a full tally of benefits and costs. This appendix provides some very simple examples of how to do that.

We begin with the standard case analyzed in the chapter, where a new project or facility lowers the price in market 1. As shown in Figure 5A.1, this facility shifts down the supply curve in market 1 by the vertical distance z and allows a new market equilibrium at (Q_1, P_1). As compared to the old equilibrium at (Q_0, P_0), the reduction in prices improves the welfare of consumers by area $A + B$. For producers, the argument is slightly more complex because their supply curve has now shifted. The presence of the facility allows them to do exactly what they were doing before but charge less for it; hence the vertical drop of z in the supply curve causes no loss in producer surplus. But the movement from Q_0 to Q_1 generates a gain in producer surplus of area $D + C$. The total gain in this primary market is the area $A + B + C + D$, and this gain, or benefit, is to be compared with the cost of the project. This is exactly the result derived earlier, except there we made things slightly easier by assuming a flat supply curve.

FIGURE 5A.1 Primary and Secondary Benefits and Costs

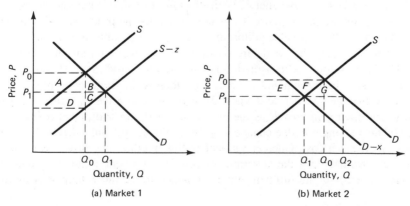

(a) Market 1

(b) Market 2

Now we consider secondary markets. Say that we introduce another good, which is a substitute for good 1. As the price of the first good, coffee, drops because of the government's new facility, the demand for the second good, tea, will be shifted down by x, as shown in Figure 5A.1(b). This shift lowers both price and quantity in the tea market to (Q_1, P_1). Producers of tea are operating under the same supply curve and therefore suffer a loss of producer surplus of area $E + F$. Consumers shift their demand to curve $D - x$ with no loss of utility; this was a direct implication of the supply shift in market 1 and results directly from the fact that the price of coffee is a determinant of the demand for tea. Hence as the price falls from P_0 to P_1, they gain area E. The net loss in market 2 then becomes area F, and this should be deducted from the gains in market 1 to measure overall net benefits.[1]

Had the good been a complement, cream, everything would run in reverse. The lower price of coffee would raise the demand for cream from $D - x$ to D, raise the price to P_0 and the quantity to Q_0. Producers gain area $E + F$, just what they lost in the previous example when prices fell. Consumers are placed on the new demand curve at Q_2 with no loss in utility, but lose consumer surplus equal to areas $E + F + G$ as the price rises. The net cost of this shift is thus area G, and this area must be deducted from the gain in market 1. The result is perhaps surprising: there is a cost in market 2 whether the good is a complement or a substitute, and whether the price there rises or falls. In fact, the only time there will not be such a cost is when either of these conditions is fulfilled:

1. The secondary demand shift is very small, resulting in no change in the secondary market price.

2. The secondary supply curve is flat, so that even a large demand shift results in no change in the secondary market price.

Next we complicate things further. Say now that there exists an excise tax in market 2, assessed at the rate of t per unit. To pay this tax, producers have already shifted their supply curve from S to $S + t$ in Figure 5A.2. We know that this excise tax has already generated a deadweight loss in this market, but we are not concerned with that because it was not caused by the program or facility we are examining. The initial equilibrium is at (Q_0, P_0), and as a result of the downward shift (say the goods are substitutes), the new equilibrium is at (Q_1, P_1). Producer surplus is measured along the supply curve S at Q_0 before the downward shift in demand and Q_1 afterward: the loss in producer surplus is thus area G. Consumers switch to the new demand curve at price P_0 with no loss in utility, and then gain area E as the price falls to P_1. In addition, tax revenues drop by the rectangle F, the change in Q times the tax per unit of t, and this tax loss is another net cost. One can rationalize this in either one of two ways: less revenue is available for the government (and for distribution back to producers and consumers), or the drop in output reduces utility more than it saves on

FIGURE 5A.2   Secondary Markets with an Excise Tax

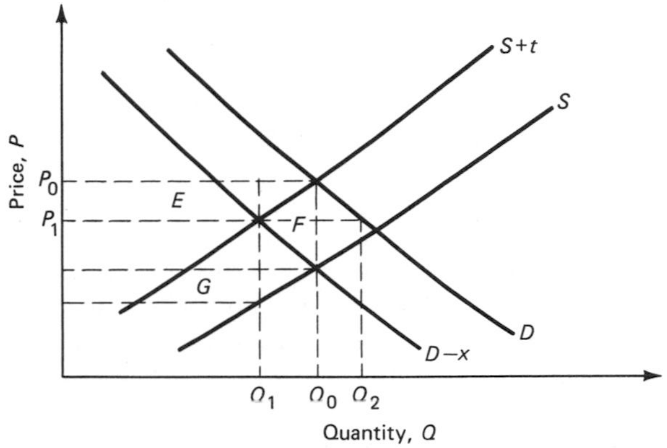

resources, because of the tax-induced wedge between utility and costs. In this case, then, the net secondary market cost is the loss in tax revenue F, plus the loss in producer surplus G, minus the gain in consumer surplus E. Had demand shifted out because the goods were complements, area G is a gain, area F is a gain, area E is a loss, and there is another consumer surplus loss represented by the parallelogram between the demand curves and P_0 and P_1 [that area is $(P_0 - P_1)$ $(Q_2 - Q_1)$ to be precise]. In general, the conclusion here is that if there is a tax in market 2, a drop in output there causes an additional loss while an increase in output yields an additional gain.[2]

APPENDIX NOTES

[1]Two of my colleagues have proved this result simultaneously, independently, and with different uses of utility maximization principles. See Richard C. Porter, "Secondary Markets in Benefit-Cost Analysis," Mimeo, University of Michigan, Ann Arbor, Mich., 1979; and Hal R. Varian, "Notes on Cost-Benefit Analysis," Mimeo, University of Michigan, Ann Arbor, Mich., 1979. The conclusion does differ, in different ways, from that reached by earlier writers on benefit-cost analysis, such as Arnold C. Harberger, "Three Basic Postulates for Applied Welfare Economics: An Interpretive Essay," *Journal of Economic Literature*, September 1971; and Edward J. Mishan, *Cost Benefit Analysis* (New York: Praeger, 1976).

[2]This conclusion agrees with that of Harberger, "Three Postulates," p. 790.

PROBLEMS

5.1 The price of a weekly bridge toll pass has varied between 5 and 10 in the past. When $P = 10$, $Q = 5$, and when $P = 5$, $Q = 10$. Compute the formula for the linear demand curve connecting these two points, and evaluate consumer surplus loss if the price is raised from 10 to 12; consumer surplus gain if the price is lowered from 5 to 3. Now compute the arc elasticity of a nonlinear (constant elasticity) demand curve between the two points, and evaluate the same loss and gain in consumer surplus.

5.2 Assume that marginal cost of supplying a material used in the construction of a government project is $MC = .01Q$. The good is sold by a monopolist, however, according to the supply curve $P = .02Q$. The private demand for the good is given by $P = 6.00 - .04Q$. The government will need 50 additional units of Q at every P. Find

  a. The expression for the new demand curve.
  b. The pregovernment equilibrium.
  c. The postgovernment equilibrium.
  d. The budget cost of the materials to the government.
  e. The consumer surplus loss of private consumers.
  f. The producer surplus gain to the monopolist on old units.
  g. The producer surplus gain on new units.
  h. The net social cost of materials.
  i. The average market price over the interval.
  j. The average marginal cost over the interval.
  k. The expansion of output fraction.
  l. The displacement fraction.
  m. The net social cost by the formula in the text.

5.3 Now you must hire labor to build the facility. The demand for labor is given by the expression $W = 92 - L$, where W is the wage rate paid per hour and L the number of workers. The supply is given by $W = .02L$. There is a minimum wage of $2 imposed on the market.

  a. Compute the initial level of labor demand, supply, and unemployment at the minimum wage.

  b. Assume that the government wants to hire five workers to build the facility. Find the budget cost, the social cost using labor's supply curve, and the social cost if there were no social value of idleness.

  c. How would your conclusions be changed if the area had an unemployment insurance system that paid workers $.5/hour when they were unemployed?

5.4 Say that economists estimate the Phillips curve relationship

$$\frac{\Delta P}{P} = -2 + \frac{10}{U} + \left(\frac{\Delta P}{P}\right)^e$$

where U is the overall unemployment rate in percentage terms, $\Delta P/P$ the inflation rate in percentage terms, and $(\Delta P/P)^e$ the expected inflation rate. In the beginning, no inflation is expected. Compute the unemployment rate that stabilizes prices, and the short-run rate of inflation when unemployment is one percentage point below and above this stable price unemployment rate.

Say that there is now a permanent policy to hold U one percentage point below the stable price unemployment rate. What would you expect to happen to inflation rates over time?

If the government project described in Problem 5.3 were carried out when the unemployment rate was at its stable price value, what is the social cost of the labor used on the project?

5.5 A typical laborer works for a wage of $6000 per year in a perfectly safe occupation. Some other occupation is not perfectly safe, having a death probability of 1 in 1000 per year and paying wages to workers of $6100 per year. Can you compute the value of a human life from this information?

5.6 Say that the utility-of-income schedule is given by $U = \sqrt{Y}$. We have a family that starts off with a certain income equal to 100. A public project is proposed that could raise the family's income to 144, with a probability of 1/2, and could lower income to 56, with a probability of 1/2.

> **a.** What is the expected income to the family yielded by the project?
>
> **b.** Compute the expected benefit of the project by subtracting initial income from this expected level. Can you come up with a better estimate of the expected benefit of the project?

6

Valuation of Resources Used or Benefits Created at Different Times

One of the most fundamental problems in benefit-cost analysis is that resources are used or benefits are created at different times. For our subway, for example, the city of Urbania must spend a large amount of money in the near term. In the immediate future, ridership will obviously be zero, but once the subway is built, there will be riders and benefits. So, as with a wide range of physical investment projects, government decision makers and evaluators must know how to compare costs borne now with benefits created later. If the community places a great weight on costs borne now, it will tend not to build the subway. If it is essentially indifferent about time, it might. In this chapter we discuss this issue.

The essence of the timing problem can be seen from a simple analogy to a common problem faced by households. Let a household have a sum of, say, $1000. If the household spends it all today, it can obviously spend $1000. If it deposits the money in a bank or savings and loan institution offering a deposit rate of 5 percent each year, 1 year from now it will have $1050. The same $1000 is worth $1000 now and $1050 next year. From this example it must be true that for the household, a dollar now is worth more than a dollar later, because today's dollars can grow into more dollars later. Further, in making any decision about when to spend the money, the household must have in mind some implicit translation factor, or rate of time preference, of its own. As with the subway, if it has a strong preference for money spent now, it will spend the money now even though there is not quite as much money to spend. If it is more patient, say indifferent between spending now and a year from now, it might as well wait and spend the greater sum.

This simple household example shows how the timing of benefits and costs can affect governmental decisions. Governments do have the option of putting their funds in banks and savings and loan institutions just like households, and earning and spending more later. Moreover, often large construction projects such as our subway will be financed by interest-bearing construction bonds. A government will borrow $1000 now and be forced to pay off the bond, for $1050, when it comes due 1 year from now (most bonds have a maturity of substantially more than 1 year—this date was used just to continue the example). So whether they are investing funds they now already have, or deciding whether to borrow funds they do not now have, governments must also come to some decision about how to compare a smaller amount of money now versus more money later whenever they undertake any project or set of projects where costs and benefits occur at different times.

Two concepts used in the chapter are quite fundamental. The first is that of *present value*. As our example has shown, a dollar now does not have the same value as a dollar later. Comparing the two without any adjustment is like comparing apples and oranges, and some translation factor is necessary before a comparison can be made. The standard one, and the one we use throughout this chapter, is to put all values, whether benefits or costs, in terms of dollars now, or present values. Hence an amended benefit-cost decision rule of the sort used in Chapter 4 would be to find the (policy) alternative that yields the greatest excess of the present value of all benefits received over the present value of all costs borne. By the same token, whenever we use a benefit-cost ratio, it will now be the ratio of the present value of benefits to the present value of costs.

The second concept is that of the *discount rate*. This is nothing more than the rate by which the present value of money received in the future can be computed. In the example used above, the discount rate was just the interest rate, 5 percent. A dollar received 1 year from now is worth 5 percent less than a dollar received now, so the present value of $1000 today is $1000 and, if 5 percent were the proper discount rate, the present value of $1050 one year from now would also be $1000.

This chapter is built around both concepts. In the first part of the chapter we inquire into the mechanical relationship between discount rates and present values: how present values can be computed from discount rates in simple and more complicated cases. Then we go on to the more interesting, but much more complicated, questions of how a community can determine what its discount rate should be and how it should use this discount rate in computing the present value of a government investment project.

THE RELATIONSHIP BETWEEN PRESENT VALUES AND DISCOUNT RATES

The relationship between the present value of a sum of money and the discount rate can be established from the example used above. If $1000 were deposited in a bank and the principal and accumulated interest drawn out 1 year hence, that sum would total $1050. If it were drawn out 2 years hence, the sum would total $(1050)(1.05) = (1000)(1.05)^2 = \$1102.50$. If it were drawn out T years hence, it would equal $(1000)(1.05)^T$. In general, then, 1 dollar now will grow into $(1 + r)^T$ dollars in the future, where r is the discount rate and T is the number of years between the time of deposit and the withdrawal of the dollar. Mathematically, $1 now $= (\$1$ in year $T)(1 + r)^T$. After dividing both sides by $(1 + r)^T$, the present value of a dollar in any year T can be seen to equal $1/(1 + r)^T$. This is the basic relationship between the discount rate and the present value.

This simple illustration has just looked at the present value of a dollar received at an arbitrary point in the future. At least with government investment projects, the more probable situation is not that there will be just one benefit payment at an arbitrary future date, but a whole stream of benefits starting when the project is completed and ending when it is no longer operational. If we denote the dollar benefits received in any future year by B_t, where t refers to the year, and if the project lasts for T years, the present value of benefits of the project is then given by the sum of all annual benefits, with each discounted by the appropriate factor to convert this annual total into present-value terms:

$$\text{(1)} \quad \begin{aligned} \text{present value of} \\ \text{project benefits} \end{aligned} = B_0 + \frac{B_1}{1 + r_1} + \frac{B_2}{(1 + r_1)(1 + r_2)} \\ + \frac{B_3}{(1 + r_1)(1 + r_2)(1 + r_3)} + \cdots + \frac{B_T}{(1 + r_1)\cdots(1 + r_T)}$$

Using more condensed notation and assuming for convenience sake that r is constant over all future periods, we get the standard equation for the present value of the benefits of a project:

$$\text{(2)} \quad \text{present value} = \sum_{t=0}^{T} \frac{B_t}{(1 + r)^t}$$

where t refers to the year. Operationally, it then becomes necessary to forecast three magnitudes to determine this present value:

1. The value of benefits in each future year.
2. The discount rate.
3. The horizon over which benefits will be paid out.

To see how this formula can be applied, say that we have two investments, A and B. As before, A yields $1050 one year from now, but we now compare it with investment B, which yields $550 1 year from now and $540 2 years from now. If r, the discount rate, is 5 percent, the present value of investment A would be $1050/1.05 = \$1000$, and the present value of investment B would be $(550/1.05) + (540/1.103) = \$1013$. In this case investment B would be more valuable: even though some of its benefits are not received for 2 years, there are enough more total benefits to make B worth more in present-value terms. But what if the appropriate discount rate becomes 10 percent, in effect lowering the present value of money received in the future? Recomputing the present values yields $1050/1.10 = \$955$ for A and $(550/1.10) + (540/1.21) = \$946$ for B. Now A is more valuable. Both present values have fallen, but that of B falls more because some of its benefits are received further in the future. If these projects were alternatives—say representing alternative types of subway cars (with a few more zeros)—the government decision maker would have to know the discount rate before deciding on the investment. If the discount rate were 5 percent and the cost of a subway car less than $1013, the government should buy the B cars; if the discount rate were 10 percent and the cost less than $955, the government should buy the A cars. Of course, as in Chapter 4, if the projects were not alternatives, the government should undertake any and all investments for which the present value of benefits exceeded the cost.

It may seem that the choice of discount rate would not matter much, but at least for long-lived investments that is definitely not the case. For benefits received in 1 year, the present value of each dollar is $1/1.05 = .952$ when the discount rate is 5 percent and $1/1.1 = .909$ when the discount rate is 10 percent, a relatively small difference. In the second year, the present values become $1/1.103 = .907$ for 5 percent and $1/1.21 = .826$ for 10 percent, a larger difference. As the time horizon grows, the difference gets greater and greater, and these greater and greater differences are cumulated in the present-value sum, making this also diverge by more and more. Apparently small differences between the discount rate are then translated into very large differences in the present value for long-lived projects.

A specific illustration of this point is given in Figure 6.1. There the present value of $10 received each year for T years is shown for different values of r and T. Note that for each of the four discount rates r, equal to 2.5, 5, 7.5, and 10 percent, respectively, the present value increases as more years of benefits are added (T grows). But the rate of addition, given by the slope of each discount-rate curve, is much less when the discount rate is high because the remote future

FIGURE 6.1   Present Value of $10 Received Every Year for *T* Years

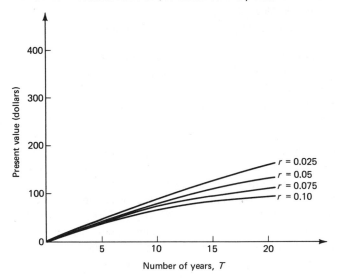

returns are discounted more in those cases. Hence the difference in present value is small when the horizon is only 5 years but much larger when it is 20 or more.

Finally, there is one approximation that is very useful in discounting. It is quite cumbersome to manipulate a formula such as (1) or (2), which could have as many as 50 terms when a project lasts this long, as a road, dam, or school building often does. Not only that, but it is somewhat unrealistic to think that government evaluators can forecast benefits and costs very precisely that far into the future. Hence it is useful to have an approximation that gives the tendency, or limit, of the present-value term as the horizon *T* approaches infinity, in effect the asymptotic limit of each of the curves drawn in Figure 6.1. If we can assume that benefits begin in year 1, that each of the numerators is constant at *B*, and that the discount rate is constant at *r*, the present value of a project lasting forever can be shown to equal B/r. More generally, as a project with a constant *B* and *r* lasts longer and longer, its present value approaches B/r in an asymptotic manner.[1] For many real-world situations, this simplification can serve as a convenient and reasonable guide.

THE PRESENT VALUE OR THE INTERNAL RATE OF RETURN

It turns out that there are two ways in which a formula such as (2) can be used. The first is to compare the present value of all benefits with the present value of all costs, and to favor the project if the sum is positive. Mathematically, this would imply accepting the project if the present value, PV, is greater than zero when

(3)
$$PV = \sum_{t=0}^{T} \frac{B_t - C_t}{(1 + r)^t}$$

where everything is just as in eq. (2) except that now each year's costs are subtracted in the numerator to give the present value of the net benefits of the project.

There is another way to do the calculation, not quite as illuminating but nevertheless worth discussing because it has often been used in actual benefit-cost analyses. Instead of *assuming* a value for r and *computing* PV as in eq. (3), say that we turned things around and tried to find the "internal rate" of return that would make an evaluator indifferent about a project. This indifference point comes where PV = 0—here the evaluator would be indifferent between recommending for or against the project. Hence we can find the internal rate of return, call it i, for which PV = 0, as in

(4)
$$0 = \sum_{t=0}^{T} \frac{B_t - C_t}{(1 + i)^t}$$

This internal rate will then be compared with the opportunity cost of capital, r, to see whether the project has positive net benefits. If $i > r$, the present value of the project is greater than zero and the project should be recommended; otherwise, it should not. Following the logic of Chapter 4, if funds are scarce, the government might array projects according to the value of i and choose those where i is the highest.

There is little difference between these methods in most real-world applications. If PV > 0 in eq. (3), we will almost always find that $i > r$ in eq. (4). There are, nevertheless, three fairly good reasons for sticking with eq. (3).

1. A mathematical ambiguity can arise in eq. (4), because it is possible to get multiple computed values for i, and nobody knows what to do then.[2]

2. Another form of mathematical uncertainty can arise when comparing projects of different horizons, T. It will sometimes be the case that one project will have a very high internal rate of return over its lifetime but last for only a short time, whereas another pays less but lasts longer. If these projects are alternatives being ranked in terms of their i, the only way to compare them is to compute the net present value for both.

3. Sometimes the government decision maker will be comparing an investment project with a consumption project that lasts only 1 year and for which there is no computed value of i. Then the present-value rule gives a clear answer (because there will be a present value of net benefits for the consumption project—just the net benefits in the first year) while the internal rate of return rule does not. For these three reasons, our discussion from now on will use the decision rule expressed in eq. (3).

Traditionally, the evaluation literature has not worried much about price inflation, simply making all calculations in today's prices, which were expected to be
tomorrow's prices. But if we expect that prices will rise over time, as we
probably should nowadays, these calculations become trickier.

Say that the general price level in the economy is expected to rise at the rate
of g percent per year. There are two ways to compute the present value of a
project, and both amount to the same thing. The first way is in nominal terms.
Using eq. (3), assume that the real value of net benefits of a project are given by
$B_t - C_t$ in each year. If all prices rise by g percent per year, in year 1 the
nominal, or current-dollar value of net benefits will be given by $(B_1 - C_1)(1 + g)$; in year 2, by $(B_2 - C_2)(1 + g)^2$; and so forth. Each term in the numerator is
appropriately inflated to put it in nominal terms.

But that is not all. The assumption made for numerators was that a price
inflation of g percent per year was expected. It stands to reason that this assumption should also be made for financial markets and discount rates in the de-
nominators. If the appropriate interest rate or discount rate were r percent a year
before the inflation was expected, once lenders and borrowers expect inflation,
they will realize that loans will be paid back in depreciated dollars. Lenders
would no longer be willing to make loans at the old interest rate r when prices are
expected to rise at g. Instead, they realize that the first year's repayment of $(1 + r)$ should also be inflated by $(1 + g)$ to keep it the same in real terms; the second
year's repayment of $(1 + r)^2$ by $(1 + g)^2$; and so forth. Under these circum-
stances the nominal, or actual money interest rate would rise to approximately $r + g$ percent.[3]

We can insert both values in the present-value expression, now stated in
nominal terms

$$(5) \quad PV = B_0 - C_0 + \frac{(B_1 - C_1)(1 + g)}{(1 + r)(1 + g)} + \frac{(B_2 - C_2)(1 + g)^2}{(1 + r)^2(1 + g)^2} + \cdots$$

It can be seen that all the $(1 + g)$ terms exactly cancel out, and the PV expression
will be the same as if no adjustment for general price inflation had been made.
This is the other way to do the calculation, in real terms. Hence the evaluator can
simply use real (noninflated) B's and C's and the real interest rate r or nominal
(inflated) values of $(B_i - C_i)(1 + g)^i$ and the actual observed nominal interest
rate $r + g$, getting the same results either way. The only pitfall to be avoided is
that evaluators should *not* discount nominal benefits by the real interest rate r,
and they should not discount real benefits by the nominal interest rate.

Although this point seems almost too obvious to mention, mistakes are often
made in practice. To take the most glaring, the U.S. government has always
required benefits and costs (in the numerator) to be stated in real terms. It should

then use a real interest rate in the denominator. But, in fact, it has required projects to be discounted by the actual nominal interest rate on long-term U.S. government bonds. Since this nominal rate does increase when inflation speeds up, the government's official evaluation procedures are clearly biased in comparing real benefits and costs with nominal interest rates—the more so the more rapid is anticipated inflation. Since the benefits of many projects are realized more in the future than when the costs are actually borne, this could lead to overdiscounting of these benefits and an unnecessarily restrictive decision rule in inflationary times.[4]

THE APPROPRIATE DISCOUNT RATE

The matters we have been discussing are relatively uncontroversial, simply dealing with how to do present-value calculations. We have assumed throughout that government decision makers or evaluators know the proper discount rate r and simply apply it to benefits and costs over time to calculate the present value of a project. But, in fact, knowing what r to use is quite a trick, one that has taken the attention of literally hundreds of economists over the past 30 years. Essentially three candidates have been proposed:

1. The gross before-tax rate of interest on private investment.
2. A weighted average of rate 1 and the after-tax rate of return on private saving.
3. The social optimum rate of discount.

In the following discussion we review the pros and cons of each candidate, digressing to show how to measure the social optimum discount rate.

The Before-Tax Rate of Return on Private Investment

The logic for using the gross rate of return on private investment is straightforward. Assume that the government investment project does not affect the overall portion of national output devoted to investment and consumption. If this is so, a dollar of public investment exactly displaces a dollar of private investment, and the benefit-cost problem is simply that of achieving the optimal allocation of this fixed pool of resources devoted to investment. The efficiency condition for achieving this optimum is that at the margin, private and public investment should be equally profitable. If they were not, total welfare could be improved by reallocating investment resources away from the less profitable use, toward the more profitable use. The way in which this standard can be met is by having public investment evaluators use precisely the same rule in making investment decisions as was used in the private sector. Private investors presumably invest up to the point where the gross before-tax rate of return on investment equals the before-tax rate of interest on private securities (rate 1 above); therefore, that should be the standard for public investment. To put it a different way, since the before-tax rate of return measures the marginal productivity of private capital, it also represents the opportunity cost of having these same funds devoted to public investment.[5]

The problem with this argument is that it is often hard to view public investment projects as mechanically displacing corresponding dollar volume private investment projects. In the first place, the same investment opportunities may not be available for public and private investors. Second, public and private projects may yield different streams of secondary private investment over time. Third, many public investment projects may ultimately be financed by taxes that reduce private consumption. Given all these difficulties, can the before-tax private market interest rate be viewed as the opportunity cost of public sector capital?

At bottom, this private market rate of interest is nothing more than a price, the price operating in financial markets to equate the demand for total national saving with that for total national investment. If at some prevailing interest rate, there is excess demand for investment, interest rates will be driven up to choke off enough investment, or induce enough savings, to equilibrate the two; and vice versa if saving demand exceeds investment demand.[6] Hence it can be argued that the market interest rate shows, by the invisible hand, how private consumers themselves balance the present versus the future. If a society is inclined to provide well for future generations, it will have a large supply of new saving, low interest rates, and a low rate of time preference. If not, there would be high interest rates and a high rate of time preference. Either way, the postulates of microeconomic consumer sovereignty would suggest that the prevailing interest rate in society shows how consumers in that society want to balance the present against the future at the margin, should determine the overall proportion of national output devoted to investment, and should also form the standard by which public-sector evaluators should evaluate public investment projects.[7]

But to argue that the private rate of interest is a price is to suggest that there could be some externalities in the market that might require correction of this price. The most important externality involves what A. C. Pigou, a British economist of the early twentieth century, first called the "defective telescopic faculty" of market interest rates.[8] The idea is simply that since public (and private) investment decisions affect the welfare of both the present generation and unborn future generations, the wishes of the latter should be represented in any investment decision. Since future generations obviously do not have any direct means for expressing their wishes about present investment policies, we might expect society to be myopic, or to demonstrate a higher rate of time preference than would be the case were future generations also saving, investing, and voting on public investment policies. We might further argue that the state, as guardian of the interests of those not yet born, might impose a lower rate of time preference for evaluating public investment projects. This argument would lower the social rate of discount below the private rate, and since for most public investments the benefits come well after the costs, raise the net present value of the public investment project and stimulate more government investment.

Although such an argument might be plausible, it can easily be carried too far. For one thing, it assumes a degree of omniscience and benevolence on the part of the state, as trustees of society, that seems a bit quaint in this modern age, where voters worry about the uncontrollability of government and the need to impose tax limitation amendments. It also assumes a lack of myopia on the part of politicians, again a dubious proposition.

Even within the market, although the interests of future generations are not directly represented in private transactions, these interests are represented indirectly. One reason is that members of the current generation are not totally selfish, in the sense that they do appear to save more than they they will ever be able to consume in their own lifetime, either because they want to leave something for their heirs or as bequests to institutions. A second is that even if the present generation were totally selfish, the "invisible hand" would still transmit signals to care for the welfare of future generations. If, for example, investors knew that the baby boom of the 1950s would generate a rising demand for higher education in the 1970s, there would be returns to be made from investing in college facilities in the 1960s. Those in the baby-boom generation had no explicit vote in this process, but in trying to maximize profits, investors were guided to do what is best for the baby-boom students. One could make a similar argument about investment today in new forms of energy, such as solar energy or processes to gassify coal. The ultimate beneficiaries of these processes are for the most part not yet born, but the investments are being made because their anticipated profitability is great. The upshot is that although Pigou's telescope may indeed be defective, it is difficult to figure out exactly how much of, and indeed whether, a correction for this externality is necessary.

A more compelling argument against using the before-tax interest rate as society's expression of how large a pool of resources should be devoted to the consumption of future generations is that the largest saver and investor in private capital markets is the government itself. In the United States, for example, the federal government has for the last decade run persistent government deficits (dissaving and driving up interest rates), whereas state and local operating budgets have generally been in surplus (driving down interest rates). Further governmental influences on private rates come from monetary policy changes, regulations, and the tax treatment of investment. Particularly for federal public investment policies, it seems a little silly to argue that public investment ought to be valued at an interest rate that is strongly influenced by what its own policies are doing.

So when the supply of funds devoted to investment is variable, the clear logic arguing in support of the before-tax market interest rate crumbles. Not only is there a possible externality, leading to higher interest rates and a lower amount of public investment than might be optimal from the standpoint of all generations, but the interest rate itself is heavily influenced by government fiscal, monetary, and tax policies. Using the private rate as a standard may ensure that a fixed pool of investment funds will be optimally allocated,[9] but it does not ensure that the pool of investment funds will be the right size.

The Weighted-Average Rate of Return

A second approach to discounting argues that since funds come from both private investment and private consumption, a weighted-average approach must be used. For that portion of the public investment financed by reducing private investment, the before-tax return on private investment gives the appropriate marginal opportunity cost. But for that portion financed out of private consumption, the after-tax return on consumer saving gives the relevant marginal cost. This is, after all, the rate actually faced by consumers as they allocate their own budgets between consumption now and consumption later. Hence this rule would be to use $\bar{r}$ as the discount rate, where $\bar{r}$ is defined as

(6) $$\bar{r} = sr + (1 - s)r_c(1 - t)$$

and where s is the proportion of the resource cost of the public investment coming from private investment, r the before-tax interest rate faced by investors, and $r_c (1 - t)$ the *after-tax* rate of return faced by consumers.[10] The logical defense of this standard is similar to that used in Chapter 5 to measure the social costs of resources supplied monopolistically, for which there was also a different shadow price on the marginal output.

We note first that if there were no difference between the before-tax investment rate and the after-tax saving rates, the two rules would amount to the same thing. What causes the difference?

The first reason is taxes. In Figure 6.2 we reproduce the diagram used in Figure 2.5, relabeling the axes to determine the supply and demand for saving, and the price, or interest rate, that equates the two. The demand for saving is really the demand for funds for investment, so the downward-sloping curve is labeled I. Taxes on the interest earnings of saving will have the same effect as taxes on the earnings of labor: since the after-tax compensation will be less if the saving curve is positively sloped, it must be shifted up to compensate savers for their taxes paid at each level of S. The new equilibrium at (S, r) will feature a before-tax rate of return to investors of r and an after-tax rate of return to savers of $r(1 - t)$, with the difference going to the government. The introduction of income taxes on interest earnings has thus placed a wedge between the before-tax interest rate influencing investors and the after-tax rate influencing savers, and now that some of our public investment comes out of private consumption, the

FIGURE 6.2   Demand and Supply for New Saving

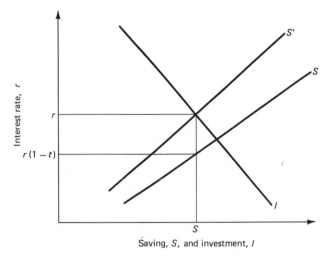

after-tax rate actually faced by savers as they allocate their own budgets between consumption now and in the future would appear to become relevant.

A second reason is institutional restrictions on the deposit rates paid small savers by banks and savings and loan institutions. For these small savers, banks and savings and loan institutional deposits form the only readily available vehicle for personal saving (at least apart from those brave souls who dare to try the stock market). In a perhaps misguided attempt to protect these thrift institutions against their own competition, the government limits the deposit rates these institutions can pay. Institutions are then prevented from competing for funds by raising deposit rates, and raise them only to the government ceiling, not to the loan rates quoted private investors. Hence financial regulation prevents small savers from realizing market returns on their saving and drives another wedge between the investment rate r and the consumption rate r_c, which goes along with the tax-created wedge between r_c and $r_c (1 - t)$.

To see how important these two wedges are in the United States, in late 1978 the before-tax interest rates on long-term corporate securities was about 11 percent, leading to a real before-tax rate of return on investment of 4 percent (if we can assume that investors expected long-term inflation rates to be about 7 percent, a common answer to surveys of the sort at the time). But the highest before-tax rate a small saver could make was about 8 percent, and if this saver faced a tax rate of one-fourth, the highest after-tax rate was 6 percent, leading to a real after-tax rate of interest on saving of -1 percent. Taxes and deposit-rate restrictions were then strong enough to ensure that savers were not even compensated for the effect of inflation on their savings, and received an after-tax rate of return $[r_c (1 - t)]$ approximately five percentage points below the before-tax investment return (r).[11] A weighted average of this rate and r would then also clearly be below r, and if s were low enough, very close to zero.

The fact that real rates of return on personal saving are negative tips us off to the major problem both with the after-tax saving rate and any weighted-average standard that relies on it. If people save at all when the real after-tax rate of interest is very low or negative, the interest elasticity of their demand for saving must be very slight. If so, the saving curve looks as it is drawn in Figure 6.3 (with the after-tax real rate on saving shown as negative).[12] Since the saving curve is quite inelastic over this range, the after-tax rate $r_c (1 - t)$ depends mainly on the wedges that hold $r_c (1 - t)$ below r—taxes and regulations that restrict the returns available to small savers. Hence it is hard to argue that $r_c (1 - t)$ is the rate savers require to compensate them for saving at the margin, as is necessary in using this rate as a standard to discount the consumption component of a public investment project. The main thing $r_c (1 - t)$ measures is what government tax and regulation policy allow consumers to realize on their saving.[13]

Thus although it sounds sensible to use a weighted-average rate, the presence of market imperfections such as financial regulations and taxes greatly diminishes the attractiveness of after-tax rate of return to savers, and any average based on it, as a standard for discounting. At least in the United States, it is even less market-determined than the before-tax investment rate. Hence we now abandon this search for what James Tobin once called the "will of the wisp" of the right private discount rate and to try to arrive directly at some judgment about the proper social rate of discount.[14] How does one do that?

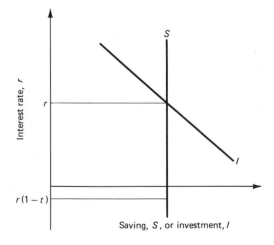

FIGURE 6.3 **Demand and Supply for New Saving When Saving Does Not Depend on Interest Rate**

The Social Discount Rate

One way to find the social rate of discount, indeed the only way that has yet been suggested, follows a suggestion of Stephen Marglin that the discount rate be inferred from a country's optimal combinations of investment and saving. It might seem that this approach is not very practical, but in fact economic growth theorists such as Edmund Phelps have developed very simple models that determine these optimal saving and investment policies.[15] The models can also be used to find the preferred capital/labor ratio for an economy and, for our purposes, the optimal discount rate to be used for public investment. Even though the models are very simple, the implied discounting rule turns out to give a reasonably sensible estimate of what a social discount rate ought to be. Hence we now spend some time going through a simple model of economic growth to see what it says about public-sector discounting.

Say that we have a society in which the labor force is growing at the rate of n percent per year, either because of population growth or the growth of technology. Total output will rise in this society both because current saving leads to the accumulation of capital and because of this growth in the labor force. If this society is trying to formulate an efficient and equitable saving policy for all generations, it will realize that it would be inequitable for any generation not to save, because that generation would be living off the capital bequeathed by previous generations and not adding to the stock (one might exempt generations which fought a war and defended the nation from this saving requirement, but it is hard to think of many other exceptions). We might go further and require all generations to devote the very same proportion of national output to new capital formation, labeling this proportion s. What we do now is find the value of s that yields the highest standard of living across all generations, and infer from it the socially optimum value of the discount rate.

The first step in the argument is to investigate the mechanics of the growth process for countries with a constant population growth rate n and a constant saving (and investment) rate s. This is done as shown in Figure 6.4. Here, the vertical axis represents the level of per capita output, denoted by y, and the horizontal axis the stock of capital per capita, k, sometimes known as the capital/labor ratio or rate of capital intensity for a society.

The top curve in Figure 6.4 is known as a production function. It shows the amount of output yielded at each level of capital. Its slope gives the increase in output for each unit increase in capital, and can be shown to equal the marginal product of capital, the amount by which output per capita increases with the addition of any unit of capital.[16] Since the entire diagram is in per capita terms, as we move in a rightward direction the amount of capital to be combined with labor gets higher and higher and the marginal product of further additions to the capital stock, shown by the slope of the curve, gets lower and lower. This reflects nothing more than the famous law of diminishing marginal returns, the law that also dictated the shape of the production-possibilities curve in Chapter 2.

FIGURE 6.4 **Relation between National Saving Rates and Capital Accumulation**

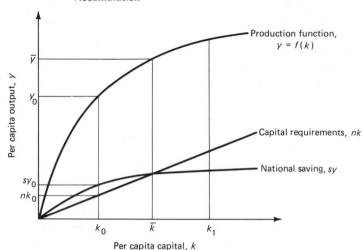

We can find the equilibrium capital intensity for any economy by comparing the two bottom curves. The first, called the national saving curve, shows the
amount of output devoted to new capital formation in any period. Since society
by assumption devotes s of new output to capital formation, this curve can be
found simply by multiplying the total output curve y by the proportion s, as
shown in the diagram. The second curve is called the capital requirements curve,
the amount of new savings necessary to maintain exactly the existing capital/
labor ratio. If the growth of labor proceeds at rate n each year, every year these n
percent new laborers will need to be equipped with k units of capital just to keep
the overall capital/labor ratio at k. Hence the capital required to preserve the
capital/labor ratio will be nk per capita. To take an example, say that there are
100 workers in society and that the labor-force growth rate (n) is .03. This means
that 3 new workers will appear next year. If the existing capital–labor ratio is 5
units of capital per worker, 15 new machines must be created to equip the new
workers at the same capital/labor ratio as the old workers and hence maintain the
average capital/labor ratio. Dividing 15 by 100 to convert to per capita terms
yields a capital requirement for this economy of .15, just n times k.

Now say that some country began with a capital/labor ratio of k_0, producing y_0, saving and reinvesting sy_0 and needing nk_0 just to maintain its capital/
labor ratio. Since the amount devoted to new capital formation (sy_0) exceeds the
amount needed to maintain the capital labor ratio (nk_0), the capital/labor ratio
will rise above k_0. This process will continue as long as $sy_0 > nk_0$, only stopping
when the two are equal. When they are equal, at $\bar{k}$, the economy has hit its
equilibrium capital intensity for this rate of saving and population growth rate.

Were any capital to be artificially removed or created, the same forces would hold and the economy would again gravitate to $\bar{k}$. The reasoning is precisely the same when the arbitrary initial value of the capital/labor ratio is above $\bar{k}$, as is shown by k_1 in the diagram. There new additions to capital would be insufficient to maintain the capital/labor ratio, and it would fall to $\bar{k}$.

The equilibrium $\bar{k}$ is a strange sort of equilibrium value because it represents an equilibrium growth *path*. At $\bar{k}$, the labor force is still growing by n percent per year. Since the capital/labor ratio is constant at $\bar{k}$, that means that the total capital stock must also be growing at n percent per year. Since per capita output is constant at $\bar{y}$, total output is also growing by n percent per year. Hence the points $\bar{k}$ and $\bar{y}$ actually refer to a growth path for an economy, with capital, labor, and output all growing at n percent per year, instead of the actual levels of capital, labor, and output.

Before considering what this diagram means for discounting, let us determine what it means for growth. As stated, the level of per capita output is assumed not to change at all, but to be constant at $\bar{y}$ along this steady growth path. This seems to be a rather dismal result: the only implication of economic growth is to generate enough capital to equip the population, but not enough to provide for higher living standards. In fact, however, the result is not nearly as dismal when we recall that n here stands for the growth of the *labor force* from either technology or population growth. If there is no technological change and growth is entirely due to population growth, as in many underdeveloped countries, the results of the model are accurate, and accurately pessimistic. But if there is no population growth and the growth of the labor force is entirely due to technological innovations that save labor, permit the existing labor force to do more, and mean that in *quality* terms the labor force has grown even if the number of workers has not grown, the results become more hopeful. Then output per quality unit of labor is constant, but output per person rises by n percent per year. To continue our previous example, say that the growth of the labor force was entirely due to advances in training and technique, so that each of the 100 old workers could produce 3 percent more this year with a given amount of capital. Hence last year's output could be produced with 3 less workers, and these workers are in effect freed to produce new output, as long as they are equipped with new machines. In equilibrium this society would have the labor force in quality units growing at n per year; output per quality unit of labor constant at $\bar{y}$ on the equilibrium growth path; but output divided by the acutal number of people, the best indicator of the country's standard of living, growing by n percent a year. Most countries lie somewhere between these two poles, with some of the growth in the labor force due to population growth and not representing an improvement in per capita living standards, and some due to technology, which does imply improving standards of living. Over the entire post–World War II period in the United States, the effective labor force has grown by about 3.5 percent per year and the total capital stock and output have also grown at about this rate, as implied by the model. Population has grown by slightly more than 1 percent per year, leaving slightly less than 2.5 percent per year for growth in output per capita.[17] Very recently, this rate of productivity change has dropped to about 1 percent, a change that will greatly reduce the rate at which living standards are improved if it persists.

We now try to see what all this has to do with optimal saving and investment policies and the rate by which public investment should be discounted. Instead of taking the saving rate as given as we did above, we must turn things around to find the constant saving rate that maximizes consumption per head for all generations. We know that in equilibrium, consumption per labor quality unit will be constant for any given saving rate, but it will vary with the saving rate. If a society were to save nothing at all, there would be no capital accumulation, output per head would be zero, and consumption per head would also be zero. That society would be clearly undersaving, as was the historical tendency of underdeveloped countries (although a most difficult tendency to correct without foreign capital, because increases in saving can come about only by restricting the already appallingly low levels of consumption per head). If, on the other hand, a society were to save all of its national output, its capital/labor ratio would be very high, output per capita very high, but none of it would be devoted to consumption: no matter how productive the society, there is no consumption and that society would clearly be oversaving. There must then be an intermediate saving and investment policy that appropriately balances the benefits and costs of capital accumulation, and this is what we are looking for.

Since we are trying to find the proper or optimal saving rate given n and the production function for the economy, we redraw Figure 6.4 without any national saving curve in Figure 6.5. We note that whatever saving rate curve is picked, in growth equilibrium it will intersect the capital requirements curve; hence in equilibrium this requirements curve will give the amount of output devoted to new capital formation. Total output is, of course, given by the production function. The difference between total output and the requirements curve is the amount of output *not* devoted to capital formation—that is, devoted to current consumption or the living standards of the population. The optimum saving rate can then be found as the one that maximizes the distance between output y and capital requirements nk. At this capital intensity, denoted on the graph as k^*, *consumption* per head is a maximum for all generations. The time-path diagram is shown in Figure 6.6. There society has chosen that saving rate, s^* (the one intersecting the capital requirements curve at k^* in Figure 6.5), that yields the highest path, recognizing that consumption per head will grow at the same rate n along all paths. If this society saved less (s_1, which corresponds to k_1 in Figure 6.5), both output and consumption per head would be less. If this society saved more (s_2, which corresponds to k_2 in Figure 6.5), output per head would be greater but consumption per head would be less.[18]

FIGURE 6.5   Optimal Saving Rate for a Society

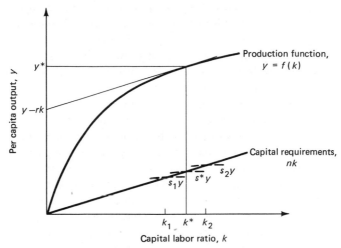

The relevance of this optimal saving and investment lesson for the evaluation of public investment projects can be drawn directly in terms of amount saved
and invested, or indirectly in terms of discount rates. Since the chapter is about
discount rates, we focus on the indirect way of looking at things. In Figure 6.5
we have drawn a tangent to the production function at k^*. Since the distance
between the production function and the requirements curve is maximized at k^*,
it must also be true that the slope of the tangent must equal the slope of the
requirements curve. Since the value of the requirements curve is nk, its slope is
nk/k or simply n, the economy's growth rate. The slope of the production

FIGURE 6.6   Path of Consumption per Head for a Society

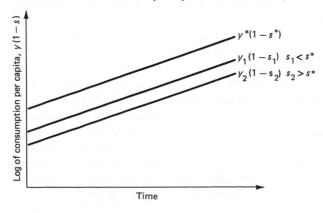

function has already been found to equal the marginal product of capital, dy/dk. If private investors are rational and capital markets reasonably competitive, they will invest to the point where this marginal product of capital equals the opportunity cost of capital, which is our private market interest rate r. Thus the optimal saving condition is simply that society should accumulate capital until the market real interest rate, r, equals the economy's real growth rate, n.[19] If an economy is undersaving, say at s_1 and k_1, capital is scarcer than it should be, $r > n$, and there would be consumption benefits to all future generations in devoting more present output to investment. Fiscal and monetary policy should be designed to encourage more saving and investment in this economy, and one could also argue that public investment should be discounted not by the actual high rate of interest r, but by the lower socially optimal rate, n. On the other hand, if society is oversaving at s_2 and k_2, there is a national interest in reducing the amount of overall and public investment, and the government might discount public investment projects not by the low actual rate r but by the higher optimal rate n.

The optimal saving policy implicit in this analysis is sometimes called the Golden Rule of capital accumulation—each generation is doing unto others (saving that proportion of national output) as it would have others do unto it. Although the logic of using the economy's growth rate as a measure of the optimal discount rate is not immediately apparent, an intuitive argument might run something like this. As an economy saves and accumulates capital, the marginal benefits of capital accumulation are given by the marginal product of capital, or r. The marginal cost is that the higher capital intensity will have to be maintained at the rate n for any level of capital intensity. Hence society should save until $r = n$ and the true social discount rate becomes n.[20] For the United States, we have seen that n has averaged about 3.5 percent since World War II, just slightly below the before-tax real investment rate (r) of about 4 percent. Hence the United States seems to have been undersaving to a slight degree in recent years.[21] But for underdeveloped countries, where the capital-labor ratio is much lower, the disparity between r and n, and the importance for discounting, would be much greater.

This growth model, elaborate as it is, has made many simplifying assumptions and one must proceed with great care in applying its results to the discounting of public investment. Alternative technology, population, and labor-force growth rates could alter its results, perhaps significantly. But despite these drawbacks, it does help us make decisions on many difficult matters. Unlike all other rules, it gives us a standard for discounting that is independent of possibly inappropriate current fiscal and regulatory policies affecting r. It also shows how a society could save too much as well as too little, and it works this right into the discounting rule. Last but not least, it does seem to give a reasonably sensible quantitative judgment about discounting. For one concerned with possibly suboptimal overall saving and investment proportions, the private rate of interest seems to be very slightly above the true social rate in the United States, where capital intensity is already high, and well above the true social rate of interest in many less developed countries, where the capital intensity is lower.

AN APPROACH FOR DISCOUNTING

These comments on the various candidates suggested for use in discounting public investment projects appear to yield something of an impasse. When the size of the pool of funds devoted to public investment is fixed, and public investment clearly displaces private investment, the before-tax investment rate of return r appears to be the proper social discount rate. When the size of the pool is not fixed, r appears to become irrelevant and some other social rate of time preference (like the Golden Rule rate n) appears to become relevant. But a logical quandary remains. If the private rate exceeds the Golden Rule rate, what does one do about a public investment project that pays less than r but more than n? On the one hand, there appears to be an opportunity for a welfare gain in this project that pays more than the social discount rate. But on the other hand, it might be possible to do even better by having these funds invested in the private sector at rate r.

The way out of the impasse follows an approach first developed by Kenneth Arrow, and later elaborated by Martin Feldstein and David Bradford.[22] When r and n differ, the procedure recommended by these authors is to use the social rate of time preference, n, as the proper discount rate for public projects. But the quantity to be discounted is the entire stream of consumption goods resulting from a project. Hence if a government project really does displace private investment that would have yielded r, the lost consumption stream is computed on the basis of r and then discounted at rate n. Generally, this will imply that the public project is a loser, unless it also creates some private investment that can earn the high rate r. The logic of this rule, then, is that high yielding private investment that really is displaced by the government investment is considered an opportunity cost of the project, while private investment that is not displaced is not considered an opportunity cost.[23]

Two things should be said about this beguiling and simple solution to the impasse. The first is that it is clearly a second best solution, only being interesting when there are differences between the private marginal product of capital, r, and the social rate of time preference, n. The best of all possible solutions would be for private investors also to invest to the point where the private return equalled the social return. To the extent that this gap is caused by government tax or budgetary policies, these should be either removed or offset so that the nation has the right amount of private and public capital. A minor externality from doing so is that this puzzling discount rate debate will be simplified.

The second statement is that all of these subtleties are not likely to make much practical difference, at least in the capital-intensive U.S. economy. A reasonable estimate of the private real interest rate r is about 4 percent; of the social optimum rate is 3.5 percent. Given the uncertainties in estimating either one of these rates, use of a real discount rate in the 3 to 4 percent range will probably yield present value solutions that come as close to being correct, or at least unbiased, as is possible in this messy area. The contrast between these recommended rates and the 10 percent real rate actually now used by the U.S. government is striking. In this area, resolving the easy question should make a big improvement in discounting procedures, while resolving the hard question should not make much difference.

SUMMARY

In the discussion in this chapter we have considered the rationales behind various procedures for discounting future costs and benefits of various public investment programs. A first point is obvious, though sometimes mistaken in practice—that all benefits, costs, and discount rates should be either in real or nominal terms. The leading violator of this rule has been none other than the U.S. government, and confusion on this count has led the government to use an extremely high real rate of return as the discount rate for government projects, well above all candidates proposed in the economics literature.

Turning to the economics literature, the main quandary regards the social value of investment in general to the country. If the nation were adjudged to be investing the proper proportion of national output, the private market interest rate r would equal the social rate of time preference, and r would also be the proper discount rate for public projects. All public projects that had a positive present value of net benefits when discounted at r should be undertaken; all that did not have a positive present value should not be undertaken. But if it is felt that the nation is underinvesting, so that the marginal private rate of return r differs from the social rate of time preference (call it n), things become more complicated. In this case the best approach for discounting public projects is to estimate exactly how much private investment is displaced now and perhaps created in the future, to use the private rate in converting that to consumption goods, and then to measure the opportunity cost of all public projects in terms of the present value of this present and future consumption. In such a way high-yielding private investment that is displaced is considered a component of the opportunity cost of public investment, but high-yielding private investment that is not displaced is not so considered. Of course, it would be even better to take measures to stimulate private investment, and thus also gain the benefits of high-yielding private investment, but that is a different question.

NOTES

[1]For those who have not had calculus, "approaches asymptotically" means that the present value gets closer and closer to B/r, although it never quite gets there. If you walk half the distance to a destination every day, you approach it asymptotically.

The proof of the proposition is straightforward. If B and r are fixed, the present value (PV) of a project in which the benefits start in year 1 and last for T years can be given from eq. (2) as

(2A) $$PV = B\left[\frac{1}{1+r} + \frac{1}{(1+r)^2} + \frac{1}{(1+r)^3} + \cdots + \frac{1}{(1+r)^T} \right]$$

Multiplying each term by $\frac{1}{1+r}$ yields

(2B) $$PV\left(\frac{1}{1+r} \right) = B\left[\frac{1}{(1+r)^2} + \frac{1}{(1+r)^3} + \cdots + \frac{1}{(1+r)^{T+1}} \right]$$

Subtracting (2B) from (2A) gives us

(2C) $$PV\left(1 - \frac{1}{1+r} \right) = B\left[\frac{1}{1+r} - \frac{1}{(1+r)^{T+1}} \right]$$

As T approaches infinity, $\frac{1}{(1+r)^{T+1}}$ approaches zero, so eq. (2C) becomes

(2D) $$PV\left(\frac{1+r-1}{1+r} \right) = \frac{B}{1+r} \qquad \text{or} \qquad PV = \frac{B}{r}$$

[2]It is possible to get up to T solutions for i for a T-year project. In the simple case where $T = 2$, let the stream of net benefits be given by $B_0 - C_0$ in the first year, $B_1 - C_1$ in the second, and $B_2 - C_2$ in the third. Using eq. (4) yields

(4A) $$0 = B_0 - C_0 + \frac{(B_1 - C_1)}{1+i} + \frac{(B_2 - C_2)}{(1+i)^2}$$

as the solution for the internal rate of return. Multiplying by $(1+i)^2$ gives us

(4B) $$0 = (B_0 - C_0)(1+i)^2 + (B_1 - C_1)(1+i) + (B_2 - C_2)$$

which is quadratic in $(1 + i)$ and therefore has two solutions for i. Often, some of the solutions are nonsensical and can be rejected, but sometimes that will not be the case and we will have to fall back on the unambiguous present-value expression. To take one not-implausible example where there will be an ambiguity in eq. (4B), let the benefits from a project equal 48 in year zero and decline by half each year, to 24 and 12, respectively, while the costs equal 38 in the first year, 46 in the second, and zero in the third as the project is fully built. The $B - C$ values are 10, -22, and 12 in the three years, and this yields $10(1 + i)^2 - 22(1 + i) + 12 = 0$, which has one solution for $i = .05$ and one for $i = .10$—both of which represent plausible values.

[3]This point was first made by nineteenth-century economists such as Knut Wicksell, and then developed more fully by Irving Fisher in *The Theory of Interest* (New York: Macmillan, 1930), Chapter 19. It has been supported in many empirical studies—for one survey, see Thomas J. Sargent, ''Interest Rates and Expected Inflation: A Selective Summary of Recent Research,'' *Explorations in Economic Research,* 3 (Summer 1976), pp. 303–325.

It should be noted that a nominal repayment of $(1 + r)(1 + g)$ is a repayment of $(1 + r + g + rg)$ times the initial value of the loan. The nominal interest rate is tnat less 1, or $r + g + rg$. When r and g are small numbers, say .1 or less, this nominal interest rate is approximately $r + g$ percent. If, for example, $r = .04$ and $g = .07$, reasonable values for the United States in 1978, the nominal interest rate is $.04 + .07 + .0028$, or approximately .11.

Finally, the impact of inflation on nominal interest rates is complicated further when the income tax law either taxes interest or allows deduction of interest expenses. As the expected rate of inflation goes from zero to 7 percent in our example, nominal interest rates rise from 4 to 11 percent. If a lender faces a tax rate of one-fourth, his or her after-tax interest rate would go from 3 to 8.25 percent, incomplete compensation for the 7 percent depreciation of the dollar. The only recourse would be to insist on an interest rate of 13.3 percent, with an after-tax rate of 10 percent, 7 percentage points higher than the previous after-tax interest rate. These intricate matters are explained in detail in Martin Feldstein and Lawrence Summers, ''Inflation, Tax Rules, and the Long-Term Interest Rate,'' *Brookings Papers on Economic Activity,* 1 (1978), pp. 61–110.

[4]Characterizing U.S. government discounting procedures turns out to be a complex job. The procedure described in the text was used until 1972 for all projects, and is still used for water resources projects. See Chap. 8 and also Raymond F. Mikesell, *The Rate of Discount for Evaluating Public Projects* (Washington, D.C.: American Enterprise Institute for Public Policy Research, 1977), especially chap. 1. Since 1972, nonwater projects have been discounted in real terms, but the government uses a rate of 10 percent, far higher than the candidates proposed in the economics literature.

[5]The best statement of this position is by William J. Baumol, ''On the Social Rate of Discount,'' *American Economic Review,* September 1968. However, after a comment by D. D. Ramsey, ''On the Social Rate of Discount,'' *American Economic Review,* December 1969, Baumol modified his position and argued for the weighted average rate of return—see ''On the Discount Rate for Public Projects,'' in Joint Economic Committee, ed., *The Analysis and Evaluation of Public Expenditures: The PPB System,* Vol. 1, 1969; also reprinted in Robert H. Haveman and Julius Margolis, *Public Expenditure and Policy Analysis,* 2nd ed. (Skokie, Ill.: Rand McNally, 1977), pp. 161–179. A more recent argument of the position can be found in Mikesell, *The Rate of Discount.*

[6]Those who have taken a course in macroeconomics will realize that national income is likely to be altered in the process, hence generating further alterations in saving and

investment schedules. The famous Hicksian *IS–LM* diagram shows how any disequilibrium will be made up in responses of *r* and output.

[7]Of course, there should be some adjustments for uncertainty and differential tax treatment—see Mikesell, *The Rate of Discount*, p. 28ff. The chapter is complicated enough without going into these matters, so we omit them.

[8]A. C. Pigou, *The Economics of Welfare* (New York: Macmillan, 1932), Chapter 2.

[9]In fact, Martin S. Feldstein will not even go this far, arguing that the choice of the wrong discount rate will lead to the choice of the wrong timing of benefits in public investment projects and the wrong allocation of a fixed-size investment pool, even when all funds are taken from private investment. See "The Inadequacy of Weighted Discount Rates," in Richard Layard, ed., *Cost-Benefit Analysis* (New York: Penguin, 1972), reading 13, p. 323.

[10]This approach was first suggested by John Krutilla and Otto Eckstein, *Multiple Purpose River Development* (Baltimore, Md.: Johns Hopkins University Press, 1958) especially Chapter IV. Richard A. Musgrave, "Cost-Benefit Analysis and the Theory of Public Finance," *Journal of Economic Literature,* September 1969, gave the conditions under which it would and would not be appropriate to use a weighted average discount rate. Robert H. Haveman, "The Opportunity Cost of Displaced Private Spending and the Social Discount Rate," *Water Resources Research,* October 1969, also uses a variant of the approach, but argues that the saving-consumption shares should be the same as the shares of different income groups in the federal personal income tax.

[11]Haveman, "The Opportunity Cost," argues correctly that the effective rate of return facing consumers is understated by looking only at after-tax rates of return on saving, because at least some consumers will be borrowing and investing at before-tax rates. He attempted to compute how important this phenomenon was and found that it raised the true rate of return facing investors and savers by only about one percentage point in 1969. Hence even adjusting for Haveman's phenomenon, the after-tax real rate of return on saving is only about zero, approximately four percentage points below the before-tax investment return.

[12]A more precise argument is needed before it is finally concluded that saving is interest-inelastic. It could be that the saving curve is upward-sloping even though there is a negative intercept. Some economists argue that there is a positive interest elasticity—see, for example, Michael Boskin, "Taxation, Saving, and the Rate of Interest," *Journal of Political Economy*, 86 (April 1978, pt. 2) pp. s3–s27. Contrary econometric evidence is supplied by Phillip Howrey and Saul Hymans, "The Measurement and Determination of Loanable-Funds Saving," *Brookings Papers on Economic Activity*, 3 (1978).

[13]Indeed, in many underdeveloped countries there are also restrictions on private capital markets for investment, requiring rationing of funds to private investors and implying that the observed before-tax rate *r* will also not be determined in the market.

[14]The terminology belongs to James Tobin, "Economic Growth as an Objective of Government Policy," *American Economic Review,* May 1964. This approach is also favored in a persuasive article by Feldstein, "The Inadequacy of Weighted Discount Rates."

[15]The Marglin article is "The Social Rate of Discount and the Optimal Rate of Investment," *Quarterly Journal of Economics,* February 1963. Some skepticism about its practicality is expressed by A. R. Prest and R. Turvey, "Cost-Benefit Analysis: A Survey," *Economic Journal,* 1965. The Phelps article is, "The Golden Rule of Accumulation: A Fable for Growthmen," *American Economic Review,* September 1961. An easy explanation of this model, now standard fare in macroeconomics textbooks, was first

given by Harry G. Johnson, "Money in a Neo-classical One-Sector Growth Model," in R. W. Clower, ed., *Monetary Theory* (New York: Penguin, 1969).

[16]The slope of the production function equals dy/dk. Using uppercase letters to denote gross magnitudes and assuming that the labor force is fixed,

$$\frac{dy}{dk} = \frac{d(Y/L)}{d(K/L)} = \frac{dY}{dK}$$

which is the general formula for the marginal product of capital.

[17]Edward F. Denison, *Accounting for United States Economic Growth, 1929–1969* (Washington, D.C.: Brookings Institution, 1974), p. 127.

[18]The axis of Figure 6.6 is written in terms of the logarithm of consumption per capita so that the growth paths can be drawn as straight lines.

[19]The other way of looking at this standard is found by extending the tangent to the ordinate, as is done in Figure 6.5. Since the slope of the tangent is r, the vertical distance between y^* and $y^* - rk^*$ on the diagram is equal to rk^*. This comes from the fact that

$$\text{slope} = r = \frac{\text{vertical distance}}{k^*} \quad ,$$

so that the vertical distance equals rk^*. The value rk^* is simply the marginal product of capital times its optimal quantity, or total profits in the economy along the optimal saving path. Because $r = n$ at k^*, rk^* can then be seen to equal sy. Total saving must equal the total profits in the economy.

[20]In fact, it is possible to introduce an additional refinement. When consumption per capita rises overtime (some of n is due to technology), the social discount rate might also be raised to reflect the higher marginal utility of lower consumption now than of higher consumption later. The more general expression for the discount rate becomes $(n' - n)e + n$, where n is now interpreted as population growth, n' as the total growth rate of the economy, and e as the elasticity of the marginal utility of consumption with respect to consumption, a number that has been estimated to lie between 1 and 2.5. In our model, when all growth is due to population, the discount rate remains at n. At the other extreme, if all growth is due to technology, $n = 0$ and the discount rate would be en', somewhat above the unadjusted Golden Rule rate n'. A derivation of this result using simple calculus is given by Layard, *Cost-Benefit Analysis,* p. 65.

[21]It is also possible to look at this disparity in terms of share of output devoted to investment. Using data for 1977, a year of reasonably high employment, corporate profits and net interest payments, the two sources of income accruing to those who have done past saving, account for 14 percent of net national product. This is the computed value for rk/y of note 19. Net private domestic and foreign investment accounts for only 5 percent of net national product, but we must also add in the share of government spending and consumption, which involve accumulation of tangible assets and should really be classified as investment. Gross public sector construction was about 2 percent of GNP and purchases of durable consumer goods (net of depreciation) about 6 percent of GNP. Hence using either test, it is not possible to find evidence of extreme undersaving in the United States.

[22]See Kenneth J. Arrow "Discounting and Public Investment Criteria," in A. V. Kneese and S. C. Smith, ed., *Water Resources Research,* Baltimore, 1966; Arrow and Mordecai

Kurz, *Public Investment, the Rate of Return and Optimal Fiscal Policy,* Baltimore, 1970; Martin S. Feldstein, "The Inadequacy of Weighted Discount Rates," *op. cit.*; and David F. Bradford, "Constraints on Government Investment Opportunities and the Choice of Discount Rate," *American Economic Review,* December 1975.

[23]Partha Dasgupta, Stephen Marglin, and Amartya Sen, *Guidelines for Project Evaluation,* United Nations Industrial Development Organization, New York, 1972, chap. 14, have developed a shadow pricing procedure for getting at the problem. To derive it, they assume that public investment yields real benefits of B per year, starting in year 1 and extending forever. The present value of the stream of benefits, discounted at the social optimum discount rate n, is B/n. The capital cost is all borne in year 0 and equals K_0. Were all funds taken from consumption, the appropriate discount rule would be to invest if $B/n - K_0 > 0$, as in the preceding section. Were all funds taken from investment, the appropriate standard would be to invest if $(B/r) - K_0 > 0$, or if $B/n - (r/n) K_0 > 0$, as we discussed in the private before-tax investment-rate case. The quantity r/n is called the "shadow price" of funds drawn from private investment—really the adjustment of capital cost needed to express capital (K_0) in terms of consumption units when society is not saving at the optimal rate (that is, when $r \neq n$). Hence we can rewrite the investment decision rule as

$$\frac{B}{n} - [sP_K + (1 - s)]K_0 > 0$$

where s is the proportion of output devoted to private investment, or the proportion of public investment funds that displaces private investment, and P_K is the shadow price of private investment. The term in brackets and the discount rate for public investment are related as follows:

VALUE OF s	TERM IN BRACKETS	IMPLIED DISCOUNT RATE
0	1	n
1	r/n	r
$0 < s < 1$	$\dfrac{n(1 - s)}{n - sr}$	$\dfrac{n(1 - s)}{1 - (r/n)s}$

In the United States, when r is only slightly above n, all values for the bracketed term are close to unity and the implied discount rates are near n or r. If, for example, $s = .25$, $r = .04$, and $n = .035$, the implied discount rate is .037; if $s = .5$, the implied discount rate is .041. If the gap between r and n were larger, however, so also would be the shadow adjustment and the deviations in the implied discount rate from either r or n. Finally, the astute (and at this point energetic) reader will note that the implied discount rate appears to be undefined for high savings rates, specifically when $s \geq n/r$. This might appear bothersome but in fact is not, for if s were to stay high enough to reduce the denominator to zero, the implied saving policy would long ago have reduced r to n, eliminating the entire problem.

PROBLEMS

6.1 Assume that you are comparing two projects, both of which cost $100 in year 0 and have the following returns 1 and 2 years hence:

	YEAR 1	YEAR 2
Project A	$114.000	
Project B		$125.40

a. If $r = .06$, which is the best project? How many and which of the two would you recommend building?

b. Same as part **a** when $r = .11$.

c. Same as part **a** when $r = .15$.

6.2 **a.** You have a project that pays a stream of benefits equaling $100 per year and lasting forever. What is the present value of this stream if the stream starts 1 year from now and the discount rate is 10 percent? 5 percent?

b. If the stream is in real dollars, 10 percent is the nominal interest rate, and 5 percent is the expected rate of inflation, find the present value of the stream. What if the stream starts this year and the discount rate is 10 percent? 5 percent?

6.3 You have two investments, both of which cost $100 this year. One pays $60 for each of the next 2 years, and the other pays $32 for each of the next 4 years. Compute the internal rate of return on each investment, and find the most desirable.

6.4 You are trying to decide whether to build a bridge across the Wabash River. The bridge will take 1 year to build, will cost $1.8 million, and if maintained properly will last forever. The net benefits to society, after deducting the cost of maintenance, will be $100,000 in the initial year's prices, growing in money terms but stable in real terms thereafter as prices rise. The long-term rate of inflation is expected to be 5 percent (hence money benefits next year will be $105,000; etc.), market interest rates are 10 percent, and the real economy has grown over the long run at the rate of 2.5 percent.

a. If you were forced to use the private interest rate as the discount rate, would you build the bridge? Why or why not? What is the logic of this means of discounting? How is your calculation affected by inflation?

b. Can you defend the use of an interest rate other than the private market rate? What might it be, why, and how does it affect your decision?

6.5 Say that an economy's production function is given by $y = \sqrt{k}$, where y is per capita output and k is the capital stock per capita. Initially, the rate of growth of population (n) is .05, with no increase in technology in this country. The initial saving rate (s) is .2.

a. Find this economy's equilibrium capital/labor ratio and level of output per capita. What will happen to capital per capita and output per capita over time? What will happen to the gross capital stock and output level over time? What discount rate is used in the private sector at this saving rate?

b. Find the optimum saving rate for this economy, the level of k and y here, and all other information asked for in part **a**.

7

Distributional Considerations: The Gains and Losses of Different Groups

To this point we have used the Kaldor–Hicks standard in our evaluations of public programs: a program is a success if it yields positive net gains, that is, if the gainers could compensate the losers and still be better off. Since we have not required the gainers to pay this compensation, however, there will be gainers and losers and we have avoided the difficult question of examining who actually receives the gains and losses. Our position has been that it does not matter whether the gain is received by group A or group B: we just add up all the gains and losses and arrive at a verdict on the program.

This procedure is oversimplified, because there are some important cases in which it does matter who gets the gains and losses. A first example, perhaps an obvious one but often confused in practice, is that of outsiders. In almost any governmental project, some benefits and costs will be felt by those outside the jurisdiction of the government making the evaluation decision: those affected by foreign trade in the case of federal government evaluations; consumers in the next state or next town in the case of state and local evaluations. Clearly, it matters to the taxpayers of community A if the beneficiaries of a project live in community B, and clearly this incidence of benefits must be taken account of in the evaluation of a project.

A second and more complicated example is also very common. In Chapter 2 we argued that governmental decision makers have valid rationales for pursuing the goal of redistributive equity as well as economic efficiency. This suggests that society will go out of its way to improve the distribution of income—actually sacrificing on efficiency grounds for the sake of equity improvements. As applied to evaluation, the same reasoning implies that as long as there is a cost to the transfer of income to low-income individuals (the cost being measured by the leaks in the leaky bucket), some adjustments in the straight Kaldor–Hicks efficiency standard may be appropriate when a project does entail changes in the income distribution.[1] The way in which these adjustments are made is to tally up the gains and losses from a project, placing an added weight on the gains and losses of low-income groups. This added weight refers in some way to the social value of the income-distribution change due to the program.

There can also be a geographical dimension to the distributional considerations. Countries with a federal structure, such as Canada and Australia, worry not only about the national benefits and costs of a project, but they also try to spread these benefits across different regions of the country. A public investment in Canada is valued more highly if it raises incomes in Ontario *and* Quebec rather than in just one or the other province.[2] A way to incorporate these considerations into an evaluation is to weight more heavily those gains that are received in different provinces or those gains that are received in lower-income provinces.

Weighting the gains and losses of different groups more or less heavily can have a dramatic impact on the evaluated net benefits of a project. To take some concrete examples, recall the Urbania subway example of Chapter 5. In the linear-demand-curve case, we found that existing commuters gained a consumer surplus of $25,000, new commuters gained $12,500, and the bus company lost $10,000. Net benefits under the Kaldor–Hicks standard were $27,500, and if the subway's annual cost were less than that, we would recommend that the subway be built.

But now we assume that all the new commuters using the subway are from a different town outside the jurisdiction of the Urbania city government. If this city government were properly trying to represent only the interests of its own citizens, it would *ignore* those benefits received by new commuters outside the jurisdiction and compute net internal benefits for the subway as $25,000 − $10,000 = $15,000. The net benefits of the subway are barely more than half of what they were before.

On the other hand, those benefits received by commuters outside Urbania might have an extra weight in the evaluation. Say that the benefits were received by residents in a very poor suburb, who now would be able to commute to areas where there were better jobs. Say also that the government considering building the subway was a regional transportation authority or a state government, responsible for the welfare of both citizens in Urbania and those in the low-income suburb. The regional transportation authority might be trying to promote development of the depressed area as well as economic efficiency and so give added weight to those gains experienced by new commuters from the depressed area. If the authority should choose a weight of 2 (that is, a dollar gain by a depressed-area commuter has twice the weight of a dollar gain or loss by those inside Urbania), the new formula for determining the net benefits of the subway would be

$$(1)(\$25,000) + (2)(\$12,500) - (1)(\$10,000) = \$40,000$$

Now the net benefits of the subway are 50 percent higher than they were in the simple case in which distributional considerations were unimportant. These numbers would be exactly the same were the added commuters simply low-income people living inside Urbania and now able to take public transportation because it was cheaper.

It can be seen from these simple examples that when allowance is made for the gains and losses of different groups—whether because they live outside the jurisdiction, have low incomes, or for any other reason—the results of an evaluation can change significantly. Indeed, one of the first tasks any evaluator must face is to decide whose gains and losses will be counted and how much they will be weighted in an evaluation. In this chapter we demonstrate a few techniques for doing that. All of the examples involve income redistribution benefits within a jurisdiction, but the very same techniques can be employed whenever differential weights of gains and losses are to be used in an evaluation, for whatever reason. Indeed, the techniques discussed here are those used to deal with any kind of uncertainty in an evaluation. After demonstrating the techniques in general, the chapter closes with a specific illustration of how benefit-cost logic can be used to estimate the cost effectiveness of various policies for income redistribution.

DIFFERENTIAL WEIGHTS

The general formula for determining the weighted net benefits of a program can be expressed as

(1) $$NB = \sum_{i=1}^{m} \frac{dSW}{dY_i} \, dY_i = \sum_{i=1}^{m} w_i \, dY_i$$

where NB is the net benefits of a program, there are m groups in society, dSW/dY_i refers to the change in an abstract overall social welfare function per dollar gain of the *i*th group, and dY_i is the real income change of the *i*th group, comprised of added consumer or producer surplus, lost profits, or whatever. For simplicity, the social welfare weights dSW/dY_i are simply called w_i on the right side of the equation. Because it is understood that net benefits summed in this way are to be compared with net costs, say paid entirely by taxpayers within the jurisdiction, the assumed weight for contributors, or taxpayers, is 1. If some group has the same social welfare weight as taxpayers, it is also set as 1; if a group has more claim to benefits because it is perhaps more disadvantaged, its weight will exceed 1; and if a group has less claim to social benefits, say because some of its members live outside the jurisdiction, its weight will be less than 1. In the Kaldor–Hicks efficiency-evaluation case, all social welfare weights are simply set at 1 and distributional questions are ignored.[3]

The most common application of weighting in the evaluation literature is to take account of the income-redistribution gains and losses of a project. If society already has an equitable distribution of income or has no limits on its ability to redistribute income (no "leaky budget" problem discussed in Chapter 2), there is no cause for tampering with the straightforward efficiency evaluation by setting differential weights. But if either of these conditions is not fulfilled, any project that improves either the relative or absolute distribution of income in society will have a side benefit in helping society to achieve its income-distribution goals, one that must not be ignored in public-sector evaluations. This side benefit can be taken account of by assigning a social welfare weight to the gains or losses of low-income families in excess of 1, as was done in the subway example. If society cares only about pulling up low incomes, that is the end of the story. If it also wishes to pull down high incomes and equalize the overall income distribution from both sides, a weight of less than 1 would be assigned the gains of high-income groups.[4]

This convention seems straightforward enough, but it does mask some important new complications in the evaluation of a project. For one thing, since distributional weights are to be applied, it now becomes much more difficult to do the evaluation. In Chapters 2 and 5 we showed a few shortcuts for finding the net benefits of a project—finding the deadweight loss triangles, eliminating all transfers between groups, and so forth. These shortcuts cannot be used if a weighting calculus is to be made. The income changes of each group must be estimated separately and a weight applied. By the same token, the social value of a project is no longer independent of its financing. If paid for by taxes on one group, which is, let us say, disadvantaged, a project is worth less than if paid for by another, more advantaged group.

Another unusual twist has been pointed out by Arnold Harberger.[5] In Chapters 2 and 5 we showed how the benefits and costs of a project might include changes for groups not directly involved. To take one example, if a project employs low-wage labor, it could push up market wage rates and yield producer surplus to a whole class of low-wage workers, not just those actually working on the project. Weighting this producer surplus gain more heavily for distributional reasons gives the not-illogical but perhaps unexpected result that most of the gains from a project go to those who have nothing to do with it directly. It is perhaps even more bizarre that a rise in the wage rate paid this labor group could raise the net benefits of the project.

Finally, we should be clear that in using distributional weights, we are introducing the possibility of economic inefficiency. In the subway example, we would be prepared to spend up to $40,000 per year on the subway, $12,500 more than we would be prepared to spend without any distributional weights. If the cost of making a simple transfer to low-income groups is less than $12,500, society should just make that transfer and forget about distributional weighting. This example illustrates an important principle: it is all right to use distributional weights, but the evaluator should also do the evaluation in straightforward Kaldor–Hicks terms so that the absolute cost of the distributional adjustment can be measured. It makes no sense to justify distributional weighting because society cannot make costless income transfers and then use these weights to defend economic waste that is far greater than the efficiency cost of a transfer.

ESTIMATING THE WEIGHTS

We now demonstrate a few techniques for actually assigning distributional weights. Although the techniques could in principle apply to distributional changes for both high- and low-income groups, in practice most observers seem to worry much more about the existence of low incomes than of high incomes. Hence we focus on distributional changes at the lower end of the scale. The techniques are all modifications of techniques that can be employed whenever there is any kind of uncertainty in defining the benefits and costs of a project. They are only brought up here because the distributional weighting of gains and losses is typically one of the most speculative aspects of any evaluation.

Displaying the Gains and Losses

A first technique is perhaps too obvious to mention. Referring to a comment made in Chapter 1, one of the great advantages of the evaluation methodology is that even if it does not give a clear answer, it shows how to ask the question. That is, it provides a framework for organizing and arraying the various benefits and costs of an evaluation. Following this, it is important for the evaluator not to get too fancy and try to arrive at only one overall weighted net benefits number. Particularly when the gains and losses of different groups are at stake, the evaluator should be sure, at a minimum, to record and display these gains and losses. Complicated techniques can later be used to weight them and add up the gains, but the policymaker using the results of the evaluation should at least know who gains, and by how much, when making any decision.

Inferring the Weights

Turning now to techniques for assigning weights, we can examine what society already does and infer from that the relative weights it must assign to improvements in the welfare of low-income people.[6] An illustration might be the U.S. personal income tax. Say that a rich person faces a marginal tax rate on the last dollar of income earned of .5, whereas a poor person faces a marginal tax rate of only .25. If we can rely on the ultimate rationality of the personal income tax as a measure of social judgment on the income distribution (this passage should not be read in April), the structure of marginal rates indicates that the rich person's sacrifice of $.50 is just as painful as the poor person's sacrifice of $.25. Alternatively, a $.50 sacrifice by the poor person is twice as painful as a $.50 sacrifice by the rich person. Carrying the logic one step further, all benefits to poor people from a program should be given a weight of t_r/t_p times the weight given benefits to rich people, when t_r and t_p are the marginal effective tax rates paid by rich and poor people, respectively.

One must be careful not to apply this logic too mechanically. When carried to its extreme, it seems to imply that all income should be equally distributed in the country: all poor people have lower marginal tax rates than all rich people, and society will always gain by making income transfers up to the point where there are no rich people and no poor people left. The reasoning actually does not have quite this strong an implication, because there are other social objectives reflected in tax laws and other external constraints against equalizing incomes. If, for example, both rich and poor people reduce work effort in response to higher taxes and transfers, society might stop making transfers far short of the equal-income point, even though the social weight on low-income gains is still above that on high-income gains. But the illustration does show the problem of trying to infer too much from the much-maligned income tax law, or indeed from any redistributive law.[7] If social preferences are inconsistent, they are inconsistent, and no single expression of them can safely be used. If, on the other hand, they are consistent, society can somehow magically come to the right decision without the aid of any analysis, and the role of evaluation advice is greatly lessened. (If you believe the latter, you probably should not waste too much more time on this book.)

Bracketing the Weights

Another approach would be to bracket the distributional weights and see if anything could be learned from that. If we divide society into low-income people and all others, and assume for simplicity that the weight to be placed on the gains and losses of others is 1, the net benefits decision rule of eq. (1) can be rewritten

$$(2) \qquad NB = w_1 dY_1 + dY_2 \geq NC$$

where group 1 is comprised of low-income households, and group 2 of all other households. The equation says that any program will be viewed as a success if its net benefits exceed its net costs (NC). The social welfare weight for low-income gains, w_1, is at least as great as 1, but let us say no greater than α, so that $1 < w_1 < \alpha$. One test focuses on the bottom bracket. Assume that w_1 equals its minimum value of 1. If NB still exceeds NC, the program is a success even if its distributional gains are ignored, and it is not necessary to estimate w_1 to make an overall verdict on the program. On the other side, w_1 can be assumed to equal a higher number α, above the highest value likely for w_1. If NB < NC, the program appears to be a failure, even if a very generous assumption is used to value low-income gains. Thus the bracketing approach permits at least some decisions to be made, and also shows how significant the weighting problem is in the overall evaluation.

Finding the Internal Weights

A third procedure is much like the internal rate of return approach discussed in Chapter 6. This time we just take eq. (2) and solve it for the w_1 necessary to make the program a success by equating NB to NC. Solving the resulting expression yields

$$(3) \qquad\qquad w_1 = \frac{NC - dY_2}{dY_1}$$

Obviously, if w_1 is found to be less than 1, the program is a success regardless of its distributional gains. But if w_1 is a very high number, the expression says that a very high weight is necessary to make the overall program a success. This is one more illustration of the point made in Chapter 1 that evaluation is better viewed as a framework for organizing information than as a final decision-making process. In this case we will not know what w_1 actually is, but we will know how high it must be to make the program a success. We can thus focus the decision on this parameter and be very explicit about how the final verdict comes out.

Specifying the Properties of the Weights

Another approach, which is more arbitrary but also flexible and useful if there are many different income groups that gain and lose from a project, is for the evaluator simply to specify some reasonable properties of the weights and find a mathematical form consistent with these properties. Rewriting eq. (1) for the case of m income groups, the weighted net benefits of a program equal $\sum_{i=1}^{m} w_i \, dY_i$. In this variant the evaluator would specify an overall social welfare function that had two properties:

1. When groups are arrayed from low to high, all w_i are greater than w_{i+1}. That is, the weight for any income group, say the sixth lowest (w_6), is above that for the next group up on the scale (w_7).

2. These weights decline as income increases according to some regular formula. There is no particular substantive reason for the latter consideration, but it does make it easier to analyze complicated problems.[8]

This approach might appear to give the evaluator a great deal of license, but in fact it may not if properly used. It can be combined with the bracketing approach to describe an entire view of the income distribution—one mathematical form can describe a set of social preferences that assigns little value to income redistribution (the extreme case would be the mathematical formula that all weights equal 1), and we can describe a set of preferences that assigns great value. Later, we review a study that uses such a technique.[9]

Cost Effectiveness

A final technique, mentioned in both Chapters 1 and 4 as a good way to get around evaluation uncertainties, is the cost-effectiveness procedure. To apply this technique to the case of income distribution weighting, it is necessary to change the rules somewhat. Now assume that we are not quantifying the distributional gains of a project for which these gains are an incidental benefit, but rather are trying to decide which of several policies designed to redistribute income maximizes social welfare. There are two ways to frame such a question:

1. The evaluator can find the program that yields the largest income gains for low-income groups per dollar of cost to taxpayers.

2. The evaluator can find the program that costs the least to raise the income of low-income groups a given amount.

In either case the evaluator is not saying whether redistribution is desirable—this social goal must be taken as given. But it is possible to say which of the many ways to implement this goal is most efficient in raising benefits most per dollar of taxpayer costs or in raising contributor costs least per dollar of benefits. The actual study reviewed in the next section, by Michael Wolkoff and this author, also uses this cost-effectiveness approach.

A COST-EFFECTIVENESS STUDY OF ALTERNATIVE INCOME REDISTRIBUTION PROGRAMS

Recent social legislation in the United States has at one time or another featured three different ways to raise the incomes of low-income groups:

1. Straightforward transfer programs, such as public assistance, supplemental security income, or "in-kind" transfers.

2. Minimum wages.

3. Job creation programs, such as public service employment.

The first program aims at raising low incomes directly, the second at raising low wage rates, and the third at expanding low-income job opportunities. It is, of course, quite true that all three programs have objectives in addition to income redistribution, but income redistribution is probably the most important rationale for all three. If it were possible to show that one of these programs formed a much better way to redistribute income than the others, at least the analytical case for this program would be quite strong. And even if the less successful programs were continued, this type of evaluation could yield valuable information about the excess costs of their continuance.

The Standards for Redistribution

A problem encountered almost immediately is the difficulty of defining the success of an income-distribution program. Upon examining U. S. poverty statistics we are struck by the bewildering diversity of the low-income problem: some families are poor because they earn very little, others because they have lots of children, others because the primary earner is unemployed, others because the primary earner is not unemployed but earns a very low wage, others because secondary earners cannot find jobs. Some families make very little in all years, whereas others alternate having good- and bad-income years. Some families gain a lot on unearned income, whereas others do not. Almost every conceivable pattern exists, and it is extremely difficult even to define what we mean by income redistribution in such a situation.

Any analysis is forced to make some simplifying assumptions in order to get anywhere at all, and this one is no different. The first assumption we made is that since life in the United States is organized basically around the family unit, in our examination of income-redistribution programs we should do the same. We define income for the family of which the worker is a part and averaging over the number of mouths to be fed in that family. The Department of Health and Human Services (HHS) makes this calculation easier because they have computed what is known as a poverty standard for families of various sizes, the amount of income such families need to be at a very minimum standard of living. This poverty standard was about $6000 per year for a family of four in 1978. Using HHS standard, we can then compute what is known as the "welfare ratio" for a family,

$$(4) \qquad Z = \frac{Y}{N}$$

where Z is this family's welfare ratio, Y its total income (including all money income after taxes and all food stamps or transfers in kind), and N the HHS poverty or needs standard for a family of that size. When the family is just at the poverty line, $Y = N$ and $Z = 1$; if the family has higher than poverty income, $Z > 1$; and if the family has income below the poverty line, $Z < 1$. To abstract from problems caused by the fact that both Y and N vary significantly over time for many families, we used a data source that kept records on families for 9 consecutive years, and computed for each family the 9-year average of Z.[10]

Table 7.1 summarizes these data for 1900 nonaged families over the 9 years from 1967 to 1975. Column (2) gives the percent of the nonaged population in each income class—there it can be seen that only .3 percent of the population has a family income that averages less than half of the poverty standard, and only 5.3 percent of the population (5.0 + .3) has a family income that averages less than the poverty standard.[11] The average income of these families obviously rises as we go up the scale [column (3)], but what is not as expected is that the poverty needs standard falls [column (4)]. This means that on average low-income families are larger than high-income families. Columns (6) and (7) deal with the labor income of the family. Column (6), entitled $2080W/N$, shows how much income (relative to poverty needs) the family's primary earner would make if he or she worked a full 2080-hour year (52 weeks times 40 hours per week). It can be seen that this full-time labor income component amounts to a fairly constant 80 percent of total family income for nonpoor families (compare $2080W/N$ with Y/N), and slightly less for poor families. Column (7) shows the average number of hours of unemployment experienced by the primary earner in a year (out of 2080). Obviously, unemployment declines with income, but note that even very high income families experience some unemployment.

TABLE 7.1 Income Distribution Statistics for 1900 Nonaged Families Averaged over 9 Years, 1967–1975[a]

(1) Y/N CLASS	% OF POPULATION	(3) Y	(4) N	(5) Y/N	(6) 2080W/N	(7) HOURS U
0–.5	.3	3,538	8,913	.397	.287	90.6
.5–1.0	5.0	5,478	6,873	.797	.518	124.3
1.0–1.5	10.0	7,639	5,996	1.274	.974	88.6
1.5–2.0	16.3	10,101	5,640	1.791	1.472	52.2
2.0–3.0	32.3	12,540	5,073	2.472	2.011	38.2
3.0–4.0	21.2	15,963	4,669	3.419	2.696	23.1
4.0–5.0	8.8	19,603	4,432	4.423	3.514	21.7
5.0–6.0	2.9	21,639	4,014	5.391	4.155	17.3
>6.0	3.2	31,908	4,205	7.588	6.531	1.1
Average	100.0	14,301	5,159	2.772	2.224	43.5

[a] Y = average family income for the class
  N = average family needs standard (HHS) definition for the class
  Y/N = average family welfare ratio, defined as in text; a value of less than 1 indicates that the family is in long-term poverty status
  W = average hourly wage of household head in the class; since 2080 is the number of straight-time working hours in a year, $2080W$ is the income the family would have if its only source were the full-time work hours of the head
  Hours U = average hours of unemployment of the family head; this figure, over 2080, would be an average unemployment rate for the family head who works full time.

FIGURE 7.1   Social Benefits of an Increase in Z

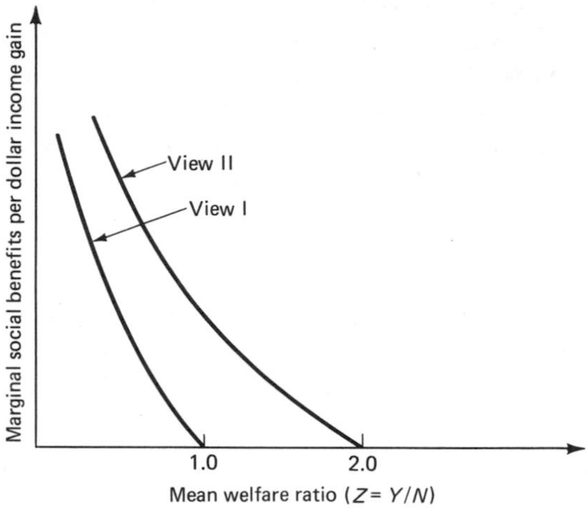

We turn next to preferences for income redistribution. Let us say that all voters favor helping most those most in need of assistance, and all can agree that the families at the top of Table 7.1, those with the lowest welfare ratios (Y/N), are most in need of assistance. But this is not the only decision that must be made, as illustrated in Figure 7.1. This graph plots the excess marginal social value of a dollar gain in income by a family (its "weight" in the discussion above less 1) against its welfare ratio. If society held view I about income redistribution, it would view favorably all the income gains going to the 5 percent of the families in the poverty status, with the value of the transfer or income change declining as family income approached the poverty line and falling to nothing as family income exceeded the poverty line. If society held view II, all income gains of the 30 percent of families up to a welfare ratio of 2.0 have some excess social value, but again there is a declining value within the recipient population as income rises toward twice the poverty level. Since these two views probably bracket true preferences for income redistribution, we have developed mathematical forms that describe each, as suggested by our discussion above of the bracketing technique and the specifying-weights technique.

The Programs

The first program is a straight transfer of income, the simplest and most direct example of which is called a negative income tax. Negative income taxes work according to the formula

(5) $$Y = G + (1 - t)\overline{Y}, \ Y \geq \overline{Y}$$

where Y is now the recipient family's income *after* the transfer; $\overline{Y}$ the income before the transfer; t the transfer reduction rate, or tax rate as it is commonly known; and G the family's guarantee level. These magnitudes are shown graphically in Figure 7.2. The parameters of the plan are G and t, and these determine post-transfer income. If, for example, the family earned nothing at all before the plan, it would receive the income guarantee G (see Figure 7.2). But as its prior income rises, its payment (shown by the shaded area) gets "taxed away" at the rate t. When taxed-away payments equal the guarantee level, $Y = \bar{Y}$ and the family is said to be at the break-even level, B. Above the break-even level, the family receives no payments.[12]

Since the guarantee level and tax rate of a negative income tax plan can be altered to target support to the appropriate families (in Figure 7.1, those holding view I should favor high tax rates and few payments to families above the poverty line; those holding view II would favor low tax rates), it might seem that this approach could not be bested as a way of achieving maximum gain per dollar of taxpayer cost. But, in fact, there are two drawbacks to negative-income-tax plans, one involving a timing problem and one involving a more basic matter of economic efficiency. The timing problem is simply that it may be administratively difficult to define an income horizon that matches the horizon over which society would prefer to make payments. Recent longitudinal data indicate that both income and family size vary widely from month to month, quarter to quarter, and year to year.[13] Voters may prefer to support the income of families who are poor in some relatively long run sense (say their income is low when measured over a several-year period), but not those who dip temporarily into poverty status for a 1- or 3-month period, even though in a more permanent sense

FIGURE 7.2   Negative Income Tax

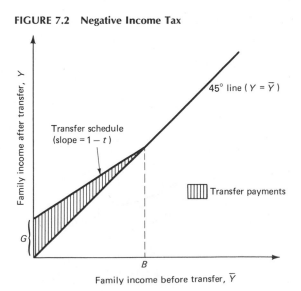

Family income before transfer, $\bar{Y}$

they are fairly well off. If, as appears to be the case, it is difficult to design a negative tax scheme based on the proper horizon from a social standpoint, the negative-income-tax scheme may support many families who should not be covered. Putting this in another way, the short-term measured income used for payments may, when income varies widely, not be a very good indication of long-term permanent income and the need for a transfer.

Perhaps a more serious difficulty is the question of leisure time. The prototype negative-income-tax formula is based on $\bar{Y}$, measured income before the transfer. If for some reason the family members choose not to work much, the family would have a misleading low measured $\bar{Y}$—valuing their leisure time would give them a higher pretransfer income and lower payments.[14] Moreover, since payments are reduced the higher $\bar{Y}$ is, families may be led to reduce their work effort in response to the transfer payment. In microeconomic terms, the negative income tax will reduce work effort for two reasons:

1. The payments raise the family's income, make it better off, and lead to an income effect raising the consumption of leisure time.

2. The tax rate lowers the family's after-tax wage, and the reduced price of leisure time leads to more consumption of it through the substitution effect.

There have been efforts to forestall this reduction in work through a work requirement (no payments unless the primary earner works), but even work requirements cannot forestall the primary earner working fewer hours, secondary workers dropping out, and so forth.

FIGURE 7.3   Work Reduction and the Negative Income Tax

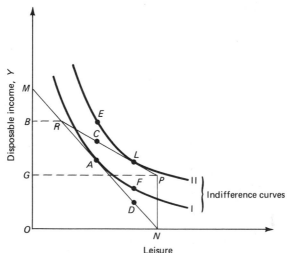

The impact of work reduction clearly makes a negative income tax less desirable on benefit-cost grounds, but it is difficult to determine by how much. The situation, in terms of a diagram dealing with the work–leisure choice of a family, is shown in Figure 7.3. The family is initially faced with a budget line of *MN* and goes to point *A*. A negative income tax is introduced, with a guarantee of *OG* and a breakeven level of *OB* on the disposable-income axis (corresponding to the same magnitudes in Figure 7.2). The budget line becomes *MRPN* and the family goes to point *L* (on the higher indifference curve II), consuming more leisure time in the process. Had the family not consumed more leisure time or reduced its hours of work, its gain in income would have been *CA* and the budget cost of this gain also *CA*. At point *L*, its gain in income is less than *CA* (and in the diagram, not even positive) and the budget cost is greater, or *LD* (the amount of income it must be given at the new level of hours worked). Using this simple comparison, it appears that the reduction in work has lowered the benefit-cost ratio for the negative income tax—the family gains less income and the program costs more tax dollars. Of course, this way of looking at things overpenalizes negative income taxes by ignoring the fact that the gain in leisure time itself has value to the family and (let us say) also to society. Perhaps it takes the form of the primary earner working fewer overtime hours and staying home with the family, secondary workers staying in school longer, or whatever. Including this gain in leisure time as a benefit means that the family's implied indifference level change is greater than the income gain evaluated at the initial level of hours (note that at *A*, the vertical distance between the indifference levels exceeds *AC*). But it is less than the gain at the final level of hours (note that at *L*, the vertical distance is less than *LD*). If there were some way to measure both *AC* and *LD*—as it happens there is (see Chapter 12)—the two amounts could be used to bracket the utility change of the family and find out how much better off it actually is when the leisure change is included.

The other way in which low-income families can be supported is by direct labor market programs. These, in turn, can work either by raising wages, as in minimum wage laws, or by raising employment demand, as in public employment. As programs for *income* support, both have the immediate disadvantage that support is given according to wage rates or unemployment, but not necessarily according to family income. Some of the low-wage workers who are helped or hurt by minimum wages will live in high-income families, if, say, the family has other earners or other sources of income, and some may have higher wages but also a greater risk of unemployment. Similarly, workers with high unemployment may earn high wages when they work, or live in families with ample sources of other labor or nonlabor income.

There can also be some losses that operate strictly through labor markets. The standard example is with minimum wages, where workers are better off because of the high wage rates but worse off because of the reduced demand for their labor. In Figure 7.4, for example, say that the worker initially worked L_0

FIGURE 7.4   **Labor Income with Public Employment and Minimum Wages**

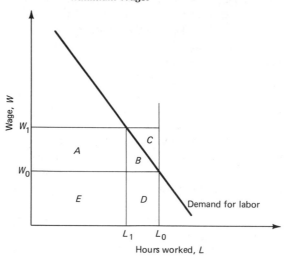

hours, earned W_0 per hour, and had a gross labor income of W_0L_0. If the government instituted a minimum wage of W_1, the worker would find demand for his or her services cut to L_1 and would now earn W_1L_1. This is greater or less than before, as area A in the figure exceeds area D.[15] The benefits of the program to the worker or his or her family can also be expressed as $A - D$, and the minimum wage law will have benefits only if this amount exceeds zero.

So much for the benefits of the minimum wage. What about its cost? It might seem that any benefits received from minimum wage legislation come free of charge, because there are no budget expenditures. But such is not the case, because the higher wage level imposes a cost of area $(A + B)$, the loss in employers' surplus, on these employers. Whether this cost is paid by the stock-holders of these firms or the consumers of their product, it is paid by some contributors and it represents the cost against which any benefits of minimum wages should be compared. For this reason, the notion of cost in this study is broadened to include consumer surplus costs and taxpayer costs, together called contributor costs.

An alternative approach to raising the income of low-income workers would be to institute a public employment plan, again paying a wage of W_1. Public employment is usually thought of as a device for employing unemployed workers, but it is logical to expect it also to operate as a magnet for low-wage *employed* workers, and here we examine its benefits and costs in that case. For simplicity, we also assume that the supply of labor is fixed at L_0.[16]

Examination of Figure 7.4 indicates that the benefit of these public jobs to workers is measured by areas $(A + B + C)$, the gain in wages on the fixed supply of hours. To determine the contributor costs of this program, we would have to know what happens to private wages. Although one can make various assumptions,[17] perhaps the most likely is that private employers try to retain their work force by raising the private wage also to W_1. In this case, the government's budget cost is $(C + B + D)$, the public wage times the amount of private labor disemployed by the higher wages, and the consumer surplus loss is $(A + B)$. Obviously, these benefit and cost calculations change as we make other assumptions about the response of private employers.

Hence each redistribution program has benefits and costs, and the determination of the most cost-effective way to redistribute income depends on a comparison of all of these benefits and costs. If labor supply reductions are small and incomes not highly variable, negative income taxes are likely to raise social benefits most per dollar of contributor cost. If labor demand reductions are small, minimum wages may. And if neither is true, public employment may.[18]

The Results

The actual calculations for the analysis were made by assuming that all families had the preprogram data shown in Table 7.1, then imagining that legislators had passed legislation for a negative income tax, a minimum wage, or a public employment program for family heads over the entire 9-year period. The employment, wages, and income statistics for each family as a result of the plans were then recomputed, and these income gains were weighted by a scheme such as that shown in Figure 7.1. To standardize comparisons in the way required by the cost-effectiveness approach, each plan was assumed to cost contributors an additional $5 billion a year for the 9-year period, and the change in overall social benefits following this standardized plan was measured.

Following the above stricture that we first display the gains and losses of any approach, the benefits, or percentage changes in income, from each plan are shown in Table 7.2. The row headings for the table are the same income-class groupings as those used in Table 7.1, and the column headings are the parameters of a $5 billion plan. For example, a negative income tax (NIT) costing $5 billion would have a tax rate of .7 and a guarantee level of .53 of the poverty line. A minimum wage (MW) with a contributor cost of $5 billion would be 10 percent higher than the present minimum ($\overline{W}$) and fully enforced. A public employment plan (PE) would pay present minimum wages, with jobs offered to only 63 percent of eligible workers ($E = .63$), to keep contributor costs down to $5 billion. The jobs were given at random to the eligible population.

Table 7.2 shows that the NIT raises the incomes of the very lowest groups much more than do the other two programs. This is because many families in these very low income categories do not benefit substantially from the other plans, either because the heads are not able to work many hours or because (for

TABLE 7.2   Percentage Changes in Income from Three Redistribution Plans, 1967–1973[a]

Y/N CLASS	NIT $t = .7, G = .53$	MW $W = 1.1\bar{W}$	PE[b] $W = \bar{W}, E = .63$
0–.5	74.1	12.1	12.7
.5–1.0	14.4	4.8	7.2
1.0–1.5	3.7	1.4	4.0
1.5–2.0	.7	.4	1.4
2.0–3.0	.2	—	.4
3.0–4.0	.1	—	.2
4.0–5.0	—	—	—
5.0–6.0	—	—	—
>6.0	—	—	—

[a]NIT = negative income tax plan with guarantee level (G) equal to .53 of the poverty line and
tax rate (t) equal to .7
MW = minimum wage set at 1.1 times the preexisting minimum ($\bar{W}$)
PE = public employment plan with the wage (W) at the preexisting minimum ($\bar{W}$) and jobs
available for .63 of eligible workers (E)
Y/N = Class is defined in Table 7.1
[b]Assuming that there is a producer surplus gain of $\frac{1}{2}$ for the vacated private jobs.

public employment) not all of the eligible workers get the jobs. Minimum wages raise income for beneficiaries less than the other plans because some workers lose employment, as discussed above.

These income changes are then weighted in line with the differing views of redistribution policy, with the results for a few of the many possible sets of assumptions as shown in Table 7.3. Since the change in the social welfare value per $5 billion increased contribution is a meaningless number, it has been set arbitrarily at 100 for the negative income tax, with gains for the other programs (per $5 billion contributor cost) expressed as a percent of the gains from the NIT. It can be seen from the table that at least in this simple case, the NIT does far outperform the other two approaches for redistributing income: higher minimum wages transfer between 33 and 37 percent to intended beneficiaries per $5 billion contribution, and public employment at the prevailing minimum wage between 49 and 63 percent.

At least under these conditions, then, a negative income tax is the most

TABLE 7.3   Changes in Social Benefits from Three Redistributions Plans, 1967–1975[a]

VIEW	NIT $t = .7, G = .53$	MW $W = 1.1\bar{W}$	PE[b] $W = \bar{W}, E = .63$
I	100	37	49
II	100	33	63

[a]All titles are defined in Table 7.2.
[b]Assuming that there is a producer surplus gain of $\frac{1}{2}$ for the vacated private jobs.

cost-effective way to redistribute income. There are a whole raft of complicating assumptions that could be made, many of which are dealt with in the paper, but this conclusion holds up fairly well under most alternatives. Notice in particular that whether society holds view I or view II about the goals of income redistribution changes, the overall results vary little, despite the radically different implications of these views. Finally, it should be reiterated that the results of Table 7.3 do not ''prove'' that minimum wages and public employment programs are failures and should be abandoned: they say only that negative income taxes seem to raise low incomes more per dollar of contributor cost. Society would still be on firm ground in continuing minimum wages and public employment if it felt that other desirable attributes of these programs outweighed the cost-effectiveness losses shown here. But to the extent the results are accurate, there might well be an additional burden of proof placed on these other programs.

SUMMARY

In this chapter we examined the very difficult and delicate issue of how to deal with gains and losses of various groups. There are some cases, the most common of which is gains and losses experienced by those outside the community, where society should ignore, or place a very low weight on, any gains or losses resulting from government programs. There are other cases, the most common being in dealing with the gains and losses of low-income people, where society might place a high weight on these gains and losses.

Regarding techniques for actually determining the weights that should be used in valuing the gains and losses of low-income groups, perhaps the most important thing to remember is that no technique for dealing with this highly subjective matter is totally satisfactory. A first comment, then, is that whatever technique is used, the gains and losses of various groups should be displayed in any actual evaluation. Beyond this, many of the general techniques for dealing with uncertainty in evaluations can be employed. Weights can be inferred from existing policies (such as the progressive income tax), the evaluation can be done by bracketing the weights, or the internal weight that must be used for the program to be a success can be found. Finally, in cases where the question is not valuing the gains and losses that do occur but rather trying to find the most efficient means of redistributing income, a variant of the cost-effectiveness procedure can be used. When this technique is applied to a comparison of the distributional efficiency of negative income taxes, minimum wages, and public employment, it seems to give a fairly definite nod to negative income taxes as the most cost-effective means of raising low incomes.

NOTES

[1]The precise conditions for using weights are spelled out by Aanund Hylland and Richard Zeckhauser, "Distributional Objections Should Affect Taxes But Not Program Choice or Design," *The Scandinavian Journal of Economics*, 2, 1979. A good discussion of the ethical underpinnings of these conventions is given by Shaul Ben-David, Allen V. Kneese, and William D. Schulze, "A Study of the Ethical Foundations of Benefit-Cost Analysis Techniques," Mimeo, New Mexico University, Albuquerque, N.M., 1979.

[2]See, for example, Walter Hettich, *Why Distribution Is Important: An Examination of Equity and Efficiency Criteria in Benefit-Cost Analysis*, Economic Council of Canada, Ottawa, 1971. For an application to United States public investment policy, see Martin C. McGuire and Harvey A. Garn, "The Integration of Equity and Efficiency Criteria in Public Project Selection," *Economic Journal*, December 1969, pp. 882–893.

[3]The convention used here is to lump jurisdictional and distributional considerations under the heading of weighting, and define the Kaldor–Hicks standard as an example of the absence of weighting. In fact, many evaluators follow a different convention where they might do Kaldor–Hicks efficiency evaluation and weight all gains and losses equally, but only consider those of groups living within an area.

[4]At this point a subtle issue arises. In this double-edged equalization case, should the weight on high-income changes simply be less than 1, or should it be negative? The answer depends on social preferences. If society would rather have low-income households gain than high-income households, but rather have high-income households gain than nothing (for they can make transfers tomorrow), as in the usual mixed efficiency-equity case, the high-income weight is between zero and +1. If on the other hand, society wants to penalize its high-income households—say by taxing them and distributing the proceeds to other communities—the implied social welfare weight is negative. The latter case is rarely, if ever, observed in practice, and does not make much theoretical sense either: any society that felt this ill-disposed toward its high-income members should have already tried to do something about the problem by a system of much more highly progressive taxation.

[5]Arnold C. Harberger, "On the Use of Distributional Weights in Social Cost-Benefit Analysis," *Journal of Political Economy*, April 1978, discusses some of the technical problems of distributional weighting. Robin W. Boadway, "The Welfare Foundations of Cost-Benefit Analysis," *Economic Journal*, December 1974, counters by showing that some weights must be used if relative prices are altered. Some of the philosophical problems of weighting are discussed by A. J. Culyer, "The Quality of Life and the Limits of Cost-Benefit Analysis," in Lowdon Wingo and Alan Evans, eds., *Public Economics and the Quality of Life* (Baltimore, Md.: Johns Hopkins University Press, 1977).

[6]Burton Weisbrod, "Deriving an Implicit Set of Governmental Weights for Income Classes," originally in Samuel B. Chase, ed., *Problems in Public Expenditure Analysis* (Washington, D.C.: Brookings Institution, 1968); reprinted in Richard Layard, ed., *Cost-Benefit Analysis*, (New York: Praeger, 1972).

[7]The problems are illustrated more graphically by Harberger, "On the Use of Distributional Weights." One successful attempt to make inferences regarding citizens' taste for redistribution in the case of public assistance laws can be found in Larry L. Orr, "Income Transfers as a Public Good: An Application to AFDC," *American Economic Review*, June 1976.

[8]Two discussions of this approach are given by Anthony B. Atkinson, "How Progressive Should Income Taxes Be?" in Michael Parkin, ed., *Essays in Modern Economics* (London: Longman, 1973), pp. 90–109; and Martin S. Feldstein, "On the Theory of Tax Reform," *Journal of Public Economics,* July-August 1976, pp. 77–103. Recently, Robert D. Willig and Elizabeth E. Bailey have developed a procedure for dispensing with the second assumption, in "Income Distributional Concerns in Regulatory Policy-Making," Mimeo, Princeton University, 1979. Their procedure is a generalization both of the Kaldor–Hicks assumption (which assumes all weights are the same) and another proposed by John Rawls, a philosopher [in *A Theory of Justice* (Cambridge, Mass.: Harvard University Press, 1971)], that a program not be undertaken unless it improves the welfare of the worst-off individual in society. This Rawlsian idea is similar to I. M. D. Little's earlier suggestion that a project must pass the Kaldor–Hicks test and cause "a good redistribution of wealth." See *A Critique of Welfare Economics* (Oxford: Clarendon Press, 1957).

[9]Edward M. Gramlich and Michael J. Wolkoff, "A Procedure for Evaluating Income Distribution Policies," *Journal of Human Resources,* Summer 1979.

[10]The data source is known as the Panel Survey on Income Dynamics, compiled by the University of Michigan's Institute for Social Research. See, for example, James N. Morgan et al., *Five Thousand American Families: Patterns of Economic Progress,* The University of Michigan, Ann Arbor, Mich., 1974.

[11]Using just the income received in 1 year, about twice as many families (about 11 percent of the nonaged population) are in poverty status. Hence averaging incomes over a 9-year period shows that many "1-year poor" are in that status only temporarily.

[12]Although eligibility and the details of the programs differ widely, both public assistance and food stamps, the major U.S. transfer programs, operate under schedules that work much like this for the eligible families. Efforts at reforming these programs usually take the form of broadening eligibility, eliminating requirements that the transfer be spent on a particular commodity, or equalizing the statewide payments schedules.

[13]See Morgan et al., *Five Thousand American Families.*

[14]See, for example, Robert H. Haveman and Irwin Garfinkel, *Earnings Capacity, Poverty and Inequality* (New York: Academic Press, 1977); and Clair Vickery, "The Time Poor: A New Look at Poverty," *Journal of Human Resources,* Winter 1977.

[15]In welfare terms, the comparison is more complicated because the added leisure time must be accounted for.

[16]It may be wondered why labor supply is fixed in the case of minimum wages and public employment but not for the negative income tax. The answer is that Figure 7.4 deals only with the labor supply behavior of family primary earners, typically rather inelastic, whereas Figure 7.3 deals with the labor supply of all family members. In Chapter 12 we see that this assumption is realistic.

[17]And we do in the original paper.

[18]Many other benefits and costs of public employment are omitted from consideration here. For one attempt to deal with them, see Robert H. Haveman, "The Dutch Social Employment Program," in John L. Palmer, ed., *Creating Jobs: Public Employment Programs and Wage Subsidies* (Washington, D.C.: Brookings Institution, 1978).

PROBLEMS

7.1 A dam costing $1 million and lasting forever will reduce flood damage for high-income property owners and also make power available more cheaply for all consumers. There are 50 high-income families in the community, each of which has real property valued at $30,000. There are 150 low-income families in the community who have no real property at all. The high-income families have an average income of $15,000 and spend 2 percent of it on electricity; the low-income families have an average income of $5000 and spend 3 percent of it on electricity. Income and population are not expected to grow in this community. The dam is expected to cut the cost of power in half and reduce the probability that there will be a flood from 1 percent a year to zero. When there is a flood, it washes everybody out (property damage is total). The discount rate is 3 percent. All families are risk-neutral.

  a. What would be the gross benefits of the dam for all families? The Army Corps of Engineers uses the net benefit rule. Would they want to build the dam?

  b. Representatives of HHS call you in to ask if the program is good for the poor. Does it help the poor at all? More than using the cost of the dam for an income transfer program to poor families?

  c. By the time a decision is made, the price of the dam has risen to $1.2 million. If this dam is to be financed by taxes paid entirely by high-income groups, and transfer payments to low-income groups are fixed whether or not the dam is built, compute the distributional weights for gains to low-income groups necessary to make the project worthwhile. Does it matter who pays the taxes?

7.2 Say we have two projects that yield the following net gains to high- and low-income groups:

	GAINS TO LOW INCOME	GAINS TO HIGH INCOME
Project A	.5	1.1
Project B	1.0	.2

Which project is preferable under the Kaldor–Hicks standard? If the income tax system is used to infer distributional weights, and high-income groups face a tax rate of .20 and low-income groups a tax rate of .15, which project is preferable? What about when marginal tax rates on rich and poor are .6 and .2, respectively? What is the relative weight for low-income groups that would leave society indifferent between the two projects?

7.3 Say that a worker had a total of 2500 hours a year to allocate either to work or leisure time, and that she made an hourly wage rate of $3. Initially, she worked 1500 hours, consumed 1000 hours of leisure time, and had no other sources of income. Her labor supply is given by the expression $H = 1500 + 50 \, \Delta W - .1 \, \Delta Y$, where ΔW is the net (after-tax) wage received by the worker and ΔY the change in income at the initial level of labor supply.

What is the worker's initial disposable income? A negative-income-tax plan is introduced that works according to the formula $NIT = 2500 - .5YD$, where NIT is the transfer level and YD is disposable income. Find the worker's subsequent level of hours worked, disposable income, and transfer payments. What would have been her level of transfer payments had she not changed her hours worked?

7.4 **a.** Say that the private demand for labor is given by $W = 7 - .05L$ and the supply by $W = .02L$, where W is the wage and L is the number of workers. Find the initial equilibrium level of hourly wage rates and employment.

b. A public employment plan is introduced that pays \$2.50 an hour to any and all comers. Say that private establishments are forced to pay this going wage to retain their work force. Find private employment, total employment, public employment, and the government's cost of this public employment plan. Is there any other cost paid by contributors?

8

Physical Investments and the Environment

The logic of evaluation and benefit-cost analysis was first developed for physical investment projects. The early benefit-cost documents of the government in the 1930s and 1950s cited in Chapter 1 all concerned physical investment projects, as did the first major evaluation studies by academic economists, such as those by Otto Eckstein and John Krutilla in 1958.[1] The field has been an active one ever since, with many physical investment evaluations being done on many diverse types of investment projects in many different countries and printed in many different languages.[2]

Physical investment projects raise most of the standard issues covered so far in this book—valuation of resources, uncertainty, discounting, and in a lesser way, the distributional question. They also raise the relatively new environmental question, and this question will be the particular concern of this chapter. Unlike many other issues dealt with in the field, where it might sometimes seem that the stakes are rather small and not of pressing national importance, environmental issues have a way of attaining rather epic proportions. Whether one is deciding whether to build a dam that will kill off an endangered species, a topic we take up later in the chapter, or to build nuclear power plants that will generate radioactive nuclear wastes that could potentially contaminate the planet for thousands of years, public-sector decision makers are being asked to make extremely significant choices. For the most part, these choices are not the stuff of economics, that marginalist discipline, and there is no pretense here that the logic of benefit-cost analysis can ever proceed very far on some of the more fundamental issues. But as with the distributional question, there are some techniques that can help focus the analysis on the fundamentals in the proper way, and we will be looking carefully at these.

The chapter begins by considering how a physical investment evaluation would be done if it entailed no environmental costs at all. Then we introduce environmental costs and see how decision rules change. Finally, we look in detail at a particular physical investment project with important environmental implications. That is the famous case of the Tellico Dam on the Little Tennessee River, the dam that seems likely to destroy the last remaining habitat of the snail darter, a small minnow that lives only in free-flowing stretches of the Little Tennessee. This evaluation was the first heard by the Supreme Court under the Endangered Species Act, the first to be appealed to the federal government's new Endangered Species Committee, and, alas, the first where brute-force political considerations overrode the recommendations of the Endangered Species Committee.

THE PROJECT WITHOUT ENVIRONMENTAL COSTS

The prototype case dealt with in this chapter is where some physical investment project yields positive benefits—cheaper electric power, cheaper oil, or whatever—but also entails environmental costs. Since by their very nature environmental costs are difficult to quantify, this standard case often forces decision makers to make rather difficult choices between the consumption needs of the present generation and long-term environmental amenities or necessities. Although it may seem that the environmental costs are more important and should be dealt with first, in fact we can probably make more headway attacking the problem the other way around. By now we have covered standard and fairly well understood ways of estimating the net benefits of a project as long as we totally ignore environmental costs. If an evaluation does not even find these net benefits (call them nonenvironmental net benefits) to be positive, including the environmental costs will make overall net social benefits even more negative and clearly indicate that the investment should not be undertaken. In such cases resolving the benefit-cost problem is relatively easy, and any inability to quantify environmental costs is no excuse for not doing the evaluation and arriving at a clear decision. Recalling Chapter 7, this would be one illustration of the bracket approach: we are taking the lower-bracket estimate of environmental costs, zero, and seeing if we can make a decision.

In other cases, however, matters will not be so clear. If the nonenvironmental net benefits are positive, they must be compared with the difficult to quantify environmental costs to see if the overall net social benefits are positive.[3] There are some techniques for quantifying these environmental costs, techniques that are covered in this chapter, but as with other instances of evaluation uncertainty, these techniques will never be entirely satisfactory. The policy choices in such cases are unavoidably difficult, and it would be naive to assert that simply going through the evaluation methodology makes them easy. However, it is still helpful to go through the evaluation exercise of trying to value nonenvironmental net benefits to know whether there is a conflict and to boil the investment decision down to its essentials.

The first task is then to determine these nonenvironmental net benefits, together with their distribution between consumers and producers. Say we have a prototype physical investment project that produces cheaper oil, electricity, or whatever. As a result of the project, the costs of producing a consumer good are reduced from P_0 to P_1 in Figure 8.1. To avoid complicating the analysis, assume also that this consumer good is supplied competitively, so that marginal production costs equal the market price.

There are two possible cases, one where the facility provides enough of the factor of production that all consumer goods can be supplied more cheaply, and one where it does not. In the first case, assume the facility generates enough electric power that the competitive supply curve in the market is shifted downward from a horizontal line at P_0 to a horizontal line at P_1. The new market equilibrium is at (Q_1, P_1), and the entire hatched area, $P_1 P_0 AB$, represents a

FIGURE 8.1 Market for a Consumer Good Where the Physical Investment Reduces Costs

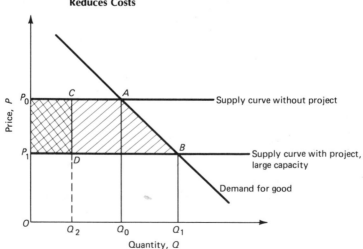

consumer surplus gain of the project. Normally, we would deduct from this consumer surplus gain a producer surplus loss, but in this case with competitive and horizontal supply curves, there is no producer surplus loss. Producer surplus was zero before the shift and after the shift. Remember, however, that with either upward-sloping supply curves or monopolistic imperfections in the market, there would need to be an additional negative entry for project benefits.

A contrasting case results when the facility cannot produce enough electric power to supply the whole consumer goods market, but only part of it, say OQ_2. In this case the new competitive supply curve becomes P_1DCA, and the market equilibrium remains at (Q_0, P_0), exactly what it was without the facility. The facility creates no consumer surplus at all because it does not affect costs or prices at the margin, but it does create producer surplus by reducing the price of some inframarginal output. This added producer surplus, P_1P_0CD, represents the benefit of the project, and it accrues just to producers.[4] Hence both the level of benefits (P_1P_0AB or P_1P_0CD) and their distribution between consumers and producers depend on the scale of output from the investment project.

We then must consider the permanence of these project benefits over time. There are many reasons why the benefits, for consumers or producers, may not be very permanent:

> **1.** If the physical investment becomes obsolete or experiences physical wear and tear, production costs of the consumer good, P_1, will rise over time even if the project is built. If P_1 in Figure 8.1 rises over time, project benefits obviously decline over time.

> **2.** In the case of a well or a mine, the most easily accessible supplies of the resource may be mined first, leaving the higher-cost and more marginal supplies. Again, production costs of the good will rise over time and project benefits will decline over time.

> **3.** There may also be technological advances for substitute factors which lower production costs without the facility, P_0. An example might be technological innovations in the supply of solar energy. If P_0 falls over time, again project benefits will fall.

For all three reasons, we might expect that the initial benefits of a project to consumers or producers will decay over time according to

$$B_1 = B_0 (1 - d)$$
$$B_2 = B_1 (1 - d) = B_0 (1 - d)^2$$

where B_0 represents the initial benefit of the project, the relevant area in Figure 8.1, B_1 represents benefits in the next year, B_2 in the following year, and so forth, and d is the annual rate of decay of these benefits. If the capital cost of the project is K_0, all borne in the initial year, and the project begins generating benefits equal to B in year 1, the net present value of the nonenvironmental benefits of the project (NB) can be expressed as

$$(1)\ NB = \frac{B}{1+r} + \frac{B(1-d)}{(1+r)^2} + \frac{B(1-d)^2}{(1+r)^3} + \cdots + \frac{B(1-d)^{T-1}}{(1+r)^T} - K_0$$

where T is the number of years the facility will be in operation. As T approaches infinity, this expression can be solved in the way shown in Chapter 6, note 1, to yield

$$(2) \qquad\qquad NB \rightarrow \frac{B}{r+d} - K_0 \qquad as\ T \rightarrow \infty$$

In the limiting case ($T = \infty$), whenever $B/(r+d) < K_0$, the project does not even have positive nonenvironmental net benefits, it should not be built, and there is no need even to deal with environmental costs. If $B/(r+d) > K_0$, it does have positive nonenvironmental net benefits, and we must compare them with the environmental costs. Note also that including the decay rate, d, can make an enormous difference in the present value of the nonenvironmental net benefits. Even if d is a relatively modest number such as .04 per year, approximately the level of the real discount rate in the United States under a few variants discussed in Chapter 6, the discounted value of the gross benefits of the project $B/(r+d)$ is cut in half by simply accounting for benefit decay.

INCLUDING ENVIRONMENTAL COSTS

Just as we can disaggregate the overall benefits and costs into a quantifiable nonenvironmental component and a more-difficult-to-quantify environmental component, environmental costs can be similarly subdivided. Some of these costs appear to be absolutely unquantifiable, such as the value of preserving a rare species or a breathtaking view. Some are more quantifiable. If, for example, a dam will flood and destroy a valuable wilderness area now used for hiking, canoeing, fishing, hunting, or bird watching, there are some commercial markets for each of these services. One might estimate a demand curve in some market where, say, the fishing is approximately as good as in the wilderness area that may be lost, adjust for differences in transportation costs, and come up with a hypothetical demand curve for this area. In such a way, at least many of the environmental costs of the investment project can be quantified and incorporated into the evaluation.

Some of the subtleties in the process are shown by analyzing Figure 8.2. Let us assume for the sake of argument that a prospective dam will flood a wilderness area that offers recreational services much the same as some "comparison" areas—areas with as many miles of hiking trails, campgrounds, birds, fish, and animals. By estimating consumers' response to the prices charged by these other areas and to the travel time to get there, it is possible to estimate a demand curve for the area to be destroyed.[5] This is the demand curve shown in Figure 8.2.

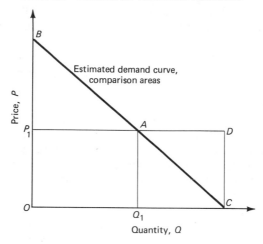

FIGURE 8.2 **Demand for Wilderness Recreation**

A common method for estimating the loss when a wilderness area is destroyed is to take the price charged in a comparison area, P_1, and the number of hikers and hunters in that area, Q_1, and multiply them together to get a measure of gross payments of recreational users of OP_1AQ_1.[6] Although commonly used, this method has very little to recommend it. Even though we measure the consumer demand curve from the demand, or willingness to pay, for a comparison area, we should generally *not* be concerned with the price charged in that area because it probably does not represent the true marginal cost of services in the area that might be destroyed.

To take a few examples, say first that the true marginal cost of providing recreational services in the area that might be destroyed is just the price charged in the comparison area, P_1. Then the rectangle OP_1AQ_1 represents not consumer losses but marginal costs foregone in destroying the wilderness area. The loss experienced by society, or the environmental cost of destroying the area, is not the rectangle but the consumer surplus triangle, P_1BA. It can be seen that this triangle is greater or less than the commonly measured rectangle, depending on the slope of the demand curve. Note further that the triangle is the true measure of loss *regardless* of the pricing policy actually followed in the comparison area. Services there could be priced monopolistically above P_1, efficiently at P_1, or inefficiently below P_1: the *potential* social loss in destroying this area is the same P_1BA every time. If, on the other hand, true marginal costs of providing services in the area that might be destroyed were zero, the entire triangle, OBC, represents the true environmental loss—this time the loss is clearly larger than the commonly measured rectangle. Note again that pricing policy for the comparison area is irrelevant—the only things that matter are willingness to pay and marginal costs of upkeep for the area to be destroyed.[7]

Just as with nonenvironmental benefits, there are also a set of horizon issues influencing environmental costs. Say that the initial environmental cost, in terms of lost consumer surplus less foregone upkeep costs, is E_0. But this environmental cost can change over time. A few likely possibilities are shown in Figure 8.3:

1. If environmental costs are related to the rate of production from the facility, such as the damage from oil spills, they will decline say at the benefit decay rate d, as shown by the bottom cost curve.

2. If environmental costs are related to the population that can use a wilderness area and the income available to be spent on hunting and fishing, they will *rise* over time, say at the rate of growth of real income in the area, n. But eventually the quantity of hunting and fishing services provided by the wilderness area will hit a peak set by the capacity of the area, and from that point on environmental costs could be constant. This is shown by the cost curve kinked at time t.[8]

3. If environmental costs are related to the population in an area exposed to certain risks, say from storing radioactive wastes, and we use either the DFE or RC standard of Chapter 5 for valuing these lives, environmental costs will grow forever at the rate of growth of real income in the area, as shown by the top curve.

4. Finally, we might imagine a case where environmental costs neither rise nor fall, but simply remain constant at E_0 forever. It is very hard to think of an example where this is strictly true in a society where population and income are growing: perhaps the closest example would be the supposed constant annual cost of killing off an endangered species, but even here the value foregone may rise as the number of biologists and environmentalists rises.

The decision rule for a project with positive environmental net benefits costing K_0 in the initial year and lasting forever now becomes

FIGURE 8.3 Environmental Costs over Time

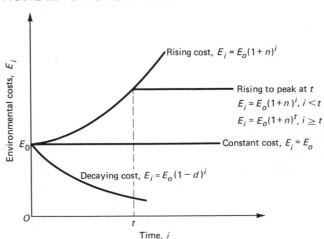

$$\text{(3A) NSB} = \frac{B}{r + d} - \frac{E}{r + d} - K_0 \qquad \text{if environmental costs decay at rate } d \text{ over time}$$

$$\text{(3B) NSB} = \frac{B}{r + d} - \frac{E}{r} - K_0 \qquad \text{if environmental costs are constant at } E \text{ forever}$$

$$\text{(3C) NSB} = \frac{B}{r + d} - \frac{E}{r - n} - K_0 \qquad \text{if environmental costs rise at rate } n \text{ forever}$$

As before, whenever net social benefits (NSB) are positive, the project is a success and should be built. In all three cases, we see, however, that including environmental costs introduces another negative factor in the evaluation decision and should make society less likely to proceed with the project. In the first case [eq. (3A)], environmental costs decay with time and are discounted at the same rate as benefits. In the second [eq. (3B)], they are constant, but in computing present values, annual environmental costs are multiplied by a larger factor than are nonenvironmental benefits because environmental costs do not decay [note that $1/r > 1/(r+d)$]. In the third [eq. (3C)], even that is not true. If environmental costs rise forever at rate n, and n equals the discount rate (from Chapter 6, remember that the two rates will be equal on the Golden Rule saving path), the present discounted value of environmental costs is infinite and there is no conceivable positive nonenvironmental benefit that could make the project worthwhile. Precisely that is what is disconcerting about nuclear power: some nuclear wastes have a half-life as long as 200,000 years (about as close to an infinite horizon as we will ever get), and the potential damage generated by poisonous wastes would appear to rise roughly with the level of real income in the country at rate n. For an r close to n and with any positive E, there is no way that such a project can ever pass the benefit-cost test.[9]

At this point, one interesting political aspect of the analysis is worth pointing out. Traditionally, environmentalists opposed to building dams have been put in the position of arguing for high discount rates to keep the net present value of the nonenvironmental benefits of a project low. This may have been a wise political strategy, but it is a mistaken analytical strategy. The proper procedure for computing net social benefits is to add environmental costs as a separate item. If they rise or remain constant over time, these costs are received even further in the future than the nonenvironmental benefits, and a low discount rate makes them even more important in present-value terms. In this proper way of framing the question, a low discount rate is the environmentalist's friend.[10]

Decaying the nonenvironmental benefits has made our decision rule for physical investment projects rather conservative, and adding environmental costs, just those that can be quantified, has made it still more conservative. There is one other factor that will not be worked into these formulas but should tend to make decision makers even more conservative about initiating physical investment projects—the irreversibility question. To understand this issue, we should recognize that any investment decision involves two distinct choices, whether to build the structure and when to build the structure. With a normal private investment, the second question is relatively benign. If the discounted net benefits of a project are positive, the private investor can build it, recognizing that he or she can tear it down when the discounted net benefits become higher for some other use of the property. But with many of these investments having environmental implications, such is not the case. If the Tellico Dam is built and the snail darter killed off, the snail darter will not be resurrected once the dam is torn down. If nuclear wastes are buried in salt domes, they will still be there long after the power plant is closed down. Some physical investments are ultimately irreversible: once done, they, or their environmental costs, cannot be undone.

To fit this consideration into decision rules such as those given in eq. (3A), (3B), or (3C) requires a number of very strong assumptions and some mathematical facility.[11] Without going through the analysis, one simple property of its results can be made clear. If we could ever imagine a case of perfect certainty over the future horizon, the irreversibility issue would vanish. Planners can compute exactly the benefits and costs every period, form the discounted sums, and pursue the optimal investment policy without any second thoughts. They do not care what happens if they should make a mistake and want to reverse themselves, because there is no possibility of a mistake in such a model. It then follows logically that as the forecasting uncertainty grows, the prospect that present decision makers will be wrong also grows, and the effective social cost of an investment entailing irreversible environmental costs does too—present decision makers should become more conservative about undertaking physical investment projects. The intuition behind this result is that some uncertainty can always be resolved by waiting: if you are uncertain about a project with irreversible costs, you should be less inclined to build it today because you can always build it tomorrow if your fears about its costs prove unwarranted. Putting it another way, irreversibility introduces an asymmetry into the decision process, and not surprisingly, has an asymmetric effect on the appropriate decision rule.

THE TELLICO DAM

We turn now from the general to the specific, and examine a particular physical investment evaluation. The evaluation is that of the Tellico Dam on the Little Tennessee River, the first Endangered Species case appealed to the Supreme Court and later to the newly established Endangered Species Committee of the federal government.

The Little Tennessee River starts in the mountains of Georgia and flows through North Carolina and Tennessee, where it converges with the Big Tennessee River in Knoxville. The lower 33 miles of the Little Tennessee flow through a region of low ridges and rolling valleys, and the river in this area is considered by trout fishermen to be one of the best fishing areas in the southeastern United States. But back in the Great Depression era of 1936, government officials had more to worry about than fishermen: responding to the high-unemployment concerns of the day, the Tennessee Valley Authority (TVA) first proposed what was then called the Fort Loudoun Dam and Extension to dam the Little Tennessee, build a canal to Fort Loudoun Lake, and add to the water pressure and power generated by the nearby Fort Loudoun Dam. Congress made funds available for the project in 1942, but activity was interrupted by World War II.[12]

Nothing happened on this project for 20 years after that, although TVA continued its building activities in the area, with the consequence that there are now 20 such reservoirs within 100 miles of the proposed Fort Loudoun Dam site. Then in 1963 TVA reproposed the project, changing very little except its name, now the Tellico Dam. The project was defended on the basis of the recreation, shoreline development, flood control, and power generation benefits it would create, although a not incidental factor was an assumed 7000 industrial and service jobs expected to be created by the project. Whereas stimulation of employment might have been a reasonable goal in the Depression years of the 1930s, by 1963 the United States was entering a long period of low unemployment (in the sense described in Chapter 5), during which time labor was also in short supply in this region of Tennessee.

The reproposed Tellico Dam was controversial from the start. Governor Frank Clement supported it, but there was much local opposition. Among other things, the dam would have flooded the ancestral home of the Cherokee Indians. They obviously opposed the project and enlisted the support of Supreme Court Justice William O. Douglas. But despite Douglas's intervention, Congress approved the project in 1966 (when the unemployment rate was at a post–Korean War low) and has appropriated funds consistently since that time. Land acquisition and dam construction first began in 1967.

Then conflicting federal legislation began to cause complications. Even though Congress appropriated funds for the project, it also passed the 1969 National Environmental Policy Act (NEPA), which required that all such physical investment projects file environmental impact statements. TVA contended that NEPA was not applicable to Tellico because the project had been started before the law was passed, but the courts held otherwise and discontinued TVA's construction activities for a 2-year period from 1971 to 1973 until the proper environmental impact statement was on file.

NEPA was a minor irritant for the TVA, but the Endangered Species Act (ESA) became a major problem. ESA was first passed in 1966, was strengthened in 1969 and then again in 1973. The 1973 amendments included a new Section 7, which prevented federal agencies from carrying out any actions that may jeopardize an endangered species in its habitat. There were at the time felt to be no endangered species in the Tellico region, but soon enough one was discovered. In August 1973, two zoologists, David Ethnier and Robert Stiles, caught and identified the snail darter, a 4-inch-long perchlike minnow known only in these waters in the Little Tennessee. Since the snail darter, like other darters, needs swift, shallow water to spawn, it would have been killed off by the completion and closing of the dam. In October 1975, the snail darter was officially registered as an Endangered Species, and a short time later a court suit was brought against the TVA for violating the ESA. Again TVA argued that its prior starting date made the law inapplicable, but the Sixth Court of Appeals ruled otherwise, later to be supported by the Supreme Court. Construction on the dam was again halted.

There was a major flap over the Supreme Court decision, and Congress came close to repealing the ESA altogether. But the forces of moderation won out, and the Act was watered down only to the extent that a Cabinet-level Endangered Species Committee (dubbed the God Committee) was set up to hear irreconcilable investment-endangered species cases. In January 1979, the Committee heard the first two such cases, the Tellico case and the Missouri Basin Greyrocks Project (which threatened the migration resting grounds of the whooping crane, a majestic wading bird well known to have been endangered throughout the twentieth century). The Greyrocks case was settled out of court—the dam will be built but water will be provided during cranes' migration season—but the Committee ruled against the Tellico Dam. Construction was suspended indefinitely, and it looked for a time like the environmentalists, trout fishermen, and Cherokees had won a rare upset victory over the TVA.

But the triumph was fleeting. Throughout 1979 various Tennessee congressmen tried repeatedly to attach riders to other bills authorizing completion and closing of the dam, and they finally succeeded. In September Congress attached a proviso to an appropriations bill funding the completion of the dam and overruling the ruling of the Endangered Species Committee. President Carter eventually signed this bill "with mixed reactions." In the early stages of his administration he had won the plaudits of environmentalists and the scorn of Washington politicos by trying to veto some pork barrel legislation for other dams, canals, and harbors. He was at that time accused of not "understanding politics." By late 1979, however, he was down in the polls, his reelection campaign was in trouble, and one of his leading contenders for the presidency seemed likely to be Republican Senator Howard Baker of Tennessee, a strong supporter of the dam. Carter found these considerations persuasive and failed to veto the appropriations measure.

In November the bulldozers eliminated the last house in the area to be flooded, and soon after the dam was closed. As an ironic postscript, it later turned out that the snail darter might not be finished after all. Efforts of the TVA to transplant the darter in the nearby Hiawassee River were extremely promising, although by 1979 it was too early to tell whether the darter would survive there.

Benefits and Costs of the Tellico Dam

With that as background, we now review the benefits and costs of the Tellico project. Most of the estimates were made by the TVA itself, in response to congressional demands for project justification, environmental impact statements, or demands for justification from the Endangered Species Committee. A few of the large number of sets of cost benefit calculations are given in Table 8.1. All numbers are in 1978 dollars, and all deal just with the nonenvironmental benefits and costs of the project. Recalling eq. (2), the decision rule when environmental costs are to be ignored is to invest when $B/(r+d) > K_0$, or when $B > (r + d)K_0$. The table gives the numbers in this form. The top panel lists the various components of total benefits (B), and the next panel gives annual interest, depreciation, and maintenance costs ($r + d)K_0$. These depreciation and maintenance costs are taken as a crude measure of the decay parameter d—expenditures at this rate are necessary to *forestall* the decay of benefits.[13] The bottom two rows of the table give our various decision concepts: nonenvironmental net benefits [they are positive if $B - (r + d)K_0 > 0$] and the nonenvironmental benefit-cost ratio [net benefits are positive if $B/(r + d)K_0 > 1$].

Four sets of estimates are shown in the table. The first is the initial estimate of benefits and costs of the dam and reservoir project, made by TVA for congressional hearings in 1968, with all numbers converted to 1978 dollars. The second set is the latest revised TVA estimate, presented to the Endangered Species Committee in 1978. The third is a further revision by the Committee staff. The fourth is the Committee staff estimate of the only feasible present alternative to the Tellico Dam, river development. Under this alternative, parts of the dam would be torn out so that the snail darter could make its spawning migration without impairment, the dam would not be closed, and ancillary development (roads, etc.) would be completed as planned.

The first thing indicated by the table is that the net benefits of the dam and reservoir vary widely depending on whether the evaluator is the early TVA, the recent TVA, or the Committee staff. Net benefits are highly positive in the first case, clearly positive in the second, and slightly negative in the third. Press reports have played the conflict up as a dispute between a highly profitable dam and a small minnow: actually, once the early corrections in the TVA's calculated benefits and costs were made, the dam never had very high nonenvironmental net benefits. On the other side, environmental groups have been arguing that the project was obviously a lemon. Although it is true that the estimates in the third column show the project to have negative nonenvironmental net benefits, they are not terribly large, there are some important uncertainties in these calculations, and even then we see completion of the dam to be the cheapest course from a nonenvironmental standpoint alone.

On the benefit side, the biggest discrepancy between the original TVA estimate and later estimates is the ''employment'' item. This consists of from 7000 to 8000 industrial and service jobs that are supposed to be created by the

TABLE 8.1 Annual Benefits and Costs of the Tellico Dam and Reservoir, Ignoring Environmental Factors (millions of 1978 dollars)

	ORIGINAL TVA ESTIMATE[a]	1978 REVISED TVA ESTIMATE[b]	COMMITTEE STAFF ESTIMATE[c]	RIVER DEVELOPMENT COMMITTEE STAFF ESTIMATE[c]
Total benefits (B)	16.53	6.85	6.50	5.10
Land enhancement[d]	1.62	.34	—	—
Flood control	1.13	1.04	1.04	—
Navigation	.89	.31	.10	—
Power	.89	2.70	2.70	—
Recreation	3.70	2.30	2.50	3.10
Water supply	.16	.05	.05	—
Agriculture[e]	—	.11	.11	2.00
Employment	8.14	—	—	—
Total costs, $(r + d)K$	5.02	3.19	7.22	6.29
Dam	5.02	3.19	3.19	2.26
Land[f]	—	—	4.03	4.03
Net benefits, $B - (r + d)K$	11.51	3.66	−.72	−1.19
Benefit-cost ratio, $B/(r + d)K$	3.29	2.15	.90	.81

[a] Taken from the General Accounting Office, *The Tennessee Valley Authority's Tellico Dam Project: Costs, Alternatives, and Benefits,* Washington, D.C., October 1977, Table 1. All numbers are converted to 1978 dollars by multiplying by 2.23, the ratio of the GNP price deflator in 1978 to that in 1968 (the base year).

[b] From the Staff Report to the Endangered Species Committee, *Tellico Dam and Reservoir,* Washington, D.C., 1979, Exhibit 3. Midpoints are used whenever ranges are shown.

[c] Ibid.

[d] For land surrounding reservoir.

[e] On land included in and surrounding the reservoir.

[f] Of land included in reservoir.

reservoir, at an average annual wage of about $11,000 per job in the early 1980s. Several criticisms can be made of this benefit entry. The first is that, as pointed out above, this area of Tennessee is no longer a high-unemployment area. The latest unemployment rate for the relevant labor market area is about 6 percent, approximately the national average unemployment rate and the typical present estimate of a prudent noninflationary unemployment target (U^* in Chapter 5). Hence if there is additional employment, it will no doubt show up as an employment reduction somewhere else, implying that this supposed benefit, were it to exist, would probably be largely a transfer from other areas instead of a net national gain. Also, fairly high wages were used in the calculation, making one suspicious that labor making $11,000 might not be persistently unemployed. Further, the entire $11,000 wage was used as a benefit, as if these workers would make nothing at all, and have no value to their leisure time, in the absence of the dam jobs. Even if the workers only made the minimum wage, they would make more than half of their assumed wages. For all these reasons, TVA was encouraged to omit this benefit item in their later calculations, and general employment gains no longer enter into the calculations.

The next largest discrepancy between the original and revised TVA estimate is land enhancement, referring to appreciation of land values for lakefront sites around (but not in) the reservoir. Originally, this item was large, because TVA allowed for very generous shoreline redevelopment benefits. Apparently, the calculations ignored the fact that some land will be taken out of existence by the reservoir flooding, that inflation will raise land prices in any case, and that there are now in eastern Tennessee a large number of similar reservoirs in very close proximity to Tellico. Also, there is liable to be double counting in including benefits for land enhancement together with recreational and other benefits. So the TVA scaled the estimates way back in its latest submission, and the committee staff went even further and reduced them to zero.

The next big discrepancy involves recreational benefits, such as boating and fishing, in the reservoir itself. These were measured in the way described above, essentially as numbers of recreational trips times average payment per trip. All of the theoretical problems raised above exist here: in principle what is desired is a measure of consumer surplus and not actual payments. On a more pragmatic level, it is questionable that residents of the Southeast would pay a special premium to boat and fish in this particular lake when there are already so many similar lakes in close proximity. In view of these factors, the TVA scaled down their estimates of recreational benefits, and the Committee staff accepted this scaled-down estimate.

The final item where the original TVA evaluation appeared to overstate benefits was barge navigation in the canal that is to be built. The initial estimate included transportation cost savings of firms that located on the Tennessee River in the early 1960s but that might have located along the Little Tennessee. But there is not much evidence that additional industries would locate on the Little

Tennessee in response to cheaper barge transportation—for one thing very few of these industries now use barge transportation. Many of the industrial parks in this area are now underutilized, and barge transportation is rarely listed as a relevant factor in location decisions. Additional, and ignored, construction expenses would be necessary to realize any navigation benefits, and some of these benefits would represent a transfer away from rail and trucking firms (remember our subway example). Again, the supposed navigation benefits were drastically cut back in the light of all of these realities.[14]

On the other side, there was one benefit that the early TVA evaluation actually underestimated. This was that of the added power from the Fort Loudoun Dam. Its benefits rose sharply as a result of the sharp rise in the relative price of electricity following the U.S. energy crisis of the early 1970s. In terms of Figure 8.1, the price of power without the facility (P_0) went up enormously, and so did the consumer surplus benefits of cheaper power.

On the cost side, the TVA's latest cost estimate is for an annual interest and maintenance cost of $3.19 million for operating the dam. This estimate is down from the initial construction cost estimate because, by 1978, many of the costs of constructing the dam had already been paid. Recalculating construction costs in this way is the right thing to do now, even it if appears to load the dice in favor of the dam, because by now the relevant comparison is between the two righthand columns under the assumption that the dam is partly completed.

There is one other exclusion from the revised TVA cost estimate that is highly controversial—the cost, if any, of land that had been purchased near the dam and reservoir and that would be submerged once the dam was closed. In its 1978 report, TVA argued that the land had already been purchased and that closing the dam therefore entailed no additional cost. But this argument hinges on a serious misunderstanding of opportunity costs. Even though the land had already been purchased by TVA, it is still there and still has economic value. Were the dam operated, the land could not be used for farming, and this would be an economic, or opportunity, cost of the project. Hence in its revision, the Committee staff added an opportunity cost of $4.03 million.

There is little doubt that some opportunity cost of the land should be included, but knowing what is a much more difficult matter. Land is obviously a capital asset yielding a stream of returns over time. Hence the Committee staff used the present-value formula backward to determine the implicit annual return on the land given its present value. The present value of the land, estimating from values of nearby farmland, was set at $40 million. Using the expression developed in Chapter 6, note 1, when the time horizon for benefits equals infinity, as it should for land, annual benefits are equal to $(r)(\text{PV})$, where r is the appropriate discount rate. The Committee staff used a rate of 10 percent to compute these opportunity costs, arriving at the cost figure of $4.0 million in Table 8.1. The 10 percent rate came from the official government standard, the same one we criticized in Chapter 6 because it deflated *real* benefits with a *nominal* interest rate. The same criticism is appropriate here. Every other magnitude in the evaluation is supposed to be in constant dollars—flood control, power, and recreational benefits from the dam are not allowed to grow over time in money terms with general price inflation. Then it biases things to use a nominal interest rate to compute the opportunity cost of land. Farmers would indeed be willing to pay 10 percent on a mortgage to buy the farmland, but that is only because they expect land prices to rise and thereby to realize capital gains. If they did not expect inflation, the nominal interest rate would be exactly the same as the real interest rate, say 4 percent, and that would determine what farmers would be willing to pay. Hence the real opportunity cost of the land, for both the dam and river development options, appears to be more like (.04)(40), or $1.6 million. Examining Table 8.1, we can see that this choice of the nominal interest rate to deflate real magnitudes makes an important difference in the result of the benefit-cost calculation for the dam: using 10 percent, the dam has negative net business benefits of $.7 million; with 4 percent, it would have positive net benefits of $1.7 million.

The fourth column in the table then shows the benefits and costs of the alternative where the dam would not be completed, termed river development by the TVA. Under this alternative none of the conventional benefits of the dam—flood control, power, water supply, navigation—would exist. An entry was included for recreational benefits, reflecting the fact that in the eyes of the Committee staff, fishing benefits would be higher were the dam not closed and the river left free-flowing than if the dam were closed. The other benefit from the river development alternative is that some of the land that would be submerged by the dam could be used for farming. It is somewhat confusing that the Committee staff included these farmland benefits as benefits rather than deducting them from land opportunity costs, but this is how the tally was made. The agriculture benefits are less than the land opportunity costs because not all of the land purchased by the TVA could be used for farming—some would be covered by a partly completed dam and some by roads.

The decision confronting the Endangered Species Committee was not whether or not to build the dam—it was already built by the time they were called in on the case. The only choice was whether to close the dam and tear out parts of it so that the snail darter can spawn. The opportunity costs of land, whether valued by real or nominal interest rates, will be the same in either case.[15] The only relevant comparison is that between the two net benefit figures: −$.7 million for dam completion and −$1.2 million for partial removal. The difference between the two, $.5 million, should be viewed as the net nonenvironmental benefit of closing the dam, given that it is already virtually built. Taking a literal interpretation of the Committee staff numbers, then, the staff has computed (perhaps erroneously) that from a nonenvironmental standpoint, the dam should not have been built, but now that it is built, it is less costly to close it than to tear down part of it.

Probably the important news in these numbers is that they are very small; $.5 million is less than 10 percent of the cost of the project (even if the real interest rates were used), and as we have just seen, it is tiny relative to some of the uncertainties, such as which discount rate to use, how to project recreational benefits, and whether to add in wages of workers who might or might not gain jobs. The sensitivity test technique of using various numbers to see if the results change lands us squarely on the razor's edge in this case—the net nonenvironmental benefits are so close to zero that even modest changes in the assumptions can tip the balance to a plus or minus verdict. So the fact that net nonenvironmental benefits are slightly less negative for closing the dam is probably not of overwhelming importance, particularly when compared with what could be the enormous—although essentially nonquantifiable—cultural and environmental costs to the Cherokees and the snail darter. This was, in any case, how the Endangered Species Committee saw it. In their first official act, they decided unanimously to pursue the river development option of the fourth column, the decision that later was overturned by Congress and the President.

Although most true evaluators were no doubt saddened by the final outcome, the evaluation conventions used by both the TVA and the Committee staff were, in fact, somewhat helpful in focusing the Tellico decision. In the end both the TVA and the Committee staff agreed that the nonenvironmental benefits were not very large in a positive or negative direction, and that they were quite sensitive to a few key assumptions. This left the way open for the decision to be made on the basis of more fundamental cultural and environmental considerations. That is exactly the role our screening procedure should play in these evaluations. But one role our screening procedure cannot play is to make political decisions, and the one that finally got made unfortunately placed very little value on these omitted environmental considerations.

SUMMARY

In this chapter we explored ways in which the nonenvironmental and environmental impacts of physical investment projects could be assessed. The easiest decision procedure to use turned out to be one that first evaluated the project by ignoring environmental implications altogether. If the project could not pass a net benefits test under these conditions, it certainly could not pass the broader social test, and it could be rejected without even dealing with the more difficult to quantify environmental costs. If the project were to pass the test, some attempt to quantify environmental costs would then be necessary. Although precise quantitative evaluations become difficult at this stage, it is still true that some headway can be made by carefully comparing the horizon for the nonenvironmental benefits and rates of increase or decrease of environmental costs.

The chapter also examined in detail a particular physical investment project, the Tellico Dam on the Little Tennessee River. This project seems likely to finish off an endangered species, the snail darter, and will certainly flood the ancestral home of the Cherokee Indians—the sort of difficult environmental and cultural issues dealt with in the chapter. In the nonenvironmental evaluation of the project done by the staff of the Endangered Species Committee, it was questionable whether the project should ever have been started, but now that it is virtually completed, the dam appears to yield slightly higher nonenvironmental net benefits if closed than if left open so that the snail darter can spawn. But all differences in nonenvironmental net benefits are very small, as compared both to the environmental costs of completing and closing the dam and to the margin of uncertainty in estimating various benefits and costs. The Endangered Species Committee then recommended unanimously that the river be developed and the dam be left open, but Congress and the President overruled this judgment.

NOTES

[1] See John V. Krutilla and Otto Eckstein, *Multiple Purpose River Development* (Baltimore, Md.: Johns Hopkins University Press, 1958); and also Eckstein, *Water Resource Development: The Economics of Project Evaluation* (Cambridge, Mass.: Harvard University Press, 1958). A recent book summarizing many physical investment evaluations is Krutilla and Anthony C. Fisher, *The Economics of Natural Environments: Studies in the Valuation of Commodity and Amenity Resources* (Baltimore, Md.: Johns Hopkins University Press, 1975).

[2] A few examples of physical investment evaluations in other countries are in: Peter Bohm, *Social Efficiency: A Concise Introduction to Welfare Economics* (New York: Macmillan, 1973), chap. 4 (Sweden); Richard Layard, ed., *Cost-Benefit Analysis* (New York: Penguin, 1972) (Britain); Partha Dasgupta, Stephen Marglin, and Amartya Sen, *Guidelines for Project Evaluation*, 1972, United Nations Industrial Development Organization, New York (developing countries).

[3] A current example of such a case is that of the Alaska pipeline. Even when international oil prices were much lower and foreign supplies much more reliable, nonenvironmental net benefits were positive (although less than for the Trans-Canada pipeline). But environmental costs were also positive. See Krutilla and Fisher, *The Economics of Natural Environments*, chap. 10.

[4] Such was the case, for example, with the Alaska pipeline, which was not expected to supply enough oil to lower the price even in the western U.S. oil zone. See Krutilla and Fisher, *Ibid.*

[5] A demonstration of the use of this travel cost method for the case of mass demonstrations is given by Charles J. Cicchetti, A. Myrick Freeman, Robert H. Haveman, and Jack J.

Knetsch, "On the Economics of Mass Demonstrations: A Case Study of the November 1969 March on Washington," *American Economic Review,* September 1971. (Many earlier citations are given there and in footnote 27, Chap. 5.) Analytically, this procedure is quite similar to the modal choice method of valuing commuter time saving, also described in Chapter 5.

[6]One example of where this is done was in the evaluation of recreational losses from the Hell's Canyon Dam. See Krutilla and Fisher, *The Economics of Natural Environments,* chap. 6.

[7]There is just one exception to the statement. Pricing policy for the other area is relevant if the demand for the area that might be destroyed depends on the price charged in the comparison area.

[8]They will not be constant even in this limited capacity case if demand and willingness to pay depend on income and income keeps rising.

[9]Obviously in this case it is presumptuous even to think that we can fit the important intergenerational issues into the benefit-cost framework: how can future generations be compensated for their losses in the Paretian sense if they are not alive to receive the compensation? The ethical issues are discussed, and a pragmatic example given, in Shaul Ben-David, Allen V. Kneese, and William D. Schulze, "A Study of the Ethical Foundations of Benefit-Cost Analysis Techniques," Mimeo, University of New Mexico, Albuquerque, N.M., 1979.

[10]A technical paper by Richard C. Porter develops this line of thinking much more completely. See "The New Approach to Wilderness Preservation through Benefit-Cost Analysis," Mimeo, University of Michigan, Ann Arbor, Mich., February 1979.

[11]See, for example, Krutilla and Fisher, *The Economics of Natural Environments,* chaps. 3 and 4. The connection with forecasting uncertainty brings up another way of framing the issue, that of option values. Consumers now and in the future do not want to lose the option of using a priceless recreation area, even if their mean forecast is that they will never commune with the snail darter. These option demands were identified by Burton A. Weisbrod, "Collective-Consumption Services of Individual-Consumption Goods," *Quarterly Journal of Economics,* August 1964.

[12]Much of the material that follows comes from an excellent and informative Staff Report to the Endangered Species Committee, *Tellico Dam and Reservoir,* Washington, D.C., January 1979. Also used are the Tennessee Valley Authority, *Alternatives for Completing the Tellico Project,* Washington, D.C., December 1978; and the General Accounting Office, *The Tennessee Valley Authority's Tellico Dam Project: Costs, Alternatives, and Benefits,* Washington, D.C., 1971. Two students, Jeannette Austin and Patrick Cooper, have provided invaluable research help on this section, and both their and my awareness of the whole issue was kindled by Zygmund Plater, a Wayne State University law professor who argued the environmental side of the case before the Supreme Court.

[13]This assumption was made in all official evaluations of the dam, and we follow it here. It ignores the possibility that the price of substitute factors of production (power from alternative sources) will decline over time.

[14]Every one of these problems with estimating navigation benefits arises in the case of another celebrated southeastern canal, the Tennessee–Tombigbee Waterway through Mississippi and Alabama. There have been numerous press stories on the questionable cost and benefit accounting for this project—see, for example, "Cost-Benefit Trips Up the Corps," *Business Week,* February 19, 1979.

[15]Under the particular accounting conventions used here, where agricultural gains are included as a river development benefit. It is, incidentally, impossible to tell what assump-

tion was made about discount rates in valuing these agricultural gains. Perhaps farm benefits were estimated directly, without even referring to the present value of the land.

PROBLEMS

8.1   Say that the cost of a dam is valued as 1000, all paid in the initial year, and the consumer surplus benefits start 1 year later at 200. The discount rate is 5 percent. Compute the present value of net benefits of the dam when the consumer surplus decays at the rate of 0, 5 percent, and 10 percent, respectively.

Now say that the benefit decay rate is set at 5 percent but that there are environmental costs equal to 20 a year in the first year. Compute the net present value of benefits of the dam if these environmental costs also decay at 5 percent per year, if they are constant at 20 forever, if they rise at 2.5 percent per year, and if they rise at 5 percent per year.

8.2   A different dam will flood a good area for hunting and fishing. Evaluators have found a similar area for which the demand curve is given by $P = 100 - Q$, where P is the price paid by users and Q is the number of users. The cost of maintaining the trails of the perhaps soon-to-be flooded area is $5 per day per user, and for evaluation purposes you can assume that this charge would have been made. Since the area is farther from an interstate highway than the comparison area for which the demand curve was measured, it costs hunters an added $2 per day to get there. Find the cost of flooding the area.

9

Human Investment
Programs

Chapter 8 concentrated on physical investment programs. The government builds a structure that yields benefits in the form of lower prices to consumers and entails the physical and environmental costs of operating the structure. A different form of investment is also a common feature of governmental policy in modern societies—investment in the population directly. Under these "human investment" programs, the nation is investing resources and the time of its citizens now in the expectation that these citizens will be more productive later. The outstanding example of a human investment program is public education, but many health programs, job training programs, and subsidies for day care and higher education can also be thought of in this light.

There are two important rationales for public support of the education of or investment in its citizens. The first is a form of paternalism: one assumption needed in establishing the optimality of free-market outcomes is that consumers are able to understand the implications of their actions. Certainly, for the public school education of children, but even for the higher education or occupational training of adults, it would be dangerous to make this assumption. How can individuals possibly be informed of the value of an education before they have it? The second, and perhaps more relevant for this chapter, regards the long-run aspect of distribution of income, discussed in Chapter 2. Whether or not society has an extensive transfer program to reduce the variance of the income distribution today, it might also try to equalize the chances of the sons and daughters of all income groups for high incomes tomorrow. The best known way to do this is to support the education, health, and job training prospects of disadvantaged individuals, in the hope that an investment now will yield a productive individual who does not need to be supported later.

It is obvious from this discussion that both individuals and the state make human investment evaluation decisions. Every time an individual decides for or against attending college one more year, he or she is weighing the benefits of continued education—higher lifetime incomes plus any increase in enjoyment due to greater awareness of cultural opportunities—against their costs—the time lost in getting an education plus the ever-present tuition expenses. Society can go through a similar calculation to find out whether an education program should be continued, this time being careful to subtract out all transfer payments at every stage so as to compare only the resources created by the program with resources invested.

In this chapter we examine evaluations of human investment programs.[1] We first determine exactly what should be considered a benefit and what a cost of a human investment program, from the individual's standpoint and then from society's. We next take a brief look at an actual human investment evaluation, of the Office of Economic Opportunity's Upward Bound program, to see how some of the difficult evaluation and measurement issues might be dealt with. From there we go to a more systematic catalogue of the types of statistical problems that can in general arise with a human investment evaluation, including in particular a digression on regression analysis to help construct a framework for understanding the potential biases that could exist. This discussion also shows that the only way many of these methodological issues can be dealt with is through explicit social experiments, hence paving the way for the discussion of Chapter 12. The chapter concludes with a look at what might be called an indirect evaluation question: how large a sample, or how many budgetary resources, should be invested in evaluating a human investment program?

THE BENEFITS AND COSTS OF HUMAN INVESTMENT PROGRAMS

Table 9.1 presents a catalogue of the benefits and costs of a typical human investment program. The table shows entries for the individuals receiving the human capital investment, for all others in society, and for the sum of the two

TABLE 9.1 Benefits and Costs of a Human Investment Program

	INDIVIDUAL	OTHERS	SOCIETY
Benefits			
1. Gain in earnings after tax	×		×
2. Future increase in taxes paid		×	×
3. Nonmonetary satisfaction	×		×
Costs			
4. Tuition costs	×		×
5. Scholarship costs		×	×
6. Higher living expenses	×		×
7. Earnings foregone after tax	×		×
8. Taxes foregone		×	×
9. Transfer payments foregone	×	−×	

columns. In this way it tries to distinguish those individual benefits and costs that reflect net social gains and losses from those that reflect only transfers from or to other members of society.

The first two items in the table record the future income gains of the individuals being invested in. For this calculation individuals are assumed to be paid what they are worth in the marketplace—hence if their income rises, their marginal product does also, and that is a benefit of the human investment program. But individuals do not reap all of the benefits of their greater productivity: since they pay higher income taxes on their higher income, individuals gain the benefit reflected by future after-tax income increases (row 1), and other members of society gain the benefit reflected in future income tax increases (row 2).

The next item in the third row records the fact that education or human investment is not valued solely for its impact on income. Education may enable individuals to get jobs they like, even if those jobs do not pay any more than the jobs they would have had without the training. In this case the individuals are clearly better off, and since nobody is worse off, society gains as well, even though the *form* of the payment is in units of enjoyment (utiles) instead of dollars. One could make similar arguments if education opens up cultural horizons for individuals, and it would not be stretching things to argue that other members of society also benefit from the individuals' education (the more college educated people there are in a community, the greater are the cultural benefits for others, whether or not they have a college education). It should be pointed out that this item is one of those that is very difficult to quantify, but we can again use our bracketing technique of doing the evaluation before worrying about row 3: perhaps the investment will pass the test even with no value at all placed on this item.

On the cost side, the most obvious one is the explicit amount paid for the education, by the students (tuition, in row 4) and by others (scholarship costs, in row 5). These payments measure the institution's resource cost of providing the education. To this is added the higher living expenses, if any, incurred when students live away from home (row 6), another resource cost.

The next three items refer not to explicit costs but to opportunity costs. When individuals attend educational institutions, they may have to give up their job or at least not work as many hours. They sacrifice current earnings to get an education, and these current earnings reductions are sacrifices in income to the individual and consumption goods to society just as much as the explicit out-of-pocket costs. Hence in line 7 we include as individuals' costs their loss of earnings after tax, and in line 9 we also include any losses in transfer payments, such as public assistance or unemployment insurance when they attend school. We also must worry about others in society—they lose the taxes students would have paid on foregone earnings in row 8, but then in row 9 they gain back the transfer payments foregone. Looking at society's account, rows 7 and 8 add to the total before-tax earnings foregone (comparable to the sum of rows 1 and 2), and row 9, being a transfer, washes out entirely.

Two other items might have been included in Table 9.1, but since these items adjust for problems of measurement and not concept, they are omitted here. The first is on the cost side. If educational institutions are operating at full capacity (in the late 1970s relatively few are, but many were earlier), expansion of the student body may move the institution along an inelastic portion of its supply curve. In such cases the marginal resource cost for admitting one more student will be much above average costs, and if for operational reasons it is only possible to measure present average costs, some adjustment must be made on the cost side to incorporate the higher average resource costs now faced by all students. Similarly on the demand side. If the professions for which these individuals are being educated are facing relatively inelastic demand curves (as aerospace engineers were early in the 1970s and humanities doctorates are today) and if it is only possible to measure average wages in these professions when tallying the benefits of the program, some adjustment must be made for the fact that the marginal products of these newly trained individuals will not be as high as the average product of present professionals.

As a final comment, in interpreting Table 9.1 it may be felt that because we have labeled the third column social benefits and costs, we should always look at it when evaluating human investment programs done for social reasons. In fact, that is not so. In computing these social benefits and costs, we have simply added up the gains and losses of all groups, just as we did when using the Kaldor–Hicks efficiency standard for evaluating programs. Should a program be done for income-distribution reasons, we may want to weight the gains and losses for the particular individuals being educated, say disadvantaged youths or adults, much more heavily than those for others in society. In this case we should redefine society benefits and costs to be a weighted average of the individual net benefits and those of others, with the weights being exactly the distributional weights we discussed in Chapter 7. As a practical matter, it may be that the weights for low-income groups are so much higher than for others that we should look mainly at individual gains and losses for those individuals.

AN ACTUAL HUMAN INVESTMENT EVALUATION

We now take a look at an actual attempt to evaluate a human investment program. The program is Upward Bound, a U.S. Office of Economic Opportunity program begun in the mid-1960s to select and send underprivileged youths to a special college preparatory education. By the early 1970s nearly 20,000 youths had entered the program at a cost of several million dollars.

The evaluation was taken from the work of Greenleigh Associates, a contract research organization, as summarized by Walter Garms and later by Robert Haveman.[2] It was based on a survey of 7236 students who had entered Upward Bound from 1966 to 1968. Because all had entered the program, it would have been impossible to tell just from this "treatment" group how much the program would raise incomes, so a control group was required. Greenleigh chose the older siblings of these treatment subjects, hence holding constant such things as race and family background—although not the time in which the subjects grew up. To keep down the costs of the evaluation, the consultants only surveyed the subjects once, using actual reported answers on whether they went to college but overall age–income profiles from the census to convert these educational attainment data into future earnings stream differentials. There are a number of advantages of each one of these choices, but also a number of possible biases, which we discuss later.

The actual evaluation presents figures for four groups: white males, white females, nonwhite males, and nonwhite females. This great mass of numbers was simplified for purposes of Table 9.2 by just showing the figures for the group suffering relatively little innate job discrimination—white males—with those for the average of the other three discriminated-against groups. Among the latter, nonwhite females seem to gain net benefits slightly greater than the average, and white females and black males less than average. Two discount rates are used in the official evaluation, 5 percent and 10 percent. Since all earnings extrapolations are taken from census data referring to a time when there was very little general price inflation in the United States (and hence all benefits and costs are measured in real terms), Table 9.2 just shows the results when the earnings stream is discounted by a rate close to the real interest rate of 5 percent. One could argue that since these individuals probably could not borrow at anything close to this real interest rate—they probably could not borrow at all—a much higher real rate should be used in discounting their individual benefits, and that would lower the net benefits shown in Table 9.2. If, for example, a discount rate of 10 percent had been used, the net individual benefits for white males would have been reduced from $5243 to $822 and that for the

TABLE 9.2 Benefits and Cost of the Upward Bound Program per Program Participant, Using 5 Percent Real Discount Rate (1970 dollars)

	INDIVIDUAL	OTHERS	SOCIETY
White Males			
Benefits			
1. Discounted future after-tax earnings	5209	1811	7020
2. Discounted future tax payments	5209	1811	5209
			1811
Costs			
4. Tuition costs	−34	3422	3388
	−294		−294
5. Scholarships and government grants		2365	2365
6. Higher living expenses	260		260
aM. Higher expenses of others		1057	1057
Net benefits	5243	−1611	3632
Average of White Females, Nonwhite Males, and Nonwhite Females			
Benefits			
1. Discounted future after-tax earnings	4445	1625	6070
2. Discounted future tax payments	4445	1625	4445
			1625
Costs			
4. Tuition costs	−43	3590	3547
	−333		−333
5. Scholarships and government grants		2482	2482
6. Higher living expenses	290		290
aM. Higher expenses of others		1108	1108
Net benefits	4488	−1965	2523

aM is an adjustment item explained in the text.

other groups from $4488 to $1197. Notice that the percentage reduction is greater for white males: that is because from census extrapolations they can expect to get greater income gains from a college education than can the other groups, who suffer more discrimination. Hence for them remote future earnings are a larger component of the discounted sum, and a higher discount rate lowers them more.

Of the items given in Table 9.1, only items 1, 2, 4, 5, and 6 are available from the articles. Items 7, 8, and 9—foregone income—are implicitly included because the consultant measured differences in discounted income streams in the with and without college patterns for the treatment individuals. Item 3 is ignored, and its exclusion should lead to some understatement of both the individual and social benefits of the Upward Bound program. Since average per student institutional resource costs were included in items 4 and 5, and the consultant felt that institutions were close to full capacity, an adjustment was included for the higher marginal than average costs, or the fact that average costs facing other students would increase. These adjustment items are denoted by M in Table 9.2. Even though the benefits item was also taken as an average product of college-trained individuals, a similar marginal-average adjustment was not included on the benefit side, because Upward Bound adds to the overall supply of college-trained individuals by such a microscopic fraction that it would not have any discernible impact on the earnings of others. Moreover, the training is so broad that both the newly trained individuals and those already with college degrees have great flexibility in allocating themselves among jobs—they certainly would not have to stay in jobs where they were driving down the wage rate.

We see that as measured here, the program is a clear success for individuals. Both white males and nonwhites and females go to college more and receive positive income gains. Both also receive scholarships that exceed their tuition costs—hence the negative entry in this cost item for both groups. Other individuals in society do lose on the program, however, since their gain in tax payments is less than the scholarship and higher expense costs. When evaluated at a 5 percent discount rate and when all gains and losses are simply added up, society then gains $3632 per white male enrolled and $2523 per nonwhite and female. All net individual gains are still positive, as stated, when the discount rate is 10 percent, but all society net benefits are negative, implying that others lose more than these individuals gain at that discount rate.

These numbers, if correct, set up a reasonably strong case for the program. If it should be viewed mainly as an income redistribution program conducted for the benefit of the individuals, individual net benefits are clearly positive when this low discount rate is used, and would be also when a much higher rate is used. Posing this alternatively, individual participants seem to be better off with the program than with a corresponding amount of dollars they can invest now at a 5 percent real interest rate (and approximately 12 percent nominal interest rate). Other members of society do make a net transfer, so they might be expected to oppose the program unless they, too, view it as income redistribution—in which case it is more cost-effective than just giving money to these youths. And even from an efficiency standpoint, where it is much more sensible to use 5 percent as the discount rate, society as a whole seems clearly to gain from the program—the gain of individuals exceeds the loss of others. Saying this in the language of Chapter 4, it would have been possible for the individual students to compensate others—by accepting less of a scholarship—and still retain enough of the gains to make them happy with the program.

The major uncertainties about the program then become two technical ones:

1. Does it make sense to use the older siblings of the treatment group as a control group?

2. Does it make sense to use past census profiles as an estimate of earning gains?

On the former, using older siblings has the advantage that behavior of the control group is not influenced by that of the treatment group, but the corresponding disadvantage that there could be an effect the other way around. Whether that effect is positive or negative is very unclear, however. All those who happen to be older siblings must wonder whether their own decisions encourage their younger siblings to imitate them, or what more often seems to be the case, to do something different. On the latter, it probably is unsatisfactory to use past profiles, but again it is hard to know what else to do. If there is now less discrimination against college-educated nonwhites and females, past profiles would understate the value of a college education for these groups. But to the extent that there is a general lowering of the value of a college education over time as more and more people get it, the use of past profiles probably overstates the gain for white males.

THE METHODOLOGY FOR HUMAN INVESTMENT EVALUATIONS

This use of the older sibling-census profile method was possible for Upward Bound because there is a great deal of past experience with the training program under study, college. It is more commonly the case in this field that there will not be such a wealth of experience with the program or that the past experience might be deemed inappropriate for this sample of the population (as, in fact, could be alleged to be the case even for the Upward Bound evaluation). In such instances, it is not possible to use census data in the way described here, and an evaluation must feature a more costly survey analysis: subjects must be asked their income, age, race, sex, parental background, and schooling information before they enter a program and after they leave it, preferably at various intervals after they leave it to measure any decay rates in the income gains from a program. The income gains of those who have been through the program are then compared with those of a control group that has not been through the program, although one that is similar in other quantifiable respects. Most commonly, the control group is taken from lists of applicants for the program who passed eligibility screening tests but for one reason or another never participated in the actual human investment program.[3]

These data can then be analyzed through a technique called multiple regression analysis. Let us say that we can express a model as

(1) $$Y_i = a_0 + a_1 X_i + a_2 Z_i{}^1 + a_3 Z_i{}^2 + \ldots + u_i$$

where the i subscript refers to the ith subject; Y_i the outcome variable, say discounted earnings of the subject over some period after the program; X_i a variable indicating whether the individual was in the program or not; and each Z_i variable ($Z_i{}^1$, $Z_i{}^2$, etc.) refers to a quantifiable controlling variable such as the individual's age, race, sex, and family background information. The parameter a_0 is the intercept of the regression, or expected value of Y_i when all other independent variables are zero, and the other "a" parameters are the regression coefficients, or partial derivatives, for the other independent variables. The u_i term, known as a residual, refers to nonquantifiable factors that also affect the individual's income. Over a whole group of subjects, this residual u_i will average out to zero—it is intended to measure just random deviations of the outcome from the regression line $(a_0 + a_1 X_i + a_2 Z_i{}^1 + a_3 Z_i{}^2 + \ldots)$.[4]

The easiest way to interpret X_i is as a binary variable that takes on a value of zero if the individual is not in the treatment group and 1 if the individual is in the treatment group. Its coefficient then measures the partial derivative of Y with respect to X, so if we change X by 1 unit by putting somebody in the program, the coefficient a_1 will measure the gain in discounted earnings. We can see this in another way by writing down the expression for discounted earnings for the treatment and control group. In the simple case where there is just one Z variable, discounted earnings for the average member of the treatment group (where all $X_i = 1$) are given by the expression

(2T) $$Y^T = a_0 + a_1 + a_2 Z^T$$

For the average person in the control group (where all $X_i = 0$), discounted earnings are given by the expression

(2C) $$Y^C = a_0 + a_2 Z^C$$

Variables with a T and C superscript refer to averages for the group, and we note that in defining these variables we have made use of the property that the residuals average zero for both groups. If values of the demographic variable are the same, $Z^T = Z^C$, the difference in earnings will be just a_1, the regression coefficient of the program variable.

From this it follows that if Z is not the same between the treatment and control group, earnings will be different for two reasons: the program and differences in Z. This can be seen mathematically by subtracting $(2C)$ from $(2T)$ to yield

$$(3) \qquad Y^T - Y^C = a_1 + a_2(Z^T - Z^C)$$

To take a concrete example, if Z refers to height, short people make higher incomes than tall people $(a_2 \neq 0)$, and there are different proportions of short and tall people in the treatment and control group $(Z^T \neq Z^C)$, any observed differences in later incomes could be generated either by the program or by the differences in the average height of the groups. To find the true effect of the program, we must hold height constant. Perhaps this can be done by randomly admitting an equal percent of short and tall people to the treatment and control groups, as in the social experiments discussed in Chapter 12. But often real-world programs being evaluated will not have done this, and it is then necessary to use a statistical device for holding height constant. By measuring the impact of height on income, this is exactly what multiple regression analysis is designed to do, and exactly why it can be naturally used in evaluation studies.

This simple example then shows how regression analysis can potentially be used to fill in the numbers in Table 9.1, particularly the difficult-to-estimate entries in rows 1 and 2. But there are still plenty of problems, both of interpretation and statistics, that can appear. In the next section we briefly review some of them in as nontechnical a manner as is possible.

INTERPRETING THE RESULTS

The discussion so far has indicated that evaluators should be interested in the coefficient, a_1, the impact of the human investment program on discounted future earnings. That should be the measure of the net impact of the program, the one used in benefit-cost tables such as Table 9.1.

There are some famous cases where some confusion arose over this issue. One example was in the case of the Coleman Report, a survey of educational attainment in the United States in the mid-1960s. The Coleman team of sociologists and educational psychologists was commissioned by Congress as part of the Elementary and Secondary Education Act of 1965 to survey student educational attainment, school district spending, and family background measures in public schools across the country. The Report reached the rather startling conclusion that school spending explained a very small part of the variance in educational achievement.[5] Does this mean that as a policy measure, spending on education is not a worthwhile program? [6]

Not necessarily. In our terms we can consider the outcome variable, Y, to be test scores measuring educational attainment in a school; the policy variable, X, to measure school spending for educational impacts, and the other intervening variable, Z, to refer to family background. The Coleman conclusion was that the proportion of variance of test scores explained by school spending was small. The equation for this proportion, call it ϕ_X, is as follows:

$$(4) \qquad \phi_X = (a_1^2)\left(\frac{S_X^2}{S_Y^2}\right)(1 - R_{XZ}^2)$$

where S_X^2 is the variance of district spending on education, S_Y^2 the variance of test scores, and R_{XZ}^2 the square of the correlation coefficient between spending, X, and family background, Z. Examining this equation, we see that there are *three* reasons why ϕ_X could be low, only one of which is sufficient to make the program fail a benefit-cost test:

1. The impact of educational spending, a_1, could in fact be low, and the schools' spending not have much influence on test scores. This is the explanation that should fail educational spending on benefit-cost grounds.

2. There could be little variance in schools' educational spending across the country, so that S_X^2 is close to zero. Even if X had a large effect on Y, one large enough to pass the benefit-cost test, ϕ_X would still be low. In this case the observed low value of ϕ_X should not imply that the spending coefficient is low. As a practical matter, of course S_X^2 is very large across schools, so this possibility exists in principle but was not of much practical importance in the Coleman case.

3. There could be a high correlation between X and Z. If all schools where family background indices were high also spent much on education, R_{XZ}^2 would be close to 1 (it would be exactly 1 if X and Z were perfectly correlated) and again ϕ_X would be low. In this case the *joint* contribution of X and Z could be explaining variation in test scores, but since X and Z vary together, it is hard to tell whether X or Z was doing the explaining. In this case, clearly a relevant one for the Coleman Report, the low value of ϕ_X does *not* indicate the program is a failure. The intercorrelation between X and Z simply makes it difficult to tell whether the program is a success.[7]

Scholars and educators are still arguing about the Coleman Report, and whether it does or does not establish the futility of spending on public education.[8] There are a whole raft of complicating technical and conceptual issues, and this is not the place to get into them (although they are fascinating issues). The only point to bring out here is that as an evaluation technique, we should be interested in the coefficient a_1 and not the percent of variance explained ϕ_X. A low a_1 would certainly imply a low value of ϕ_X, but the reverse is not the case. If either reason 2 or 3 were true, ϕ_X could be low even though spending was very influential in raising test scores, and would therefore pass a benefit-cost test. To go back to the point raised in Chapter 1, an evaluation should only require the program to make a net improvement (have an a_1 large enough to outweigh costs), not to be a panacea (have ϕ_X large enough to overcome all of the factors that make for low achievement levels in certain schools).

THE IMPLEMENTATION PROBLEM

A second issue that arises in interpreting the results of a human investment evaluation is the implementation question. Social scientists are now waking up to the fact that just because Congress legislates a program, that by no means assures that the program is operating properly. There are hosts of bureaucratic, institutional, and organizational reasons why programs do not operate according to the books or are not being implemented as planned.[9]

The big quandary for evaluators is not to identify poor implementation of a program but to know what to do about it. One approach would be to say that since certain sites have not implemented the program properly, their subjects will not be included in the treatment group for the analysis, so that the program is not penalized at all for the fact that it was not implemented properly at certain sites. The alternative would be to consider the implementation of a program part and parcel of the whole program, to include the subjects from these poor implementation sites in the treatment, and to measure program effectiveness from the regression in the usual way. In this case the program is penalized for the fact that it was not implemented properly: indeed, programs can now fail a benefit-cost test either because they are not effective programs or because they are not implemented well. Convincing arguments between these two positions can be made on either side. Why penalize a good program because of a few jokers at the Peoria site? Or, why do you think a national scale program will be implemented well when the Peoria version could not be? The only sensible compromise positions might be for the evaluators to wait a decent interval and allow program managers to get the bugs out of the program before subjecting it to a formal analysis. In any case, following our usual bracketing approach, the evaluation should be done twice, with subjects from the Peoria site in and out, to see how much impact the choice has on the overall results.

MEASUREMENT PROBLEMS

A related issue refers to the measurement of X, Y, and Z. Often these variables cannot be measured very precisely. In the standard human investment case, we may not have good measures for the dependent variable, income, or for either of the independent variables, say school spending on the classroom or family background.

The difficulties raised by measurement error turn out to depend critically on which variable is mismeasured. If measurement error is random, the case usually treated in the literature, and it involves the dependent variable, there is no problem. The random residual in eq. (1) now has a larger variance, and the entire regression will explain less of the variation in the dependent variable, but as long as we are concerned with the value of a_1, there is no reason why a straightforward application of statistical regression techniques will not give as accurate an estimate of a_1 as is possible. But if measurement error affects either one of the independent variables, and if Z and X are even slightly correlated, problems can be raised. The intuition behind this is that whatever value we record for X or Z, we are not recording the true value of the variable but just some proxy that is randomly related to the true value. If we used exactly the true values for X and Z, our technique would yield the correct estimates of a_1 as the program impact and a_2 as the correction for Z. If we used absolutely random variables for X and Z, our technique would yield zero as the estimate for both impacts. Hence when we have measurement error, our estimates of both a_1 and a_2 will be weighted averages of zero and the true parameters—or biased toward zero. This discussion emphasizes the critical importance of measuring these independent variables as well as possible, and also of trying to get information on the reliability of program data to know when adjustments should be made in program effects.[10]

We note the subtle difference between the implementation problem and measurement error in the program variable X. In both cases something is watering down the influence of the program variable—for the implementation case it is the fact that a program cannot be implemented without difficulty; for measurement error it is that we cannot measure a program variable without error. In the implementation case, it is not clear whether any correction should be made, but in the measurement-error case it is clear that a correction should be made. Why the difference? The answer involves the role of evaluation. For the implementation case, one can argue for not making a correction because the actual program is not implemented properly, and that is a defect in the program that must be penalized in an evaluation. In the measurement-error case the program might be doing just fine—the only problems are those of finding evidence that it is. So a correction in the analysis could be necessary to undo the sins not of the program itself, but of the technique for evaluating its success.

SELECTION PROBLEMS

Perhaps the greatest difficulty in human investment programs of this type involves what is known as the selection problem. It was asserted above that a regression-type study was needed to correct for the influence of the quantifiable variable Z on the results—were that not done, the program impact would be confounded with the impact of Z, height in the example used, and we could not be sure whether it was really our human investment program or height that was altering income. Precisely the same difficulties exist with our random residual u, except that this time they are much harder to solve because u, unlike Z, is unmeasurable.

Referring to eq. (1), say that there is some nonquantifiable variable, call it ambition, that raises income. Every subject that has ambition will have slightly higher income for any set of X and Z variables. If somehow magically our evaluation had exactly the same proportion of ambitious and lazy people in both the treatment and control group, ambition would cause no interpretation problems. But if not, it would cause problems. If the ambitious people realized that to get ahead they had better get in the program, they would "self-select" themselves into the program. In statistical terms, X would be correlated with u, violating one of the important regression assumptions. In pragmatic terms, it will look like the program is good because those in it are getting higher incomes, but in fact that is at least partly because those in in the program are the more ambitious ones who would have done better anyway. Self-selection has biased the results in favor of the program.

There are many examples of this type of problem in the evaluation literature. If the subjects themselves do the selecting, as in the example above, the bias is called self-selection bias. Or the program administrators may do the selecting: if they can sense who will do well in the program in a way that cannot be controlled by the quantitative data, they might choose the cream of the crop for the program, a phenomenon known as "creaming." This will again bias the results in favor of the program. But the bias can also go the other way. Sometimes program administrators will have such a strong social consciousness that they will only select for the program those who are really down and out—we might term this phenomenon "dregging" and expect that dregging will bias the evaluation against the program. Selecting control subjects from the waiting list for a program, one of the techniques discussed above, might also create a negative bias. Say that all unemployed workers in an area sign up for a training program and are put on the waiting list. But by the time the program starts, some of the unemployed workers, the more ambitious ones, have already gotten a job and have taken themselves off the waiting list. Hence the program is left with those who are, on average, less ambitious than those in the control group, the ones from the waiting list who got jobs, and the evaluation will be biased against the program.

WHAT TO DO ?

This long list of difficulties could lead an aspiring evaluator into a state of prolonged pessimism—almost everywhere one turns there seem to be problems. There are problems in measuring the program impact when X is correlated with Z, when the variables are not implemented properly, measured properly, or when the nonquantifiable residual is positively or negatively correlated with the program variable. Although in many cases it is possible to make statistical corrections for these problems, and in many other cases the problems will not be terribly serious, sometimes the problems will be serious and it will not be possible to make very good corrections. Is there anything that can be done?

In fact, there is. One of the promising new techniques for doing evaluation studies, particularly in the human investment area, is called social experimentation, the topic dealt with in Chapter 12. Instead of taking real-world programs as given and trying to evaluate them, in a social experiment the government actually creates the program and the evaluation technique so as to minimize some of the problems that we have been discussing. We will see in Chapter 12 that social experiments are costly, complicated, and time-consuming. But it is important to recognize that they do offer a way out of many of the evaluation difficulties considered here.[11] A partial listing of some of these difficulties that social experiments might help solve is:

1. The evaluator may have trouble in measuring the impact of a certain program (X) because there are not enough real-world examples of it. In a social experiment the evaluating agency would simply set up the requisite number of programs.

2. The evaluator may have trouble in distinguishing, say, the impact of spending on classrooms (X) from that of parents' background (Z), because the two are so highly correlated. In an experiment the evaluating agency would simply break the pattern by including some cells where there was high spending when parents' background was low.

3. The evaluator may have various kinds of self-selection problems. In an experiment subjects can be randomly allocated to treatment and control group, hence ensuring that the program variable (X) is uncorrelated with the nonquantifiable residual term (u).

4. The evaluator may have trouble in quantifying some Z variables, measuring X variables or whatever. An experiment can be set up which devotes sufficient resources to the proper measurement of the variables, at a point in time and over time.

THE SCALE OF THE EVALUATION

Whether an agency is doing a standard human investment or a social experiment, a final matter that must be decided is the scale of the project. If you are in charge of conducting a survey to evaluate program X, do you interview 200 subjects, 400, or 1000? How much of the agency's scarce evaluation budget do you invest in evaluating this program? It turns out the analysis is very similar to that of the program in general: as with any government program, you allocate funds to the evaluation until the marginal benefit of the additional dollar spent, or person interviewed, exactly equals the marginal cost. Also, as with any government program, it is not so easy to figure out what these benefits are, and we must examine the matter.[12]

Our estimate of the program impact, a_1, can be thought of as a sample statistic. If we have a very small sample of subjects, the statistic may not be a very good estimate of the true program impact for the entire population of subjects. But as we add to the sample, the law of averages implies that the sample estimate will become an increasingly more accurate estimator of the true impact. This is precisely the reason for getting a larger sample.

An illustration of this property is shown in Figure 9.1. Say that the true program impact on outcomes is given by α_1. We are trying to estimate this true

FIGURE 9.1   Sample Estimate of Program Impact for a Small Sample, N₁, and a Large Sample, N₂

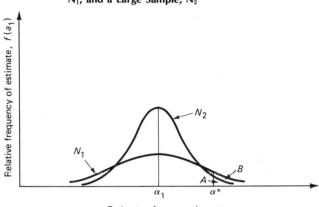

Estimate of program impact, a_1

program impact by sampling subjects from from the treatment and control group. If our total sample is of size N_1, a small sample, the relative frequency distribution of outcomes for our evaluation is as shown in the diagram. The height of the distribution for each value of a_1, called the relative frequency of that estimate $[f(a_1)]$, rises to a peak at α_1 and then declines again. But as we add sample observations and get a bigger sample, N_2, the relative frequency distribution becomes more compact about the true estimate α_1. As a convention, the area under both relative frequency curves is set to equal 1, so the frequency between any two a_1 points can be viewed as the probability of getting an estimate in that range.

Next, let us say that we estimate from program cost data how large the program's impact on outcomes would have to be to make it yield positive net benefits. Call this value α^*. In Figure 9.1, α^* is placed above the true estimate α_1, as if the program would *not* pass the benefit-cost test if we had a large enough sample to make a precise estimate of α_1. This is done just for illustrative purposes: the entire analysis could be turned around for the case where $\alpha_1 > \alpha^*$.[13]

The benefit from sampling can then be defined as the greater probability of making a correct evaluation. Referring to Figure 9.1, if we have a sample size of N_1, the probability of a miscall—saying a program yields positive net benefits when it does not—is the area $(A + B)$. As the sample expands to N_2, this probability of a miscall falls to that denoted by area A. The area B then represents the marginal gain, in reduced probability of a miscall, from expanding the sample. It can be shown from statistics that if we label this probability of a correct evaluation as π, π will rise with N, but at decreasing rates, a statistical law of diminishing marginal returns.

The next task, as with any evaluation, is to put π in dollar terms. It can be shown that the benefits of an evaluation are given by the expression

(5) $$\text{BEN} = (p)(\text{PV})(\pi)$$

Here BEN stands for the total benefit of doing an evaluation, π is the probability of a correct call referred to above, PV is the discounted present value of program costs, and p is the probability that political decision makers will listen to the results of the evaluation. In addition to reduced uncertainty, we have included two other principles in defining this total benefits function:

1. Do not spend scarce evaluation dollars evaluating a program that has small costs. Evaluations have their value in potential cost savings to society, and these are largest where the costs (PV) of the program are largest.

2. Do not spend scarce evaluation dollars evaluating programs where nobody will listen to or act on the results. If a program is a sacred cow, other things equal p will be lower and fewer evaluation dollars should be devoted to the program.

We can then compare this benefits function with the costs of doing the evaluation survey:

(6) $$\text{COST} = c_0 + c_1 N$$

where c_0 is the fixed cost of hiring the survey firm even before they interview anybody at all and c_1 is the marginal cost per interview. The efficiency condition, or optimal scale of the evaluation, is determined by equating marginal benefits $d\text{BEN}/dN$ to marginal costs, c_1, as is shown in Figure 9.2 at point N^*. At N^*, the benefits curve is parallel to the cost curve, implying that the slopes $d\text{BEN}/dN$ and c_1 are equal. We can see that this optimal sample size will rise to N' as either p or PV rise—the stakes of the evaluation get bigger and it has more

FIGURE 9.2 Optimal Scale of the Evaluation

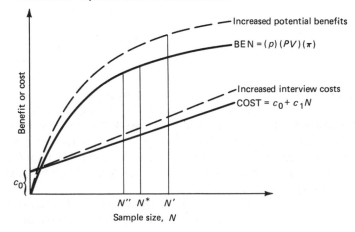

potential benefits. Conversely, the optimal sample size falls to N'' if interviewing costs rise.

Although this is a nice conceptual framework for knowing how large a sample to draw, the procedure is not that easy to operationalize. The reason is that to get anywhere at all, you must know the frequency distribution for a_1, and how can you know that before you have done any surveys? This is a good question, but there are two answers. For one thing, you can estimate the mean and variance of a_1 from that of other articles evaluating other similar programs in the literature. With knowledge of the frequency distribution, you can do the evaluation. Another procedure, more generally applicable, involves an iterative approach. Any sample survey done by a reputable surveying firm will be carefully pretested to get the bugs out of the questionnaire. There is no reason why the evaluating agency could not commission a small pilot survey, get some preliminary estimate of the mean and variance of a_1, find N^*, do the evaluation, and estimate a_1. Having done this, it would be possible to reestimate the frequency distribution of a_1, recompute N^*, and add observations if that is suggested by the new computations. One can iterate in this manner until the assumed and estimated frequency distributions of a_1 converge.

SUMMARY

In this chapter we analyzed the benefits and costs of human investment programs. Benefits consist of later earnings gains from a human investment program, costs as explicit costs paid or as the opportunity cost of time not spent in the labor force now. Both benefits and costs could be viewed either from the individual's perspective or society's, with the appropriate choice depending on whether the program is intended to promote income redistribution for certain individuals (in which case the individual perspective is closer to the truth) or as an overall efficiency-type program (in which case the unweighted social perspective is the proper one). The one actual program looked at, the Office of Economic Opportunity's Upward Bound Program, appears to pass both tests, although there is a strong transfer element implicit in the program such that the social gain is clearly less than the individual gain.

The chapter went on to discuss a number of technical problems that arise in human investment evaluations, problems that could interfere with precise evaluation judgments. Many of these problems can only be solved by having the evaluating agency step in and control certain aspects of the program to be evaluated, such as ensuring that there is random selection of subjects into the treatment and control group. Finally, the chapter looked at how to evaluate an evaluation, really how to determine the extent to which an agency's scarce budgetary resources should be put into evaluating programs. In general, there is a way to solve this problem: other things equal, the evaluation sample should be larger the more uncertainty can be resolved by the evaluation, the greater the budget of the program itself, the more policy decisions are dependent on the evaluation, and the lower are interviewing costs. Just as with a program itself, the optimal sample size can then be found by sampling until the marginal benefits of an additional observation equal the marginal costs.

NOTES

[1]This is not the only attempt to survey the principles of benefit-cost analysis as applied to human investment programs. See also Glen G. Cain and Robinson G. Hollister "The Methodology of Evaluating Social Action Programs," and Thomas K. Glennan, Jr., "Evaluating Federal Manpower Programs: Notes and Observations," both in Peter H. Rossi and Walter Williams, eds., *Evaluating Social Programs* (New York: Seminar Press, 1972). The Cain–Hollister piece is updated and reprinted in Robert H. Haveman and Julius Margolis, *Public Expenditure and Policy Analysis* (Skokie, Ill.: Rand McNally, 1977).

[2]In fact my data are taken from a survey article by Haveman summarizing the article by Garms. The citations are: Walter I. Garms, "A Benefit-Cost Analysis of the Upward Bound Program," *Journal of Human Resources,* 6, no. 2 (Spring 1971); and Robert H. Haveman, "Benefit-Cost Analysis and Family Planning Programs," *Population and Development Review,* 2, no. 1 (March 1976).

[3]An example of such an evaluation is also given by Einar Hardin and Michael E. Borus, *The Economic Benefits and Costs of Retraining* (Lexington, Mass.: Lexington Books, Heath, 1971); quoted in Haveman, "Benefit-Cost Analysis". For a good discussion of some of the statistical difficulties that can result, in particular regarding unexplained swings in income before the program started, see Orley Ashenfelter, "Estimating the Effects of Training Programs on Earnings," *Review of Economics and Statistics,* February 1978.

[4]It may not be clear why u_i serves two roles, being both the residual after the influence of X_i and all of the Z_i are accounted for *and* being a random deviation term that averages out to zero. The reason is that the regression coefficients (a_i) are estimated under the assumption that the residual is a random deviation. Any component that is systematically related to movements in any of the Z_i will be adjusted for in the relevant coefficient; any constant component in the regression intercept.

[5]See James S. Coleman et al., *Equality of Educational Opportunity,* Washington, D.C., 1966. Later analyses of the same data are contained in Frederick Mosteller and Daniel P. Moynihan, eds., *On Equality of Educational Opportunity* (New York: Random House, 1972).

[6]The following argument is taken from Glen G. Cain and Harold W. Watts, "Problems in Making Policy Inferences from the Coleman Report," in Peter H. Rossi and Walter Williams, eds., *Evaluating Social Programs* (New York: Seminar Press, 1972).

[7]Students who have had econometrics know this disease as multicollinearity, and the diagnosis of it to be indicated by a low statistical significance level for the coefficient a_1.

[8]A recent article which explains pupil and not school achievement test scores with a more carefully chosen set of independent (X and Z) variables, and also more carefully formulated interactions between them, in fact finds that certain inputs do have important effects on educational attainment. See Anita A. Summers and Barbara L. Wolfe, "Do Schools Make a Difference?," *American Economic Review,* September 1977. For those interested in this field, that article also gives a long list of citations of previous studies on this topic.

[9]See, for example, Walter Williams, ed. *Special Issue on Implementation, Policy Analysis,* Summer 1975. A graphic example of the shortcomings of program implementation can be seen with the minimum wages, perhaps the most straightforward of all laws to implement. It turns out that there appears to be quite widespread noncompliance with the minimum wage, as measured either from employee or employer reports. See Orley Ashenfelter and Robert Smith, "Compliance with the Minimum Wage Law," *Journal of Political Economy,* April 1979, and my own "The Impact of Minimum Wages on Other Wages, Employment, and Family Incomes," *Brookings Papers on Economic Activity,* 2 (1976).

[10]For those who know some econometrics, these issues are discussed in Arthur Goldberger, "Selection Bias in Evaluating Treatment Effects: Some Formal Illustrations," Discussion Paper 123-72, University of Wisconsin Institute for Research on Poverty, Madison, Wis. For a specific illustration of the types of corrections that can be made in an actual real-world evaluation, see Irwin Garfinkel and Edward Gramlich, "A Statistical Analysis of the OEO Experiment in Educational Performance Contracting," *Journal of Human Resources,* Spring 1973.

[11]There are also less costly ways of dealing with some of these problems. Regarding selection bias, some investigators have used a discriminant function method. In this they fit an equation explaining the probability of selection into the program as a function of some set of Z variables. The predicted probability is then used as an independent variable in explaining the dependent variable—in effect, controlling for probability of selection into the program. For an illustration of this technique, see Gerald G. Somers and Ernst W. Stromsdorfer, "A Cost-Effectiveness Analysis of In-School and Summer Neighborhood Youth Corps: A Nationwide Evaluation," in David Nachmias, ed., *The Practice of Policy Evaluation* (New York: St. Martin's Press, 1980).

[12]This analysis follows that of George E. Johnson, "The Optimal Scale of Program Evaluation," Institute of Public Policy Studies Discussion Paper 86, University of Michigan, Ann Arbor, Mich., 1976. An application of the technique can be found in Ashenfelter, "Estimating the Effects of Training Programs on Earnings."

[13]Since α^* exceeds α_1, we are concentrating here on reducing the probability of calling a program good, given that it is not good. If α_1 exceeded α^*, we would try to reduce the probability of calling a program bad, given that it is good.

PROBLEMS

9.1 An educational program costs students $10,000 in tuition and living expenses, but it generates for them $20,000 in extra discounted earnings after tax. The rest of society pays costs of $14,000 for scholarships but receives $2000 in discounted added tax revenues. Would this program pass the Kaldor–Hicks net benefit test? Is that the right test?

9.2 The Evaluation Office in the Department of Labor figures it costs $100 to put heads of poor families through a 1-month training program (a short enough time that sacrifices of alternative earnings can be ignored). They have analyzed the income of 100 graduates of the training program and they find that graduates earn $14 more than a control population in the first year after the program, declining by 5 percent in every following year. The standard error of this coefficient is $2 (if you have not had statistics, this is the square root of the sampling variance of this coefficient—you can do the rest of the problem without worrying about this part), but whether or not the subject has been enrolled in the project explains only 10 percent of the variance of earned income among the populations of all enrollees and control groups. There is no correlation between whether people are in the program and any other independent variable, and the appropriate rate of discount is .05.

> **a.** Some statisticians argue that since the program explains only a trivial proportion of the variance in income, it should be dropped and the money should be given directly to poor people as income support. Is this argument correct? How confident are you of your verdict?

> **b.** Right now, for every 10 people in the population of potential enrollees, the program is administered to 5 (hence a zero–one variable explaining enrollment can be computed to have a variance of .28). If this program were extended to 8 out of 10, how much of the variance in the income of potential enrollees would it explain (assume the coefficients remain the same)? To 10 out of 10?

> **c.** OMB circulates a memo telling all agencies that because market interest rates have risen to 10 percent, agencies should now use that rate in all benefit-cost calculations. Does this change your verdict? The Secretary of Labor is livid: why do market interest rates have anything to do with whether DOL trains people or pays income support?

9.3 Recent health legislation mandates that some program money be put into evaluating the program. Assume that you are in charge of both the evaluation and the operation of a small program. Consultants tell you that to evaluate the program it will cost $3 million to hire the analysts and print up the surveys, and that it costs exactly $20 for every subject surveyed. Your staff figures the benefits of the evaluation, in terms of improving knowledge about how the program works, to be given by the expression TB = $4020N - $2N^2$, where N is the sample size.

> **a.** Find the sample size (N) and the amount you will spend on the evaluation. Explain.

> **b.** Would you do the evaluation if it were not mandated? Explain.

9.4 An instructor at East Podunk University never knows whether to give his students open-book or closed-book exams. He finally decides to find out once and for all. Being concerned with only how well students learn the material, he is prepared to consider an outcome a success when the students do better on the exam (he has other, more malevolent colleagues with a different set of objectives). Hence he sets up the following experiment:

1. An identical test is administered to all students.

2. All students must choose an open- or a closed-book examination. They are warned that the instructor will grade the open-book test harder in exactly the appropriate amount to compensate for the openness. Hence test scores are a perfect indication of how well students learned the material.

The instructor has 40 students, exactly half of whom chose the open-book and half the closed-book test, the average score on the closed book was 90 and on the open book 80, and the standard deviation within each group was 3 points.

a. Did the closed-book exam appear to the instructor to be the better testing mechanism? By a statistically significant amount?

b. The instructor was bragging about his results to a colleague, who informed him of a fatal defect in his experiment. What was it?

c. The instructor is a persistent type and next year he repeats his procedure, making one alteration suggested by his colleague. What is that? Now he gets average scores of 85 and 84 for the closed- and open-book exams, respectively, with no change in the standard deviation. Is this difference statistically significant? What does the instructor do then?

10

Intergovernmental Grants

The typical evaluation study assumes that a government is simply spending money on project X. The benefits of X to the society are then compared to its resource costs and the project either passes or does not pass the benefit-cost test. But in fact this classic prototype is coming to be an increasingly unrealistic description of most government expenditure programs. As shown in Chapter 3, the United States (together with other countries) is gradually developing a different and more complicated federal structure. In the middle is a central government, conducting some programs on its own (defense, social security), but many more by way of grants to lower levels of government. Next are state governments, receiving grants from the federal government, conducting some projects on their own (highways, natural resources, welfare), but giving still more grants to local governments. Most actual domestic government services (education, police and fire, street maintenance, snow removal) are then produced by local governments, with grant assistance from both the state and central governments.

This federal structure sets up new evaluation complications from the standpoint of both the donor and recipient governments. From the standpoint of the donor government, if the grant were intended to stimulate local spending on some project, it may not do that. There are, as we will see, a number of complications involved in the transfer of funds from one government to another, and these complications could greatly weaken the impact of the grant on spending for a certain intended program. From the standpoint of the recipient government, if receipt of the grant depends on undertaking a certain program, the evaluation question becomes whether to accept the grant and undertake the program or not. Do the local benefits from the added funds outweigh the local costs not paid for by the central government grant?

In this chapter we raise both of these questions. We review briefly the theoretical rationale for grants of various types, and then we consider how evaluations of grant programs might be done at both the federal and state or local level. We conclude with a number of specific examples showing how the provisions of the grant can make a difference in the impact of programs in such diverse areas as federal highway construction, food stamps, special revenue sharing, and public service employment.

THE RATIONALE FOR INTERGOVERNMENTAL GRANTS

There are three broad rationales for intergovernmental grants, and each implies a grant with a particular set of provisions.[1] The first, and most common, justification cited in the economics literature involves what are known as benefit spillovers. Referring to Figure 10.1, say the cost of a unit of government service (for

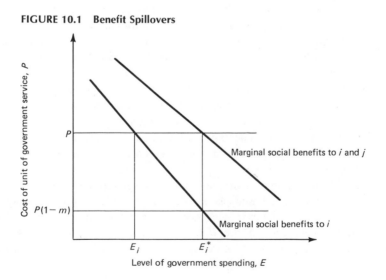

FIGURE 10.1 Benefit Spillovers

example, the output of one government worker) to community i is P and that the social benefits to the ith community of public spending on this service are given by the lower demand curve. This might be thought of as the vertical summation of the marginal utilities of individual voters in the community, as in the public goods example of Chapter 2. Doing a marginal benefit-cost calculation, community i will find its optimal level of spending to be where the net benefits of further expansion of public spending are just zero, or where the social benefit curve cuts the cost curve at E_i.

Say, further, that expenditures on this function by community i "spill over" into community j and benefit citizens there. This might be true for water pollution prevention expenditures, public health programs, road construction, or an integrated public transportation system, to name a few examples. We could then add the marginal utilities of citizens in the other community, j, to our sum to derive society's overall demand curve for public spending in community i. Optimum spending in i from this broader social perspective is E_i^*. Of course community i by itself will not typically go to E_i^*, because the net benefits of expansion past E_i are negative for its own citizens. The case of benefit spill-overs then leads to possibly suboptimal behavior, requiring some form of intergovernmental transfer in the same analytical sense that the existence of the public goods problem can lead any particular individual to underconsume public output and make desirable some governmental fiscal action.

There are two types of intergovernmental transfers that would work in this simple case. The first is for the citizens in community j to bribe those in i to spend more, paying their own benefit share of the costs at E_i^*. This arrangement is perfectly feasible in our example, but probably not in real life. The reason is the sheer magnitude of the complicated arrangements necessary—there are 75,000 local governments in the United States, and if a large number of them had to make these bribes to a large number of other communities for a large number of different programs, incredible confusion would result. Perhaps a more feasible arrangement is for the central government simply to make price-reduction subsidies generally available to all local governments for spending in this functional area, paying m percent of the cost of public output, reducing costs to the ith government to $P(1 - m)$, and increasing local spending to E_i^*. This, then, is a rationale for what is known as an open-ended price reduction grant, which we will call a case A grant. The federal government pays m percent of the cost of all local expenditures on a program or in a functional area, and the local government can spend as much as it wants.

In analyzing the impact of grants on local government expenditures, it becomes very important to know whether this price subsidy is limited or not. If it is unlimited, that is, if the local government can spend as much as it wants on the public good and still get the subsidy [the new price line is horizontal at $P(1 - m)$ in Figure 10.1], the grant is considered a case A grant. If the subsidy is limited, so that local governments get the subsidy up to a point but not beyond, the grant may not lower relative prices *at the margin* for the local government (the price line may kink at some point to the left of E_i), and its impact could be entirely different. Hence in later discussions it is important to keep this limit in mind and to identify case A grants as only those grants that reduce prices for a certain type of expenditure, and where there is no limit on the expenditures that can qualify for the price subsidy.

Although case A grants are common in other countries and at the state level in the United States, they are not common for the U.S. federal government. In fact, there are only two U.S. grant programs that might be considered case A types—one for public assistance (welfare payments) and one for medicaid (health insurance for welfare recipients). Even the public assistance program is a somewhat impure strain of a case A program, because the federal matching share, or price subsidy, declines as welfare payments (E_i in Figure 10.1) rise.

Why the U.S. Congress has seen fit to use A grants in this manner is something of a mystery. On the one hand, for all those programs such as pollution prevention and transportation where there are obvious benefit spillovers, the federal government does not use open-ended case A grants and, as a consequence, may not be making price reductions at the margin. On the other, the federal government does use A grants for programs that are really income redistribution programs and should probably not be dealt with by grants at all. Conducting public assistance policy by grant still leaves decision-making authority about the level of benefits in the hands of states, and results in welfare benefits that differ for recipients living in different states. This difference, in turn, leads to inequities within the welfare system and may set up migration incentives.

A second justification for grants deals more formally with the question of income distribution and migration incentives. It has been shown empirically that the benefits of local government expenditures accrue more or less proportionately to all income groups and may even be disproportionately focused on low-income groups.[2] Taxes, on the other hand, are slightly higher for high-income groups—although not high enough to make the overall tax system progressive.[3] These two phenomena are shown graphically by the solid lines in Figure 10.2.

If all communities started with the T and B functions drawn and had the overall mean income in the country $\bar{Y}$, the situation could possibly last indefinitely. Within every community, high-income groups would be making transfers to low-income groups through the local budget, and there is no reason why that situation could not persist. But if for some reason community income differentials were to arise, the situation might not be so desirable from a social standpoint. If, for example, we had a high-income community with mean income Y_h and a low-income community with mean income Y_1, the high-income community would be running a budget surplus ($T > B$) and the low-income community a deficit ($T < B$) were they to operate on these original schedules. But it is

FIGURE 10.2 **Taxes Paid and Expenditure Benefits for
Various Income Groups**

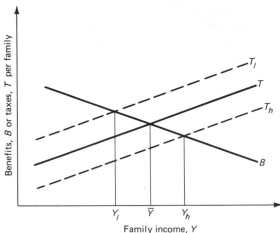

illogical for communities to run persistent surpluses (why tax more than you have to?) and illegal to run persistent deficits (state constitutions do not allow it). Hence both communities will shift their schedules.

In principle, either the B or the T schedule could be shifted and it does not matter which for the following argument, but let us suppose that each community responded to its fiscal imbalance by shifting the T schedule entirely. The high-income community cut taxes per family to the T_h schedule, and the low-income community raised them to the T_l schedule. Notice, then, that for a family of any income, it is more expensive to live in the low-income community. For a constant menu of expenditure benefits, given by the B schedule, low-income community residents of any income have to pay a higher tax price, given by the difference between T_l and T_h for that income. Nor is that the end of the story. It then becomes more desirable to live in the high-income community: richer people in the low-income community will try to move there, drive up property values there, making it less possible for poor people to move there, and tending to raise Y_h and lower Y_l again, causing new shifts in the curves.

If pure consumption goods such as yoyos were financed by public budgets, it would be inequitable to force residents of low-income communities to pay higher prices, but it would perhaps not harm the long-run income prospects of the poor in any very obvious sense. But when services that have a strong influence on the long-run distribution of income, such as education, are financed by public budgets, it is not only inequitable in the short run, but there can also be great damage to the long-run income opportunities of low-income groups. We saw in Chapter 3 that education spending accounted for just about half of total local government spending in the United States. Hence in addition to all of the other

problems facing low-income groups, the existence of community income differentials implies that poor community residents have to pay more for schools
that are worse than in wealthy areas. This clearly is a social problem.

There are several potential solutions to the problem:

1. The whole line of reasoning starts from the existence of downward-sloping
benefit functions and upward-sloping tax functions, leading to what James Buchanan
first called "fiscal residua" (positive $T-B$) for high-income groups.[4] Local governments themselves could even out these differentials by making both the B and the T
functions flat, eliminating all fiscal residuals, all price differences across communities,
and all fiscal incentives for migration. Of course, that action would also eliminate all
local government income redistribution, which itself would hurt lower-income groups.

2. There could be efforts to consolidate the governments, or at least finance
important "merit want" services, such as education, throughout larger areas. In the
nineteenth century, the urban problem was not quite as serious as it is today because
many of the northeastern cities consolidated by annexing their high-income suburbs,
an option that is typically precluded by law in most northeastern states today. A more
relevant current example of this consolidation solution is the existence of statewide
equalization plans for educational finance: since education is now financed statewide
in many states, all residents of a state face the same average T schedule.

3. There could be redistribution grants from high- to low-income communities.
Unlike case A grants, these need not be tied to any particular type of spending, but
simply available for any priority need of local governments—even cutting taxes to
eliminate tax price disparities across communities. We will label these unconditional
grants—money with no strings attached—case B grants. Note that unlike case A
grants, case B grants do not alter relative prices at all. By the same token, the success
of a case B program does not depend on what the local community does with the
money.

In the United States there are some examples of case B unconditional grants,
but very seldom are they redistributive across communities in the way that the
foregoing rationale would suggest they should be. Some states have unconditional
revenue-sharing programs for their localities, but the plans usually look more like
per capita distributions than like community income redistributions. The national
government had no unconditional grants at all until 1972, but the general revenue-
sharing program passed in that year did provide a first national case B grant.
Again, however, the money is distributed essentially on a per capita basis, with
very little attempt to direct more funds into poorer areas.[5] If there is any redistribution implicit in the program, it is only to substitute the very slightly
progressive federal tax system for the very slightly regressive state and local tax
system as a means of financing state and local expenditures.

The third rationale for grants involves less economic reasoning and more
political science. There are very good democratic reasons to try to keep political
power close to the people by having strong and vigorous local governments actually producing most public services. At the same time the federal government has

increasingly become more ambitious in trying to establish minimum service or spending levels for various government-provided goods and services. It has compromised these partly conflicting objectives by settling on a hybrid form of grant, called here a case C grant, that is used in the overwhelming majority of present-day grant programs. This grant is like a case A grant in that it is categorical; that is, it only matches spending or reduces prices for a certain kind of state or local expenditure. But it is unlike case A grants because the amount of the grant is limited: the post-grant relative price of Figure 10.1 kinks at some point. To the left of the kink point the relative price of spending on a particular service is $P(1 - m)$; to the right, it is P.

Federal policymakers believe that limits on the size of the grant are necessary because without them, states and localities would spend very large amounts and require very large federal matching expenditures. These fears are usually quite well founded, because in the typical federal case C grant program, the federal share of program expenditures (m in Figure 10.1) is so high—about .8 on average and for many programs .9 or more—that local governments view these services almost as free goods and will indeed spend large amounts on the programs. What has never been made clear is why Congress has forced itself to limit its liability by writing grant programs with such generous matching ratios.[6] It makes no obvious sense to argue that the externalities for a particular local expenditure form 90 percent of the marginal benefits of a program up to a certain expenditure level, and zero beyond that. Moreover, we will see below that the existence of limits on the size of the grant permits it to have quite unintended effects on local public spending.

THE IMPACT OF DIFFERENT TYPES OF GRANTS ON SPENDING

Before we can evaluate the various types of grants, we should consider their impact on the budgets of local governments. For this analysis we use the same indifference curves dealt with in Chapters 2 and 7, except that now the decision maker we are dealing with is the recipient government itself. Assume that this government is forced to choose between expenditures on a certain program and all other uses of the community's funds, including property tax cuts so homeowners can spend on private goods. There will be some relative price ratio between program expenditures (denoted by E) and all other expenditures: other things equal, the higher this relative price is, the less will be spent on E. At the same time, the richer the community is, the more funds there will be to spend both on E and on all other goods, the implicit budget line will shift out, and expenditures for both types of goods will increase. Since the three types of grants we have listed influence the relative price of program services, community income, or both, we can analyze their probable impact through the same kinds of price and income effects that the normal indifference curve analysis deals with.[7] Finally, to keep things simple, we analyze just and only the community's response to the grant; in a full general equilibrium analysis we would also have to worry about its response to the higher federal income taxes necessary to finance the grant.

This analysis is shown in Figure 10.3. The initial budget line is shown by MN, and the community initially moves to point I, spending E_1 on the program and Z_1 on all other types of expenditures and private goods. The first grant to be analyzed is a case A grant, where the federal government pays m percent of the cost of the program regardless of the level of expenditures, the effective price to the community is lowered, and the budget line shifts to MR.

The community could go anywhere on this new budget line, but in practice it is likely to raise spending on the program as a result of the grant-induced price reduction. The exact response of the community is found by reading from its price-consumption path, which shows its level of spending as relative prices are changed. Let us say that the community goes to point A, spending E_a on the program and still spending Z_1 on all other goods. In this instance exactly the amount of the grant, $E_a - E_1$, is spent on the program, a result that occurs if the price elasticity of demand for the program is equal to 1.[8]

Now say that we took away this case A grant, moved the community back to I, and instead gave a case B grant. For case A grants the federal government changes the relative prices facing local governments: for case B grants it just changes the spendable income of local governments by giving an unconditional grant, leaving relative prices unaffected. The result is a parallel shift in the budget line to PQ, drawn as intersecting point A to keep the size of the grant constant. The community will now move along its income-consumption path, the

FIGURE 10.3 Effect of Various Types of Grants on Local Budgets

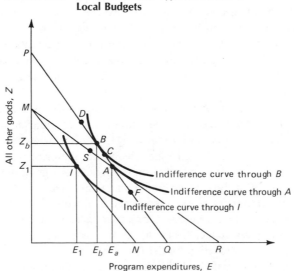

locus of points that shows the community response to income changes. Say that the movement takes the community to point B on the diagram, to the left of point A because now there is no reduction in prices. This time not all of the grant, only $E_b - E_1$ of it, is spent on the program, whereas with the A grant the entire grant was. Note also that the local indifference curve through this new point B is higher than that through point A, indicating that the local government would rather have no-strings-attached money than the same amount of money that could only be gotten by spending on E. This sets up an important evaluation quandary for grants. From the standpoint of the recipient, whether a government or a consumer, unconditional grants are clearly preferable, since the recipient gets the money and is free to spend it in any desired way. But from the standpoint of the donor, if the donor is interested in spending on a particular program, categorical grants are better because more of the grant will be spent on the program. We will come back to this point later when we try to evaluate grants.

Now we consider close-ended categorical grants, or case C grants. These are just like case A grants except that the size of the grant is limited, implying that the new budget line is kinked. But unfortunately this kink point introduces additional complications because it matters where the new budget line kinks. If we are dealing with grants of the same maximum size as the B grants analyzed above, all possible kink points will lie on line PQ, the B grant budget line. Should the kink point be to the left of point B, say at D (giving an undrawn budget line of MDQ), the community will move to point B just as with the B grant, and the case C grant will operate just like a B grant. Prices for the program in question are reduced, but only in a very small range: in the relevant range between points I and B there is no effective price reduction and no effective difference between noncategorical B grants and supposedly categorical C grants.

Going to the other extreme, say now that the kink point is to the right of point A, perhaps at F (giving an undrawn budget line of MFQ). We know from the results of our A grant experiment that the price-consumption path for this government includes segment IA, implying that the government will respond to this grant by going somewhere along this segment. Hence in this case the kink point will not be reached, the grant limit is irrelevant, and the C grant has effects that are identical to those of A grants. Before we noted that when the funds limit is very tight (line MDQ), the price reduction becomes irrelevant. Now we see that when the funds limit is loose (line MFQ), the limit becomes irrelevant.

A true case C grant, then, is one where both the price reduction and the funds limit are relevant. This is shown on the figure as a grant that kinks along segment BA, say at C (giving an undrawn budget line of MCQ). Here the government will go to point C, spending more than with a case B grant and less than with a case A grant.[9] Hence case C grants are in some sense the intermediate case: relative prices are reduced, but the locality is prevented from taking full advantage of the price reduction by the funds limit.[10]

It appears, then, that the limit on the size of the grant does more than simply limit federal grant expenditures; it also limits the expenditure response of local government for a given-size grant. On the right side of the diagram, tightening the limit tends to turn case A grants into case C grants, with lower per dollar impacts on local spending. On the left side, furthering tightening of the limit tends to turn case C grants into case B grants, with still lower per dollar impacts on local spending. For grants we have a property that is the reverse of the law of diminishing returns; if the grant has no limit, the per dollar impact of the large grant on program spending is maximized, but as the limit tightens, both the size of the grant and its per dollar impact decline.

In analyzing actual cases it is sometimes more convenient to think of the limit on grant funds in a different way. We have seen that if the limit implies a kink point to the left of point B, the grant operates like straight noncategorical assistance where the government is free to do as it wants with the money. Another way of saying this is that if the size of the grant and its kink point are small relative to the level of spending the government would have undertaken anyway, the federal grant has become a "drop in the bucket." For this drop in the bucket, it is impossible for the federal government to categorize the grant and ensure that spending is taken on the program in question, because the locality is already spending enough on the program in question that it can easily claim its other spending as evidence that it has satisfied the categorical restrictions of the grant.

EVALUATING GRANTS

The evaluation decision for recipient governments is to decide whether or not to take the grant. This decision is not hard for a B grant because there the jurisdiction is simply given no-strings attached money, and rational communities will simply take it and make optimizing decisions on how to spend it. For an A grant, the recipient's evaluation problem is to find the new point where net benefits at the margin from added spending are zero, point E_i^* in Figure 10.1. For a case C grant, where the central government is making only a limited amount of money available but under quite attractive terms (a high federal share m), normally the local government will again take as much as it can, although sometimes in this case a project application is required, and that may add to the transactions cost of getting the money. There are also some cases, such as desegregation grants for public schools, where the locality might find the net benefits of any expenditures to be negative, and decide not to participate in the program.

Decisions about whether the overall grant program has positive net benefits are left to the federal government. In making such decisions, federal planners must tally up the following program benefits:

1. The gain felt by the local community from added consumption of the aided good.

2. The gain felt by the local community from added consumption of all other goods.

3. Any social benefits resulting from the locality's added spending on the aided good.

It may seem strange that federal evaluators should worry about localities' added consumption of all other goods, but clearly they should if these benefits are to be compared with program costs, which are nothing more than the reduced consumption of all goods of taxpayers in all jurisdictions.

In general, of course, it is difficult to know how the evaluation will come out, but there are two familiar cases where we know that a categorical grant program will not have net benefits that are greater than those of noncategorical assistance, and where the categorical program should be discontinued. The first is the obvious one where item 3 is zero—that is, there are *no* social externalities at all from local spending on the grant-aided program. In this instance we have already shown that a categorical grant (of case A and C) will be less efficient than an untied case B transfer, because per dollar of grant, the B type leaves the local community on a higher indifference level. Hence if there is no reason rooted in social externalities to categorize a grant, doing so leads to an inefficient constraint on local choices, and the categorical grant will always show up as having smaller net benefits than a noncategorical grant.

The other instance involves the funds limit, the "drop in the bucket" problem referred to above. If the limit on the size of the grant is set so tight that the grant operates like an unrestricted B grant, or is "cashed out" in the jargon of grantsmanship, the net benefits rule also says that the categorical grant is worse than a noncategorical case B grant. The reason is administrative costs. The recipient community is able to cash out the grant, or treat it just like an equivalent-sized income transfer. But taxpayers are paying for the fiction of a categorical grant—resources are used in checking applications, defending budgets in Congress, and trying to police the apparently unworkable categorical restrictions of the grant. These resources could be saved by just giving the ith community a case B grant. The evaluation question is then to see if this is so: to see if the limit is so tight that the recipient locality is cashing out the categorical grant, in which case the central government donor might as well also.

We turn now from the general to the specific and examine a few real-world grant programs with these considerations in mind.

FEDERAL ROAD BUILDING

There are two important federal road-building programs. The first, called the ABC program, was started back in 1926 to construct interurban highways. The federal government pays two-thirds of the cost of road construction to states, which then build highways along predetermined connecting routes. These roads are usually well-paved four-lane highways but not limited-access highways. The second, called the Interstate Highway System, was started in 1956 to build limited-access throughways along predetermined routes. There the federal government pays 90 percent of the cost.

The big difference in the two grants is the size of the funds limit relative to what states would have spent anyway. Taking the Interstate system first, in Figure 10.4(a), before the grant, and presumably even now in the absence of the grant, there were virtually no interstate highways. Initially, states were then at point I and as a result of the grant, they moved to point C, spending a total of E_c on the grant, E_0 of their own money (to match the federal grant) and $E_c - E_0$ federal money. Diagrammatically, what has happened is that the reduction in price is sufficient that the states are only too happy to take the entire grant and devote it to building highways, the grants are almost fully subscribed, and expenditures on the program are slightly more than the grant. From the federal perspective, net benefits of the program equal all discounted future benefits of the highways less the present cost of the roads, E_c. If the program passes this test, federal authorities should be content to continue the categorical grant program. From the state perspective, net benefits of the program are the discounted net benefits of state residents only, and the costs are only $(1 - m)E_c$, the matching contribution state taxpayers must make (reflected in the slight drop in Z in the diagram). If these net benefits are positive, state authorities should accept the grant, and indeed in most instances they have eagerly done so.[11]

But precisely the opposite is the case for the ABC program. There a careful examination of highway building plans has turned up the startling fact that all but nine states spend more than the amount necessary to satisfy the federal spending conditions for receiving the grant.[12] For these 41 states, the situation is as shown in Figure 10.4(b). The state begins at I, already spending more than the E_c necessary to satisfy the federal restrictions, and it gets the grant. As can be seen, the grant does not change relative prices at the margin, and only affects highway

FIGURE 10.4 Federal Road-Building Grants

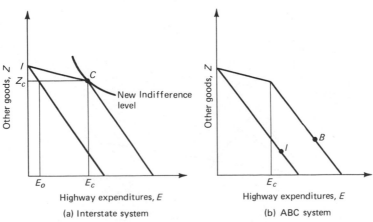

(a) Interstate system

(b) ABC system

construction by the amount that a general rise in income in the state would. This is exactly the drop in the bucket problem. This program clearly fails the net benefits test—not because road building is a poor idea but because the grant limit is so tight that states are treating the funds as an unconditional grant, and resources are being wasted to preserve the fiction of a categorical grant program.

FOOD STAMPS

Another federal program in which the provisions of the grant are quite instrumental in determining the impact of the program is that of food stamps. This program was begun in the 1960s as a grant from the federal government to low-income households in an effort to raise their consumption of food. The program has been expanded throughout the 1960s and 1970s and now pays benefits to almost 20 million individuals. Although the program is a transfer to individuals, it is one of the few federal transfers that is tied to consumption of a specific commodity and hence is analyzed in this section.

Before an important change was made in 1977, the program worked as follows. On the basis of family size, the government would establish a minimum subsistence needs level of food consumption for a family. The family would then be allowed to buy this amount of food stamps at a cost of $(1 - s)$, where s is the federal subsidy rate (like m in the previous examples). The subsidy rate is 1 for families with no other income, but it declines toward 0 as family income rises. Food stamps could then be used as currency in supermarkets. The result of all this was that the government lowered the price of food for low-income people.

Diagrammatically, this situation is shown in Figure 10.5. Take a poor family whose pre-food-stamp consumption of food was F_1 and of other goods

FIGURE 10.5 The Food Stamp Program

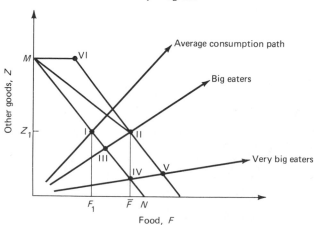

Z_1. Say that the minimum food standard assigned by the government for this family is at $\overline{F}$, and the government allows the family to buy $\overline{F}$ of food stamps for a sacrifice of MZ_1 in its consumption of other goods. Before the program the family could only have gotten F_1 of food for this same sacrifice, so the family should participate in the program. Assuming for simplicity that its price elasticity of demand for food is 1, the family will move from point I to II, spending the entire grant, $\overline{F} - F_1$, on food. In food stamp lingo, the size of this grant is called the "bonus value" of the stamps.

All of this is computed for a family with an average propensity to consume food. But if the government sets these parameters on the basis of an average family, there will always be families of big eaters, who consume food along the "big eater" line. These families would have been at point III before the grant and at point II after. In moving to point II, they only raise food spending by part of their grant, or bonus value (although they do spend all of their stamps on food because they consume $\overline{F}$ after the grant). Then we might have a family of very big eaters, who consumed $\overline{F}$ even before the grant. For them, the food stamps simply pay for food the family would have bought anyway; they are a drop in the bucket, and the family can in effect use the food stamps to release other income to be spent like an unconditional grant. Note also that with the stamps, this family would move to point V, to the right of its maximum allowance of stamps. Hence if it could find a family of small eaters who would otherwise not use all of their stamps, it could offer to buy the unused stamps of these small eaters, hence cashing out the grant for both families (there was alleged to be a black market in food stamps). It would be in the interests of the small-eater family to sell, because both families are better off when they can cash out the grant and treat it as an unrestricted source of funds.

The income-conditioning aspect of the program also becomes relevant at this point. Other things equal, as an average-food-consuming family gains in income and moves out along the average consumption path, F_1 rises, the distance between predicted and subsistence food consumption ($\overline{F} - F_1$) falls, and the bonus value ($\overline{F} - F_1$) falls. For these upper-income poor families, the graph shows that it takes a much smaller deviation of its consumption propensity from the average to put the family in the range where it is cashing out its stamps and treating the food stamp bonus as a general income gain.

In terms of evaluation, food stamps ironically risked failing the net benefits test on both sides. Champions of the poor families who felt that the program was effective in influencing the spending patterns of low-income families worried about the utility losses of recipients from the fact that the transfer was tied. These analysts pointed to budget studies which indicated that poor people do not spend their money frivolously, and asked why the poor could not simply be given the cash equivalent of their bonus value as cash?[13] They were also bothered by the fact that the poor had to spend time and energy procuring the stamps, and then had to bear the humiliation of spending stamps, and not money, in the supermarket. The whole program had overtures of second-class citizenship for recipients, and many wanted to do away with the categorical part of it—this was, in fact, why all the welfare reform provisions submitted by both Republican and Democratic administrations in the past decade have proposed such a cash-out.

Another set of program analysts could have argued that the program failed the net benefits test from the standpoint of taxpayers. Since many families could cash out the stamps and treat them as untied grants anyway, the program wasted administrative resources—paid partly by the poor (time spent waiting in line) and partly by taxpayers in general (expenses of printing the stamps, running the food stamps office, etc.). Many of the poor were using their stamps as dollars, so it would make sense just to give them dollars.

The matter was tentatively resolved in 1977, when Congress made a little-noticed but far-reaching change in the program that essentially cashed the program out. Under this change, families no longer would have to buy their entire allotment ($\bar{F}$) of stamps: they could just receive their bonus value ($\bar{F} - F_1$) in the form of stamps. The kink point of the price then shifted up to VI in Figure 10.5, ensuring that just about all families were already spending more than their stamps on food, and allowing them to cash out the stamps on their own. Any utility losses due to food-stamp-induced alterations in consumption patterns are now much less for low-income families, although they still have to wait in line for their stamps. And, of course, taxpayers are still paying the apparently unneeded expenses of printing the stamps to maintain the fiction of a program.[14]

SPECIAL REVENUE SHARING AND PUBLIC SERVICE EMPLOYMENT

We can apply a similar analysis to two other grant programs of current interest. One is special revenue sharing. In 1970 President Nixon proposed converting many of the existing categorical grants for social programs—in areas such as education, transportation, human resources, community development, and law enforcement—into special revenue-sharing grants. These grants eliminated many of the categorical requirements of existing case C grant programs, and merely required local governments to spend in certain areas to keep on receiving the federal money. The advantage of the approach was that it consolidated many small and obsolete grants into these larger packages, cut down on red tape, and gave localities more freedom of action in deciding how funds should be spent. The disadvantage was that in greatly broadening the definition of eligible program spending, it became much easier for states and localities to claim spending they would have made anyway as the way they spent the federal grant, totally diverting the grant to their own purposes and assuring that grants would not raise program spending at all. In terms of our drop-in-the-bucket analogy, the drops (grant) were the same size but the bucket (eligible types of spending) was made much larger, and the possibility of cashing out the grant much greater. Gradually, these special revenue-sharing plans have been adopted by Congress, and it is perhaps no surprise that empirical attempts to estimate the degree of state and local spending due to the grant now find much lower responses than before the special revenue-sharing changes.[15] In the interests of consolidating and streamlining programs, special revenue sharing risks killing them off altogether.

A second example is public service employment. In Chapter 7 we compared this approach with that of negative income taxes as a means of redistributing income: now we are concerned just with the grant aspects of the program. Originally, U.S. public employment programs were not operated through grants—in response to the massive unemployment of the 1930s the federal government initiated the Works Progress Administration and Civilian Conservation Corps to hire workers directly, to build bridges and roads and improve the national parks. While precise evaluations of the programs have not been made, general impressions are positive: even today visitors to the national park system are walking on trails and ramps built then (the service flow has not decayed rapidly), and since labor was unemployed with little prospect of getting jobs (that was before the government learned how to stabilize employment demand through macroeconomic policy), the social cost of the resources used appears to have been low.[16] But today, in line with prevailing federalist tendencies, public employment programs are operated through grants to state or local governments. Under various titles of the Comprehensive Employment and Training Act (CETA), local governments are given grants to employ low-wage or unemployed workers. But as with many of the grants examined in this chapter, it is very difficult for the federal government to make sure that local governments are using grants to expand employment, particularly when state and local employment is already so large and expands so steadily even apart from CETA. Once again, if local governments can claim that employees they would have hired anyway were hired under CETA, they get the federal CETA grants with no strings attached and will use only a small portion of it (given by the overall income effect) for employment increases of low-wage workers. Whether there is or is not a big expansion of state and local employment due to CETA then becomes essentially an empirical question, and regression studies that try to control for trend changes in wage rates, income, and demographic factors typically find that CETA has a rather low impact on state and local employment. Again we have a grant that appears to be cashed out.[17]

SUMMARY

This chapter has tried to show how the provisions of a grant matter in the determination of the net benefits of a program that attempts to raise spending indirectly by grants to lower levels of government. If the grant program works in the way it is intended, as, for example, the interstate highway program appears to, funds are spent on the program by both federal and state governments. At the federal level, the program is evaluated by comparing net benefits of all citizens with total program costs, the sum of the federal and state-local costs. This is the usual type of evaluation, and the fact that the program works through a grant is of no particular consequence. From a state perspective, the evaluation question is whether to accept the grant, and this is decided by a comparison of statewide benefits and costs.

But there are a large number of grant programs that do not work as intended, usually because the federal funds limit is set so tightly that there is no effective reduction of relative prices at the margin. In these cases—characteristic of the ABC highway construction program, food stamps, special revenue sharing, and public service employment—it appears to be easy for recipient governments and individuals to claim their initial spending as evidence of fulfillment of the conditions necessary to get the grant, and then use the grant as they would use any source of untied funds. The only spending on the program generated by the grant is that due to the general rise in income following the inflow of grant funds—a magnitude that often is very small. In such cases the federal program does not really exist—there is a federal grant, but it does not get spent on the program area. This outcome appears clearly to be worse than simply turning over the funds to local governments, because resources are wasted in trying to administer the grant. In such cases, then, the net benefits of the program are clearly less than those of a simple alternative. The upshot is that when a program works through a grant, one must make a careful analysis of the budgetary actions of recipient governments to ensure that the money was in fact spent in the appropriate way. Often the answer to this question can determine the results of the benefit-cost calculus all by itself.

NOTES

[1]Much of this discussion of the rationale for grants follows (in less detail) that of Wallace E. Oates, *Fiscal Federalism* (New York: Harcourt Brace Jovanovich, 1972), particularly chap. 3.

[2]The downward-sloping benefit schedule is drawn as if benefits are disproportionately focused on low-income groups, but the argument works as long as the benefit schedule's slope is *less positive* than that of the tax schedule. Notice also that the analysis equates the value of benefits received from government spending with the cost of government spending, as if there were no efficiency gains of the sort described in Chapter 2. Were there such gains, we would need two B schedules, one describing the value of government services to people and one describing the budget cost of government expenditures.

There have been a great many analyses of the incidence of government expenditure benefits. One that finds a downward-sloping *B* function under most assumptions is by W. Irwin Gillespie, "Effect of Public Expenditures on the Distribution of Income," in Richard A. Musgrave, ed., *Essays on Fiscal Federalism* (Washington, D.C.: Brookings Institution, 1965). Some recent research that indicates the function may be upward-sloping is described in Robert P. Inman and Daniel L. Rubinfeld, "The Judicial Pursuit of Local Fiscal Equity," *Harvard Law Review,* June 1979.

[3]See Joseph A. Pechman and Benjamin A. Okner, *Who Bears the Tax Burden?* (Washington, D.C.: Brookings Institution, 1974). If local taxes were proportional, the tax *rate* would be the same for all income groups, so that actual tax payments would rise proportionately at the same rate as income and the *T* schedule would be a ray from the origin. Pechman and Okner find that taxes rise, but not quite as much in proportional terms as income. Hence local taxes are slightly regressive, although high-income taxpayers still pay more tax dollars.

[4]See James M. Buchanan, "Federalism and Fiscal Equity," *American Economic Review,* September 1950.

[5]See Richard P. Nathan, Allen D. Manvel, and Susannah E. Calkins and Associates, *Monitoring Revenue Sharing* (Washington, D.C.: Brookings Institution, 1975) for a detailed discussion of these "formula" issues.

[6]One attempt to rationalize the structure of these grants, although not without criticism of them, can be found in Charles L. Schultze, "Sorting Out the Social Grant Programs: An Economist's Criteria," *American Economic Review,* May 1974.

[7]The first person to do this was A. D. Scott, "The Evaluation of Federal Grants," *Economica,* November 1952. A complete summary of the ensuing raft of articles is given by James A. Wilde, "Grants-in-Aid: The Analytics of Design and Response," *National Tax Journal,* 1971. Later I tried to see to what extent the predictions of these types of models were borne out in practice—see Edward M. Gramlich, "Intergovernmental Grants: A Review of the Empirical Literature," in W. E. Oates, ed., *The Political Economy of Fiscal Federalism* (Lexington, Mass.: Lexington Books, Heath, 1977).

[8]This assertion can be argued intuitively in the following way. When the price elasticity of demand is 1, total dollars expended by the community on the program are always constant—any reduction in price is balanced by an equal percentage increase in quantity of services purchased. It follows, then, that total dollars spent on all other goods are also constant. In this case the community has received a grant and spent it all on the program, maintaining constant expenditures on all other goods and a constant expenditure of its own dollars on this good as the effective price was reduced—the elasticity is 1.

[9]This can be shown as follows. For B grants we must compare the spending effects of grants of the same size. If the grant line kinks at point *C*, the grant is the same size as a B grant and the impact on program spending is obviously greater, as point *C* is to the right of point *B*. When comparing with A grants, however, we can only isolate the impact of the funds limit by comparing grants of the same matching ratio. Say that the matching ratio is given by *MR*, except that the grant kinks along segment *SA*. Comparing with point *A*, we see that the reduction in expenditures as we go to the kink point (along *AM*) is greater than the reduction in the grant (along *IM*), so that the expenditure impact of the grant is reduced by the funds limit.

[10]The paragraph described case C grants by holding the maximum size of the grant constant and varying the matching rate and kink point along *PQ*. We could also have held the matching rate constant and varied the maximum size of the grant along *MR*. To the left of *S,* the price reduction is irrelevant and the grant is like a B grant; to the right of *A,* the limit is irrelevant and the grant is like an A grant; and on segment *SA*, the grant is a true C grant.

[11]It might be wondered why we do not add a component reflecting the added state taxpayer cost for the federal share in E_c. The reason is that these taxes are fixed by law (to be precise, they are paid as a federal excise tax on gasoline). If one state did not accept the grant, the money would be given to some other state and no state taxes would be saved.

As one other comment on these grants, the 90 percent matching ratio on construction is somewhat misleading as a true cost-share proportion because states are entirely responsible for later maintenance expenditures. Presently, many states are finding these to be nontrivial.

[12]See Edward Miller, "The Economics of Matching Grants: The ABC Highway Program," *National Tax Journal*, June 1974.

[13]See, for example, John L. Palmer and Michael C. Barth, "The Distributional Effects of Inflation and Higher Unemployment," in Marilyn Moon and Eugene Smolensky, eds., *Improving Measures of Economic Well-Being,* Institute for Research on Poverty Monograph Series (New York: Academic Press, 1977), particularly Table 1, p. 203, for one such budget study.

[14]An even more bizarre way in which food stamps can be cashed out can be found in the country that is normally a model of enlightened, rational social policy, Sweden. To maintain equity between workers who receive untaxed income in the form of employer-subsidized lunches and those who do not, the Swedes have created their own food stamp program, one that subsidizes the restaurant lunches of high-income business people otherwise unable to get subsidized lunches. The categorical restriction of this program should be that these stamps must be spent in restaurants at noon on working days, but in fact there is no way to police this provision. Hence stamp recipients can use the stamps in restaurants at any time and on behalf of anybody (wives, dates, etc.). In fact, until regulations were recently changed, one would often find that restaurants would give change in kronor. The possibilities for cashing out the grant now become immense.

[15]One piece of evidence on the apparently reduced impact of grants on state and local spending can be found by comparing the results of two of my own articles on state and local governments. In "State and Local Fiscal Behavior and Federal Grant Policy," *Brookings Papers on Economic Activity,* 1 (1973), Harvey Galper and I found that case C grants raised state and local spending by about $.70 per dollar of grant. By 1978, essentially the same estimation technique had lowered the impact to only $.20 per dollar of grant—see Gramlich, "State and Local Budgets the Day after It Rained: Why Is the Surplus So High?" *Brookings Papers on Economic Activity,* 1 (1978). Other evidence on the same point is given in U.S. Advisory Commission on Intergovernmental Relations, *The State and Intergovermental Aids,* Washington, D.C., 1977, p. 67.

[16]See Jonathan R. Kesselman, "Work Relief Programs in the Great Depression," in John L. Palmer, ed., *Creating Jobs: Public Employment Programs and Wage Subsidies* (Washington, D.C.: Brookings Institution, 1978).

[17]Two estimates featuring low-employment impacts are George E. Johnson and James D. Tomola, "The Fiscal Substitution Effect of Alternative Approaches to Public Service Employment Policy," *Journal of Human Resources,* Winter 1977; and my own "Stimulating the Macroeconomy through State and Local Governments," *American Economic Review,* May 1979. Two that leave the matter more up in the air are Michael E. Borus and Daniel S. Hamermesh, "Study of the Net Employment Effects of Public Service Employment—Econometric Analysis," Mimeo, National Commission on Manpower Policy, Washington, D.C., 1978; and Laurie Bassi and Alan Fechter, *The Implications for Fiscal Substitution and Occupational Displacement under an Expanded CETA Title VI,* The Urban Institute, Washington, D.C., 1979.

PROBLEMS

10.1 Two equally large communities have identical local expenditure benefits functions that can be written as $E = 1000 - .02Y$, where E refers to the benefits from public expenditures and Y to family income in the community. Both communities derive all their revenue from proportional income taxes, and average family income is $5000 in the poor community and $10,000 in the rich community. Find the income tax rates that will be assessed in each community.

A family with an income of $6000 is considering moving to one of these communities. Determine the taxes paid and benefits received in each. Do the same for families with incomes of $12,000 and $18,000.

Where would you expect all families to try to locate? What would you expect this to do to property values in both communities? Who will make it into the rich community? What will this do to average incomes in both communities?

Design a revenue-sharing program that will eliminate the whole problem—that is, equalize fiscal residuals for given income groups across communities.

10.2 In the food stamp program the government used to fix the minimum food standard for a family and allowed the family to buy that amount of stamps below cost. These stamps are accepted as currency in the purchase of food but not for anything else. Say that the minimum food standard for a four-person family is $1000. All four-person families with annual incomes below $3000 are then allowed to buy $1000 worth of stamps, with an implicit subsidy rate (S) of $S = 1 - Y/3000$ per stamp, where Y is this family's annual income. Consider three four-person families, each with incomes of $2400 and income and price elasticities of 1 (to get the calculations to come out right, you will need to use arc elasticities).

> **a.** The family of middle-sized people initially spends $800 on food. What will be their total expenditure once the food stamp program is introduced?
>
> **b.** The family of skinny people initially spends $600 on food. What will be their total expenditures on food under the program?
>
> **c.** The family of fat people initially spends $1000 on food. What will be their expenditure on food under the program?
>
> **d.** Agriculture Department evaluators place a very high weight on the increase in food consumption generated by the program. What do they find objectionable in the present structure? What could they do to correct this objectionable feature?
>
> **e.** HHS welfare reformers simply want to raise the utility or indifference levels of poor people. What do they find objectionable in the present structure? What could they do to correct that objectionable feature?
>
> **f.** In 1977, Congress votes to suspend the purchase requirement. Hereafter poor families simply get their maximum bonus value in the form of stamps. Who won the bureaucratic fight, and why?

10.3 You are managing a program for manpower training for poor persons. Your agency gives a grant of $1 billion to local governments to "induce" them to conduct these training programs, and they select the client population in accord with your guidelines. They then fill out reports on the program and return them to you. Before your grant started, local governments had no programs at all of this sort.

A new president is elected who promises an all-out war against federal bureaucrats telling local governments what to do. She proposes relaxing the conditions on your grant to allow local governments to use the money either for manpower training or public employment, with no further conditional restrictions. Your grantee governments now have a total wage bill (gross amount spent on wages) of $50 billion.

Predict what will happen if this change in the conditions on the grant is made. Are the net benefits of the program computed by weighting only the utility gain for poor persons likely to rise or fall? Do you see any way to compromise your interests or hers? What?

10.4 Say that the counties of Arizona spend $2 billion on education. Legislators want to increase spending and pass a bill which provides that the state will pay one-fourth of the cost of all spending on education, up to a total state outlay of $.6 billion. Total income in these counties is $20 billion, the income elasticity of demand for education expenditures is 1.0, and the uncompensated price elasticity of demand is .5 (that means it includes both income and substitution effects). For these computations you can use initial values as the base of the elasticities.

  a. Find the first-year effect of the grant on total spending and grant levels. Is it an A, B, or C grant? What would be the level of spending if the same amount of money were given out in the form of noncategorical assistance?

  b. The grant program languishes in the legislature until 1984. Over this time community income rises to $25 billion, and the underlying income and price elasticities remain the same. What will be the level of spending and the grant now?

  c. Does the grant have as high a benefit-cost ratio as it did before? Why or why not?

  d. For those who are really on their toes: can you find for this grant in 1984 the funds limits that make the grant case A, B, and C respectively?

11

Government
Regulatory
Activities

All of the evaluations considered thus far have involved explicit government expenditures. Funds are allocated from the government's budget, private resources are hired to produce some public output, benefits are created, and the program either does or does not pass the net benefits test. In making this test, we have learned not to focus just on budget costs but on true resource costs. These could be less than budget costs if the good or service is supplied monopolistically, or greater than budget costs for activities with adverse environmental impacts.

Focusing on costs in this way leads to the realization that benefit-cost analyses of government activities need not be limited to government expenditure programs. There is no reason why the same logic could not be extended to the social regulation activities of government, activities where the government simply requires the private sector to do or not do something. To comply with these restrictions, normally in areas such as the environment, worker safety, consumer product safety, or antidiscrimination, the private sector must use extra resources—these are the costs of the regulation. Of course, there are benefits, too, in the form of a cleaner environment, a safer workplace, or whatever. As with any expenditure program, if the net benefits outweigh the costs, the regulation can be said to pass the net benefits test.

Regulation is an important area today because it is so widely used. In the past decade Congress has created a whole set of agencies to regulate the activities of the private sector—the Environmental Protection Agency (EPA), the Occupational Safety and Health Administration (OSHA), the National Highway Transportation Safety Board, the Consumer Product Safety Commission, and the Equal Employment Opportunity Commission, to name the most famous examples. These and related agencies have promulgated regulations estimated to have cost private business $100 billion to comply with in 1979—leading to predictable cries of outrage and alarm from that sector.[1] But private business is not the only group complaining about excessive regulation—lately, economists on the President's Council of Economic Advisers and the Council on Wage and Price Stability have become concerned about the inflationary impact of social regulation. Regulation drives up the costs and prices of certain consumer products and raises the consumer price index. The output of the regulations—cleaner air or a safer workplace—is not measured anywhere as a benefit. Hence the apparent cost of living (ignoring the offsetting improvements in air quality or worker safety) is raised, and since many wages in the economy are now tied to this apparent cost of living, regulation can cause wage increases which can cause further price increases and an inflationary spiral. The proper solution to this problem is not to eliminate all social regulation, but rather to try to write wage adjustment clauses that do not depend on regulation-induced relative price changes. Until that is done, however, social regulation can be inflationary.[2]

Because some regulations may not pass a reasonable benefit-cost test, and are inflationary to boot, there is a growing feeling that regulatory procedures should be modified to try to incorporate a benefit-cost test.[3] In this chapter we see how such a test might be formulated. We review a model of worker safety decisions that shows how one might answer the question in the abstract, discussing the role of worker compensation policy and subtopics such as whether performance or procedural standards are optimal, the pros and cons of taxes and standards, and the wisdom of imposing universal standards. We then look more carefully at one such regulation, OSHA's noise standard, to see how the costs and benefits can be ascertained in that case. Although the chapter uses examples drawn mainly from the health and safety area, the same analysis could be easily applied to other topics in social regulation.

A THEORY OF REGULATION

There are several types of government regulation of private activities, and several aspects of firm or individual behavior that might be regulated. For this chapter we confine our attention to the newer social regulation activities of government—the province of agencies such as EPA, OSHA, and others listed earlier. We are not dealing with some of the older price regulation activities, such as those of the Civil Aeronautics Board, Interstate Commerce Commission, and Federal Communications Commission. This is not because these older agencies are unimportant—they are estimated to generate even larger costs to consumers than do the newer social regulation agencies. The reason for not dealing with them is that for the older price regulation agencies the efficiency or benefit-cost questions do not seem to be as difficult. The market externalities are not great, and the benefit-cost question involves the relatively straightforward question of equating marginal benefits to marginal costs, so that deadweight losses of the type discussed in Chapter 2 are minimized.[4]

The newer social regulation activities raise much more difficult questions because parties other than the firms and consumers are involved. For environmental protection, society in general has an interest in whether the production activities of firms create adverse environmental impacts, and any benefit-cost calculation must include any such gains in the form of cleaner air. For worker safety, workers benefit from greater regulation, and these worker gains must be compared to firm and consumer losses. For antidiscrimination efforts, minority groups gain. In each case the issue is not a straightforward computation of a deadweight loss triangle, but a comparison of these deadweight losses with important but difficult to quantify externality-type benefits. It becomes harder to make the net benefits test, and more important to see if we can come up with at least a framework for asking the question.

Regarding social regulation, the theory used here is applicable to the case where a producer is producing a private good and generating some social "bad" in the process—pollution, worker accidents, or whatever. A social regulation will force the firm to change its procedures to reduce the adverse implications of its actions, but it will also raise firm and consumer costs. In the most general case it is probably true that even without regulation there is some market incentive already for the firm to avoid producing the bad—worker injuries force the firm to pay higher wage rates and/or worker compensation premiums, unsafe consumer products will not sell as well, and environmental degradation risks the firm being zoned out of more and more jurisdictions. So the regulation question dealt with here in the general case involves not whether the regulation will finally make the firm worry about the adverse implications of its behavior, but whether the costs of preventing these implications are appropriately balanced at the margin.

Using occupational safety as the main example, in Chapter 5 we saw that a careful examination of wage differentials was one way to value a human life— workers seem to be compensated for undergoing risks, and the value of this compensation can be used to infer their own implicit valuation of their life (although perhaps this procedure would yield only a lower bound estimate). The same argument suggests that they will also demand higher wages to compensate for risk of injury, and again empirical studies bear this out, although less strongly than when the injuries involve fatalities.[5] These risk differentials imply that worker accidents are costly to firms, and that firms will have a motive for preventing them even in the absence of any regulation. Whether firms engage in the optimal amount of accident prevention is, of course, another matter. To examine this more carefully, we try to construct a simple model that provides a framework for analyzing accident prevention.[6]

Say that there are two firms, one that is perfectly safe and paying a wage of W_2, and one that is not safe and paying a wage of W_1. Apart from the risk of injury, jobs in the two firms are exactly alike, requiring the same skill, having the same other working conditions, and so forth. Every time a worker gets injured she loses h percent of her wages in the form of medical costs or days out sick, and for now we assume that she bears the entire cost of that loss. Hence the three possible outcomes for the worker are:

1. Work in firm 2 and not be injured; gain W_2.
2. Work in firm 1 and not be injured; gain W_1.
3. Work in firm 1 and be injured; gain $W_1(1 - h)$.

If the accident rate in firm 1 is π, the expected wage in that firm—called $E(W_1)$—is the weighted-average outcome. The wage if uninjured, W_1, is multiplied times the probability of that outcome $(1 - \pi)$ and that product is added to the product of the wage if injured, $W_1(1 - h)$, times the probability of that outcome, π:

(1) $$E(W_1) = W_1(1 - \pi) + W_1(1 - h)\pi = W_1(1 - \pi h)$$

Intuitively, you can convince yourself of this formula by assuming that $\pi = \frac{1}{2}$. Then the expected wage is just the simple average of W_1 and $W_1(1 - h)$.

If all workers are neither risk lovers nor risk averse but simply try to compare their expected earnings in all firms, the market will equilibrate at a point where at the margin workers will be indifferent between going to work in firm 1 or 2. This implies that the expected wage will be the same in both firms, or that

(2) $$W_2 = W_1(1 - \pi h) \quad \text{or} \quad W_1 = \frac{W_2}{1 - \pi h}$$

What has happened here is that because of the risk of an accident in firm 1, the wage in that firm is bid up by an appropriate amount. Workers for that firm are compensated for undergoing accident risk. When we reported on the RC estimates of the value of a human life in Chapter 5, we were just using this formula in reverse—knowing wage differentials (W_1 and W_2) and death probabilities (π), we were using the formula to figure out the implicit h workers placed on their own lives.

The cost of having an unsafe workplace, then, is simply the extra wages that must be paid to get workers to work in it. If the firm hires L_1 workers, this "consequences" cost (CC) is

(**3**)
$$CC = L_1(W_1 - W_2)$$

After substituting for W_1 from eq. (2), we have

(**4**)
$$CC = L_1 W_2 \left(\frac{1}{1 - \pi h} - 1 \right) = \frac{L_1 W_2 \pi h}{1 - \pi h}$$

This curve is drawn in Figure 11.1 as the consequences cost, or CC curve.[7]

Before going on, we inquire about the things that would shift this CC curve. If either the size of the work force or the general level of wages in firm 2 went up, the consequences of injury and the CC curve would shift up. The reason is that firm 1 is being forced to pay differentials either to more workers (if L_1 went up) or on a higher base wage (if W_2 went up). More important for our theory, if workers became more risk-averse and began insisting on a higher "psychic" premium for bearing injury risk, their own psychological h would rise and the curve would again shift up. It takes more to bribe a reluctant than a willing complicitor.

Paying for the consequences of accidents is of course only one of the options open to the firm, the other being to prevent them from happening in the first place. If the firm also spends on accident prevention, we can define its total accident-related costs, TC, as the sum of consequences costs, CC, and prevention costs, PC.

FIGURE 11.1   Accident Costs and Rates

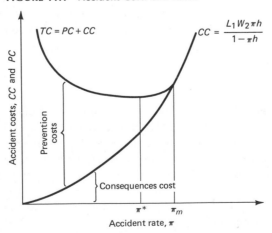

(5) $$TC = CC + PC$$

These prevention costs are then added onto the consequences costs in Figure 11.1. Say that π_m is the maximum accident rate the firm would have if it spent nothing at all on prevention. There PC = O and TC = CC, as shown on the graph. Moving left from that point, TC is higher than CC by just the amount spent on prevention, as shown. Notice also that both the PC and the TC curves are drawn as if there were decreasing marginal returns to accident prevention: it is easy to prevent the first few, but as the firm tries to prevent enough to get the accident rate (π) down to zero, prevention costs begin rising rapidly.

From Figure 11.1 it is obvious what the profit-maximizing firm will do. If all other aspects of its behavior (output, product prices, factor demands, etc.) are unaffected by worker accidents, it will go to the point where total accident-related costs are minimized, or π^* in the diagram. At any accident rate to the right of π^*, the firm would save much on consequences costs by reducing accidents; at any point to the left, it could save on prevention costs by allowing a few more to happen. The accident rate π^* is the one that minimizes firms' accident-related costs and thus maximizes the firms' profits.[8]

Some of the matters dealt with in this chapter are easier to see if we talk about minimum-cost accident rates not in terms of total costs, as is done in Figure 11.1, but in terms of marginal costs and marginal benefits. The marginal cost to the firm of preventing an accident is just the absolute value of the slope of the PC curve at any accident rate, or

(6) $$MC = -\frac{dPC}{d\pi}$$

where MC refers to marginal prevention costs and the negative sign is to make the expression positive, since PC will always decline with higher accidents. The marginal benefit to the firm of preventing accidents is that it will not have to pay workers so much extra wages to work there, and thus will save on its wages, or

(7) $$MB = \frac{dCC}{d\pi}$$

where MB refers to the wage costs the firm saves by accident prevention, in equilibrium the same as the worker benefits from greater safety (or the amount it is no longer necessary to bribe workers). These two curves are drawn in Figure 11.2, again showing the firms' optimum at π^*.[9] These curves must also be read from the right. Beginning with an expenditure on accident prevention of zero and an accident rate of π_m, the firm finds that as long as $\pi > \pi^*$, it pays to prevent more accidents. In this range prevention (from the MC curve) costs less than paying the consequences (from the MB curve). But once the firm hits π^*, that is

FIGURE 11.2   Marginal Costs and Benefits of
Accident Prevention

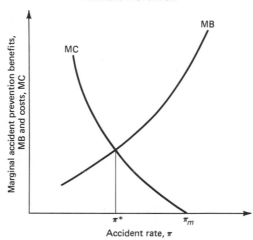

no longer the case. Below π^* prevention becomes very costly and it is cheaper for the firm simply to accept and pay the consequences of whatever accidents occur in that range.

   Before thinking about whether π^* is a socially optimum solution to the accident-prevention problem, the impact of worker compensation laws should be added to the model. The United States, together with most other industrial countries, has a worker compensation law. The theory behind the law is to set up a trust fund which makes full monetary compensation of the accident costs for injured workers, although not the psychic costs. It can then turn around and charge firms an ''experience-rated'' premium—forcing the firms causing the accidents and compensation payments to reimburse the trust fund, and the safe firms to pay nothing at all. The U.S. worker compensation law does not quite fit this model, neither paying full compensation to workers nor charging fully experience-related premiums for firms,[10] but to make the argument clear let us assume that we had an ideal system so we could see how that would change the results. For workers who are risk-neutral, they would now earn a wage of W_2 even in the risky firm 1, since worker compensation now takes care of their accident costs. But the cost of a worker to firm 1 is exactly what it was before, $W_1 - W_2$, since the actuarial payment for accident compensation is added on as a payroll tax for the firm. Hence there is no change in the MB curve facing the firm or in the wage received by the worker, and the firm still allows π^* accidents to happen. For risk-averse workers, where $W_1 - W_2$ exceeds the actual monetary costs of accidents, there is no change either. These workers get fully compensated for accidents by the government, so their W_1 declines but not all the way to W_2, because the workers still charge a psychological risk premium. Again there should be no change in π *. But there will be a change for the workers who either did not realize the true accident cost of working in firm 1 and hence did not raise W_1 appropriately, or for the daredevil workers. Now even if the workers do not charge the full accident premium, the worker compensation trust fund will, and presumably even these workers will bid the after-tax wage up to W_2. Hence there is a rise in consequence costs for these insufficiently risk-averse workers, an upward shift in the MB schedule in Figure 11.2, and a reduction in the number of accidents. An ideal worker compensation law then either has no effect at all if workers already charge actuarially appropriate accident premiums, or it reduces accidents if workers do not charge actuarially appropriate premiums.

IS THE MARKET SOLUTION OPTIMAL?

The interesting question in all of this is whether the result of the market system's invisible hand, for the firm to go to π^*, is the socially optimum result. If it is, obviously any regulation that changes things will impose positive net costs on society: if not, there may be net benefits to regulation. The answer, not surprisingly, turns out to depend on whether all those perfect market assumptions we made in developing our model were correct. A few cases where they would not be correct are listed as follows:

1. Workers may not have good information on injury risks. Many occupationally related diseases are not known at the time and take years to develop—it takes 30 years for asbestos-related cancer to appear, normally about this long for black lung disease, and 10 years for beryllium-related diseases.[11] In such cases we would hardly expect workers to charge the right premium for working in risky jobs, and there would be a presumptive case for regulating worker health-risk exposures.

2. Workers may not have the ability to find an alternative job that pays as well. The case of coal mining may again be an example—workers either work in the mines or they do not work at all. In such cases employers may have monopsony power and workers would not have the ability to earn their opportunity wage of W_2 because alternative jobs do not exist. Again, there is a good case for regulation.

3. The worker compensation arrangements may compensate workers inadequately, and charge insufficiently experience rated premiums to accident-prone firms. When this is true, and when workers themselves are either poorly informed or not risk-averse, the consequences schedules confronting firms may not reflect the true social costs of accidents, and again there is a case for regulation.

These three points are similar to the corresponding points made in Chapter 5 for possible drawbacks of the RC means of valuing human lives. The first two points are exactly the same as made there, the third is modified to reflect the explicit compensation mechanism in existence, and the other points made about human-life valuation are not relevant here because they refer to imputations of market values to other individuals—something we are not doing here. Here we are valuing the costs of injury to the particular workers being hired, so we do not have to worry about whether these workers' tastes are representative. But our general conclusion is the same as was reached there: the market will clearly induce some injury prevention of its own, and under a rather tight set of assumptions the right amount. But it is not hard to think of examples where the free market will underprevent injuries and where some additional regulation of firms will be beneficial.

The situation where there is a case for regulation is shown in Figure 11.3. The marginal cost of prevention is a physical concept, unaffected by the workers' psychological or true social valuation of their accident risks: hence this is exactly as drawn in Figure 11.2. But there are three MB curves. The first is that given by the free market, leading to a high injury rate of π_0. Then, on the assumption that at least some workers are insufficiently risk-averse, the next curve shows the solution with a worker compensation law added. The higher risk premiums for these insufficiently averse workers shift up the MB curve for avoiding accidents to the firm and lower the accident rate to π_1. But even this rate may not be the social optimum if there are still some workers who do not have the information or bargaining power to protect themselves from the psychic costs (not compensated by worker compensation laws) of extreme injury (losing an arm or a leg) or even death. The true social optimum curve is given by the social MB curve, and the social optimum injury rate by π_2. The free market has prevented some injuries, worker compensation has prevented some more, but it is entirely plausible that both together have not prevented enough accidents and that the true social optimum accident rate is π_2.

From these marginal cost and marginal benefit curves we are now in a

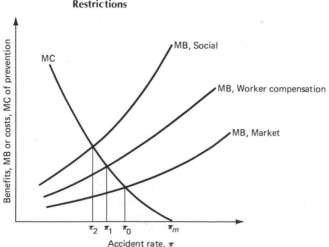

FIGURE 11.3   Should the Government Impose Worker Safety Restrictions

position to find the net benefits or costs of social regulation. These are shown in Figure 11.4, where for simplicity we include only the market MB curve and the social MB curve. Taking the positive case for regulation first, say that the firm responding to market incentives will go to π_0 but that the true social benefits of accident prevention are given by the higher social MB curve. If the regulation is exactly right, it forces the firm to reduce its accident rate to π_2. The physical costs of this move are given by the area under the MC curve, area $A + B$. This area is just the number of accidents prevented times the cost of preventing each accident. The social benefits of the move are given by the area under the social MB curve, or area $A + B + C$. Subtracting one from the other, as we would do under the Kaldor–Hicks principle, we see that in this case the regulation has a net benefit defined by the triangle C.

But, of course, the regulation may not always be just right. Let us say now that the regulators get carried away and try to reduce the firm's accident rate to π_3. In this case the physical costs of the new regulatory change are given by area $D + E + F$, while the benefits are only $D + E$. Here there is a net cost of this new regulation, or deadweight loss, given by the triangle F. With this framework we see that it is possible either to over- or underregulate. Whether there are net benefits or net costs of regulation depends both on the physical costs and on the social valuation of the resources devoted to accident prevention, just as with most other types of government expenditure programs.

Before leaving this section, it should be stressed that the degree to which there is over- or underregulation hinges very much on how efficient the market is in setting up incentives for firms to prevent social ills on their own. It could be argued that the labor market, for all its imperfections, may be fairly good at setting up such incentives—firms' accident rates are compiled, they are used in

FIGURE 11.4   Benefits and Costs of Regulation

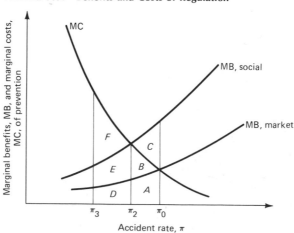

industry wage negotiations, there are mechanisms for firms to feel the cost of allowing these accidents to occur, and most industry and firm labor supply curves are quite elastic. The same may soon be the case for consumer product safety. Journals such as *Consumer Reports* publish extensive product information, and alert consumers may be able to bid down prices, or not buy at all, when products have questionable safety records. But there are other cases where the market is not as efficient in translating social consequences into market incentives. For environmental regulation most of the costs of pollution are borne by surrounding residents, groups that may not have any formal market transactions with the firms, and no price that can be bid up or down. The same would be true of antidiscrimination regulations—minorities may have few ways to strike back at firms within the market. In these instances the case for some social regulation will generally be much stronger, although it will be just as possible for regulators to overdo it and impose regulations that entail more costs than benefits.

SUBTOPICS IN REGULATION

The preceding section developed the overall case for placing some constraint on the activities of business, even a business that has some market incentive to engage in accident prevention or environmental cleanliness. But it did not discuss the important question of how such constraints might be implemented. This section takes up a few aspects of that issue.

A first question is whether regulatory constraints should be placed on the procedures or the performance of firms. In the worker safety example, OSHA could either regulate firms' safety procedures—by setting restrictions on the types of railings, the ways in which ladders should be constructed, and so on—or it could simply use a performance standard and regulate accident rates, forcing firms to take additional safety measures if these accident rates are too high. Something can be said for either approach. Economists usually favor performance standards because they give profit-maximizing firms an incentive to find the cheapest way to reduce accidents. On the other hand, regulatory agencies often find it easier and cheaper to determine compliance with the regulations by monitoring actual procedures. This avoids answering the difficult question of whether a firm is in compliance if it has adopted the right procedures even if accident rates have not yet been reduced, or whether it is in compliance if it has not adopted the right procedures even though accident rates dropped for some mysterious reason.

A more general issue is the question of whether the firm should be taxed or regulated. Typically, economists are in favor of taxes, but politicians usually end up writing laws that impose specific regulations.[12] Again, an argument can be made for either side. In Figure 11.5 we show the case for a comparison of an accident tax with a performance standard regulation. The lower MB curve in the figure is that set by market wage differentials, and the higher one, labeled "MB,

FIGURE 11.5   Taxes or Performance Standards ?

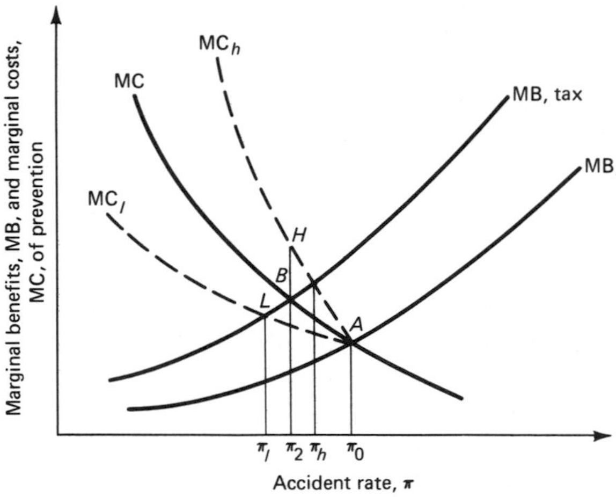

tax,'' is that if the firm is taxed or fined according to the accidents that occur on its premises. By contrast, OSHA could levy no tax at all, but simply impose a performance standard that the firm must reduce its accident rate to π_2 or be closed down.

If there were no uncertainty about the physical costs of accident prevention, there would be no difference at all in the results of the two approaches. Say that the true cost of accident prevention is known to be given by the solid line denoted by the MC curve. A tax or fine that shifted the MB schedule as shown would lead the firm to accident rate π_2, with added prevention costs given by the area $\pi_0 AB\pi_2$. A regulation limiting the firm's accident rate to π_2 will have exactly the same results and entail the same added prevention costs.

But differences between the two approaches result if there is uncertainty about how much it will cost the firm to prevent accidents to the left of π_0, a range where the firm might never have been and where it is very possible that neither the firm nor the government will know the cost schedule. Say first that the performance standard forces the firm to an accident rate of π_2 and that the costs of prevention in this range turn out to be higher than expected, given by the MC_h curve on the graph. Then the cost of compliance for the firm is given by the area $\pi_0 AH\pi_2$, larger than before. On the other hand, the tax will lead the firm to an accident rate of π_h, higher than π_2. Which situation is preferable depends on the underlying social costs of accidents: if any deviation of injury rates from π_2 has extremely grave social consequences, an exact performance standard that tries to place an absolute ceiling on the level of injuries will be the preferred policy. If, on the other hand, the social costs of deviations of accident rates from π_2 are relatively minor, taxes will be the preferred approach because performance regulations may impose extremely high compliance costs on firms (the area under the MC_h curve between π_h and π_2).

The reverse situation obtains on the low side, if prevention costs turn out to be less than anticipated. Taxes will lead to an accident rate of π_1, regulation to π_2. This time a performance standard risks underregulating if the costs of accident prevention turn out to be very low.[13]

A related question is whether accident standards should be uniform across industries or particular to industries. Here our analytical apparatus can arrive at a more definite conclusion. Say that we have two firms, one in which it is very cheap to prevent accidents and one in which it is very costly. These firms are shown in Figure 11.6, with both facing the same market and social benefits-of-prevention schedules, but having different MC schedules. Before government action, the firms were operating with the high accident rate of π_e in the expensive firm and the low rate of π_c in the cheap firm. Were either a tax or a *particular* firm standard that equates marginal benefits and costs to be imposed, both firms would prevent more accidents and the new rates would be π_e' and π_c'. The expensive firm would spend $\pi_e AB\pi_e'$ more on prevention and the cheap firm would spend $\pi_c CD\pi_c'$ more, for a total reduction in accidents of $(\pi_e - \pi_e') + (\pi_c - \pi_c')$. As an alternative, let us say that the government tried to impose a *uniform* performance standard forcing the expensive firm to lower its accident rate to that of the cheap firm. Then the cheap firm would spend no more on accident prevention and the expensive firm is forced to spend $\pi_e AE\pi_c$ more for a reduction in accidents of $\pi_e - \pi_c$. If accidents in the two firms are equally grave, in this case it is clear that imposing uniform standards is a very costly way to improve worker safety. As compared with the taxing approach, or with an approach that just imposed differential regulations of π_e' and π_c', the uniform

FIGURE 11.6   Uniform or Particular Standards ?

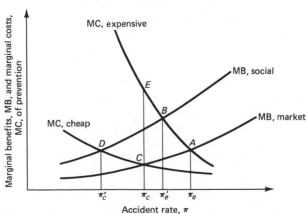

standard costs are essentially the same (area $\pi'_e BE\pi_c$, the added prevention costs of the expensive firm under uniform standards is drawn to be equal to area $\pi_c CD\pi'_c$, the unrealized prevention costs of the cheap firm) but prevents many fewer accidents (compare $\pi'_e - \pi_c$ with $\pi_c - \pi'_c$). Uniform standards are forcing high-cost firms into accident prevention and letting low-cost firms off the hook, violating the important marginal provision of economics. It is much more effective, in terms of accidents prevented per dollar spent, to tailor particular restrictions for particular firms, trying to hit the optimum prevention rates for each firm. One easy way to do this is by accident-rate taxation. Otherwise, regulations will be trying to force safety improvements just where it is more difficult to make them, and not inducing them when it is easy.

The argument in favor of uniform performance standards is that it is not fair to subject workers in different industries to different accident risks. But this is a strange argument because before either one of the standards was imposed, workers were already volunteering to work for different risks, doing so because their wage was higher in the expensive firm. We argued that these "preferences" could be viewed with some skepticism if there were gaps in information or imperfections in the labor market, but these problems should have been corrected along the social MC curve—there firms are fined and workers compensated appropriately, the workers in the expensive firm still receiving higher wages, now on the basis of proper market information. As long as the social costs are properly reflected in the incentives facing the two firms, and equally competent workers voluntarily choose to work in one firm or the other, it is incorrect to argue that these workers are being treated differentially just because one component of a whole job package is different.[14]

A SPECIFIC CASE STUDY: THE OSHA NOISE STANDARD

We move now from the general to the specific, examining one case of an attempt to regulate the behavior of private firms, the OSHA noise standard.[15] This is an example of an excessively strict set of regulations that may entail excess costs; others could easily be found where the benefits of regulation appear to be positive. We take up just one to show how benefit-cost analysis might be applied to a regulatory standard.

One of the first standards handed down by OSHA was its interim noise standard. This standard limited the average noise level to which workers could be exposed to 90 decibels, with a maximum exposure to noise at any time of 140 decibels, to noise over a 2-hour period of 100 decibels and over a 4-hour period of 95 decibels. In layman's terms, a noisy subway train has about a 90-decibel sound level. This standard has been in effect since 1972, although there is alleged to be a substantial amount of noncompliance.

But this 90-decibel standard was only an interim standard, and the National Institute of Occupational Safety and Health (NIOSH), an agency set up to conduct research on occupational health, also recommended an 85-decibel standard, with the maximum exposure not to exceed 115 decibels, for 2 hours not to exceed 95 decibels, and for 4 hours not to exceed 90 decibels. When noise levels are at 85 decibels, workers standing a yard apart could converse without shouting. Numerically, the NIOSH standard may not appear to be much more stringent than the interim standard, but 85-decibel noise has only half the energy and sounds three-fourths as loud as 90-decibel noise.

OSHA then commissioned a prominent noise-consulting firm—Bolt, Beranek, and Newman (BBN)—to estimate compliance costs for the 85- and 90-decibel standards through engineering measures alone (not earplugs). These costs came out to be $31.6 and $13.5 billion, respectively, for all manufacturing firms. It is obviously difficult to estimate cost figures like this, but the BBN numbers are still used both inside and outside government.[16]

On the benefit side, there are at least four ways to measure the benefits of both sets of noise standards. None of these ways are perfect, but all lead to the same conclusion, setting up a reasonably strong empirical case against the standards. A first approach is simply to argue that if workers for noisy firms were well informed about the risk of hearing loss and had sufficient bargaining power to gain a well-paying quiet job, the social benefits of noise prevention could be read directly from the market wage differential schedule. Since firms facing this market wage differential did not prevent noise before the regulations were handed down, we might infer that the benefits of noise prevention are less than the prevention costs, and that the standards have negative net benefits.

If we cannot rely on the market wage curves to yield a proper solution, a second way to infer the benefits of noise prevention is to try to infer RC values from other aspects of people's behavior. One possibility is housing values: it is well known that house values are lower, other things equal, in noisy areas around airports. Robert Smith has looked at a number of studies estimating house price differentials and he finds, through the procedure laid out in Chapter 5, that the present value of housing values is about $130 per decibel reduction in noise.[17] Translated into aggregates for the manufacturing sector, this yields a marginal benefit from the 90-decibel standard of $6 billion and an additional benefit of another $6 billion for the 85-decibel standard. There are many reasons (all mentioned by Smith) why these figures are upper-bound totals—if people care about noise at home but not so much in the workplace, if the price differential includes the risk of a plane crash. But even using the upper-bound estimates of Smith, the marginal benefits of noise prevention are less than the marginal costs and both standards would fail the net benefits test.

A third method involves direct estimation of the value of hearing loss. There is general agreement that workers exposed to noise levels over long periods of time will suffer some hearing loss, but the loss appears to be slight (in most cases the worker only has trouble with faint speech) and the exposure must be prolonged, 20 years or more. Both NIOSH and BBN made estimates of the percentage of retirees with hearing loss were they to work their entire career in noisy workplaces under the various standards, and came up with the following estimates:[18]

	BBN	NIOSH	AVERAGE
Unregulated system	36	38	37
90-decibel standard	31	33	32
85-decibel standard	25	22	23

Hence the incidence of hearing loss for long-term employees declines by *five* percentage points with the 90-decibel standard and an extra *nine* percentage points with the 85-decibel standard. Although no figures are given, these estimates are certainly overestimates of the benefits of imposing standards, because most employees do not work at one job for anything close to an entire career. But even were they to do so, as could be assumed under the upper-bracket approach, multiplying by the number of employees involved yields a saving of hearing losses for 700,000 employees for the 90-decibel standard and 1,300,000 employees for the 85-decibel standard. Putting a monetary valuation on these losses is, as usual, difficult, but we might use the average workers' compensation award for hearing losses paid in New York State, the only state that now makes such payments. This figure is in the $2000 to $3000 range for cases that appear to be on average at least as serious as the ones we are dealing with.[19] Again using the upper-bracket figure of $3000 per employee, we get implied benefits of $2.1 billion ($3000 times 700 thousand) for the 90-decibel standard and $3.9 billion ($3000 times 1300 thousand) for the 85-decibel standard. These estimates are again very much less than the costs of the standards, even though upper-bracket values have been used at every point where there was uncertainty. Again, the net benefits from either set of standards appears to be negative.

A final means of estimating benefits is less quantitative but linked more closely to workers' actual behavior. The OSHA noise standards refer to engineering changes within the firm to lower noise levels, but another way to prevent hearing loss is simply to have workers wear earplugs. While wearing earplugs is not pleasant, perhaps not hygienic, and lowers the ability of employees to communicate with each other, the noise level experienced by workers with specially fitted earplugs is much below that for either of the OSHA standards. But workers will not wear earplugs. Almost every attempt to outfit them with free earplugs has had to be abandoned soon after inception due to workers' lack of interest. It could be that wearing plugs is just so unpleasant that workers will not do it, but another way to interpret the experience is that workers are not willing to pay for an almost costless way to prevent hearing loss. If so, why force them to pay (in possible job losses or lower wages) for a set of standards that could be much more costly?

So each approach for estimating the benefits of both sets of noise standards, each of which is less than perfect in its own way, comes out with an estimate of benefits that is much less than the estimated cost. Neither the observed behavior inference nor the earplug inference yields a quantitative estimate, but comparing the two quantitative estimates with the cost estimates leads to the following tabular summary of the results, in billions of 1974 dollars for the manufacturing sector:

	MOVING TO 90-DECIBEL STANDARD FROM PRESENT SYSTEM	MOVING TO 85-DECIBEL STANDARD FROM 90 STANDARD
Cost	$13.5	$18.1
Benefits, home value inference	6.0	6.0
Benefits, hearing loss inference	2.1	3.9
Net cost, home value	7.5	12.1
Net cost, hearing loss	11.4	14.2

For both sets of standards, then, the net benefits appear to be negative—even if we add the two separate means of estimating costs (which we should not do because that would be double counting). One is perhaps never sure of anything in benefit-cost analysis, but all of these computations do make a reasonably strong case against the noise standards.

As a final note, OSHA did impose the 90-decibel standard in 1972, although it is alleged to be imperfectly enforced. Although NIOSH recommended the 85-decibel standard at that time, OSHA had still, as of mid-1979, not decided whether to go ahead with it or not. Supposedly a decision will be made some time in 1980.

SUMMARY

In this chapter we tried to determine how one would do a benefit-cost analysis for government regulatory activities. The logic and methodology are very similar to that used for explicit expenditure programs, with only the budget cost absent from the picture. The cost of such regulations is in the expenditures made, or resources used, by firms in modifying production processes to yield greater worker or product safety or environmental cleanliness. The benefits are in terms of the values of the worker safety or environmental cleanliness.

As with the evaluations of direct expenditure programs, it is particularly difficult to quantify the benefits of regulation. To some degree they are already included in market transactions, because firms pay lower wages when the workplace is safe, or can charge higher prices when the product is safe. But knowing the degree to which this is true is very difficult, especially when workers or consumers may not have good information about risks. It is easy to argue the case that sometimes some regulation of the activities of private firms will be necessary; and also easy to argue that regulations requiring absolutely safe workplaces or clean environments will be very costly and generally quite infeasible. So the general degree to which there should be regulation depends essentially on a case-by-case analysis where the benefits—difficult as they are to estimate—must be compared with the costs. This is exactly the aim of present efforts to limit excessive regulation.

In the one specific case we looked at, OSHA's noise standards, the cost of imposing those regulations seems to be substantially greater than the benefits, in any of four (admittedly imperfect) ways of estimating those benefits. But there are other cases, such as OSHA restrictions on worker exposure to asbestos or beryllium, where regulation of private activities seems clearly to be in the public interest. There is no way workers could have had the information they needed to protect their health. The only general statement one could make about regulation is that it is neither always desirable nor always undesirable, but that its desirability depends on a careful comparison of benefits and costs.

NOTES

[1] The cost estimate comes from Murray L. Weidenbaum, "The Costs of Government Regulation of Business," A Study for the Joint Economic Committee of the U.S. Congress, Washington, D.C., 1978.

[2] See the *Economic Report of the President,* Transmitted to Congress, January 1979, Washington, D.C., p. 68, for another statement of this position.

[3] A good argument along those lines can be found in Richard Zeckhauser and Albert Nichols, "The Occupational Safety and Health Administration—An Overview," Report to Congress, Washington, D.C., 1979.

[4] For an interesting discussion of the issues, see Alfred E. Kahn, "Applications of Economics to an Imperfect World," *American Economic Review,* May 1979, pp. 1–13.

[5] See Robert S. Smith, "Compensating Wage Differentials and Public Policy: A Review," *Industrial and Labor Relations Review,* 1979. His Table 1 finds six studies reporting positive wage differentials when industry injury rates are high, and 10 when death rates are high.

[6] This model follows that developed by Walter Oi, "On the Economics of Industrial Safety," *Law and Contemporary Problems,* Summer-Autumn 1974. Essentially the same

model is described in Edward J. Mishan, *Cost-Benefit Analysis,* 2nd ed. (New York: Praeger, 1976), chaps. 22, 23.

[7]Just looking at the numerator, we see that CC is proportional to π; hence the numerator would be drawn as a ray from the origin. But as π increases, the denominator falls, so the quotient, CC, rises at an increasing rate, as the curve is drawn. Those of a more mathematical bent can verify that both the first and second derivatives of CC with respect to π are positive; hence the curve will slope up at an increasing rate.

[8]This turns out to be the standard first enunciated, from a social standpoint, by a lawyer, Guido Calabresi, in *The Cost of Accidents: A Legal and Economic Analysis* (New Haven, Conn.: Yale University Press, 1970), Chapter 3.

[9]Those who know calculus can do the differentiation implied by eq. (7). From eq. (4), it is

$$ MB = \frac{dCC}{d\pi} = L_1 h W_2 \left[\frac{(1 - \pi h) + \pi h}{(1 - \pi h)^2} \right] = \frac{L_1 h W_2}{(1 - \pi h)^2} $$

This is clearly positive and rises with π, as can be seen by differentiating MB again with respect to π (getting the second derivative). The MB curve in Figure 11.2 has these properties.

[10]See Robert S. Smith, *The Occupational Safety and Health Act: Its Goals and Achievements* (Washington, D.C.: American Enterprise Institute for Public Policy Research, 1976), p. 29.

[11]Ibid., p. 30.

[12]See Allen Kneese and Charles L. Schultze, *Pollution, Prices, and Public Policy* (Washington, D.C.: Brookings Institution, 1975). A good discussion of the various alternatives for cleaning up the environment can be found in William J. Baumol and Wallace E. Oates, *Economics, Environmental Policy, and the Quality of Life* (Englewood Cliffs, N.J.: Prentice-Hall, 1979), part III.

[13]These pros and cons are discussed in more detail by Baumol and Oates, *Ibid.*, chap. 20; by Russell F. Settle and Burton A. Weisbrod, "Governmentally Imposed Standards: Some Normative Aspects," in *Research in Labor Economics,* 2 (1978), pp. 159–189; and by Christopher A. Nash, "The Theory of Social Cost Measurement," in David W. Pearce, ed., *The Valuation of Social Cost,* (London: Allen and Unwin, 1978), p. 15.

[14]One could make a stronger argument for uniform procedural standards because it will be very costly to tailor procedural requirements to the production processes of individual firms.

[15]Most of the following review comes from an excellent summary by Smith, *The Occupational Safety and Health Act,* chap. 3. The figures here are presented differently from his, but they are his figures.

[16]This original report was Bolt, Beranek, and Newman, "The Impact of Noise Control at the Workplace," Report 2671 submitted to the U.S. Department of Labor, OSHA Office of Standards, January 1974. It is cited and used extensively by Smith in his summary. As an indication that the cost figures are still used, see "OSHA's Deaf Ear to Tighter Noise Control," *Business Week,* March 26, 1979, p. 30.

[17]Smith, *The Occupational Safety and Health Act,* p. 48.

[18]See the U.S. Department of Health, Education, and Welfare, NIOSH, "Occupational Exposure to Noise," 1972, Table XII; and Bolt, Baranek, and Newman, "The Impact of Noise Control," p. D-2.

[19]Smith, *The Occupational Safety and Health Act,* p. 56.

PROBLEMS

11.1 Fancy Wheels Skateboard Company employs 50 testers who occasionally fall and break their arms. The workers could earn $9800 in perfectly safe occupations, but when they break their arms, they lose an average of 20 percent of annual wages. The company could repave its sidewalks with special extra-soft asphalt, and lower the probability of an arm break, according to the following schedule:

π (PROBABILITY OF A BREAK)	ANNUAL COST OF REPAVING
0	$80,000
.1	40,000
.2	20,000
.3	10,000
.4	4,000
.5	0

a. If workers are risk-neutral, how much will FWSC spend on repaving? What would be the extra cost to FWSC if OSHA regulations required repaving until testing was absolutely safe?

b. A new generation of daredevils comes along, and they love skateboarding so much that they are willing to test for $9800—despite the fact that some occasionally fall and break their arms. What will FWSC do now? What is now the extra cost of OSHA regulations?

c. The city council is thinking of enacting an ordinance to outlaw skateboarding on city streets. The costs of this legislation would be the loss of personal freedom; the benefits, the fact that the city would no longer have to treat the broken arms of daredevils suffering skateboarding accidents. Can you use the information given here to estimate, or bracket, benefits? Why or why not?

12

Social

Experimentation

Most of the preceding chapters have focused on the question of how one evaluates different types of government programs. In this chapter we change the focus somewhat and ask about information—how does an aspiring evaluator ever come up with the information needed to measure the benefits and costs of various programs. We have seen that information is often the key stumbling block in estimating benefits and costs, and often it may be worthwhile for the government agency just to spend funds, or resources, to yield the information so that it can make better program decisions.

One of the interesting new techniques in this regard is the idea of running large-scale social experiments with programs. Of course, physical scientists and psychologists have been doing experiments for decades, but the idea is rather new to social scientists. And what is very new is the idea of experimenting with a social program—consciously setting up a small-scale replica of a national program, organized not to make the subjects better off but essentially to gain information about how such a program would work. The first one of these social experiments was started back in 1968 by the Office of Economic Opportunity (OEO), when it experimented with a negative income tax (NIT) in five cities in New Jersey and Pennsylvania. This was followed by several more income-main-tenance experiments, a health insurance experiment, some housing allowance experiments, and some educational experiments, together with several smaller and less publicized experiments in crime prevention, drug abuse, and other areas.

One can think of several intrinsic advantages of social experiments. On the political side, the experiment is designed as an experiment—that is, not as national policy. If it turns out that certain aspects of the plan need to be adjusted to make things work better, that can be done without stirring up vocal interest groups. If it turns out that the plan does not work at all, it can be scrapped without alarming such groups. If it turns out the plan works well, it can be implemented at a sensible rate, avoiding some of the initial startup difficulties that may have plagued the experiment itself, and certainly would have plagued a full-scale national program. In terms of statistical measurement, Chapter 9 closed with a list of innate advantages of experiments—policies that do not exist can be observed, better control groups can be formed, and better measurements taken.[1]

For all these benefits of social experimentation, there are also some costs. Social experiments take a lot of time—the shortest one on record took 2 years from start to finish, but that one was strongly criticized for being done too hastily. A more reasonable estimate of the time an experiment will usually take from start to finish is somewhat in excess of 5 years. If some policy question is not of very enduring interest, it is not a good topic for a social experiment. Experiments also cost a good deal more money than most government evaluations—to pay subjects, to run the program, and to do the analysis. If subjects are paid, this is only a transfer and should not count as a true resource cost, but most of the budget expenditures for experiments go for operation and analysis and do comprise a true resource cost. Hence if some policy question is not of very great importance, it is probably not good material for an experiment.

This chapter reviews some large-scale social experiments. We first classify different types of experiments and then different types of experimental designs. We then review two different experiments—the NIT experiments recently completed by the Department of Health, Education, and Welfare, now the Department of Health and Human Services (HHS), in Seattle and Denver, and the OEO experiment in educational performance contracting (EPC). The chapter concludes with a discussion of the question of whether social experiments can in some sense be said to be unethical.[2]

DIFFERENT TYPES OF SOCIAL EXPERIMENTS

There are at least four different types of social experiments, and it is hard to talk about the issues involved without making distinctions between the types. They are:[3]

1. *Individual response experiments.* These experiments attempt to discover how individuals or households will respond to changes in their income or relative prices occasioned by some government program. Examples are all of the OEO and HHS income-maintenance experiments (to be discussed later), which altered the income and the tax rates on earnings facing recipient families; the health insurance experiment currently being carried out by HHS, which alters the cost of medical care for recipient families; and one of the housing allowance experiments of the Department of Housing and Urban Development (HUD), which alters rents.[4] The point of the experiment is to measure the change in income or consumption patterns for recipient households, the unit of observation is the household, and there typically will be a set of experimental and a set of control households. The regression model framework used in Chapter 9 is ideally suited for analyzing the results of this type of experiment.

2. *Market response experiments.* In this type of experiment the goal is to find out both how the individual households respond to a policy change, and how a whole market responds. If demand for a good or service is raised by a government program, the experiment might attempt to find out whether this added demand pushes up prices or not—implicitly then the goal of the experiment is to trace out the market supply curve. We can see this in Figure 12.1. Assume that the demand schedule for a good or service is raised from D_0 to D_1 by, say, a food stamp or rent supplement program. Will this higher demand raise prices to all consumers (along S_2) or will it not (along S_1)? Since these experiments try to trace out the response of a whole market, the budget cost is many times the cost of the individual experiments of type 1. The reason is that it is impossible to sample with type 2 experiments. All consumers in a market must be given the consumption subsidies in order to see if the general response of everybody induces price changes. Since such experiments cost more of an agency's funds, they are less common (there is a demand curve for social experiments, too). The only one ever done in the United States is the housing allowance supply experience, which is making

FIGURE 12.1 Market Response Experiments

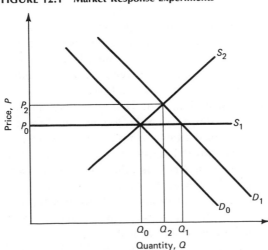

housing allowance or rent supplement payments throughout the low-income housing markets of Green Bay, Wisconsin, and South Bend, Indiana.[5] Another problem, then, is that even with the enormous budget costs, the number of site responses observed is very limited. If Green Bay and South Bend are not typical, a lot of HUD's money has been wasted.

3. *Production function experiments.* These experiments are not with responses to price and income incentives, as in type 1, but with various ways of providing government services. The main examples until now have been the Head Start and Follow Through experiments of HHS—the aim is simply to find better educational programs and ways of teaching. Obviously, these experiments have to be done classroom by classroom rather than household by household. In addition, it is much more difficult to assure that the instructional program is kept intact and operating as it should be than when households' relative prices are changed—in terms of Chapter 9, the implementation problem is much more serious for these types of experiments.[6] But in terms of the analysis itself, students can be treated as individual observations, either in a group (classroom) of experimental subjects or a group of control subjects.

4. *Production incentive experiments.* These experiments are in many ways similar to the production function experiments of type 3, except that the policy question is not a method of teaching or training but a new type of incentive. Both examples of such experiments, the school voucher plan of HHS and the EPC experiments of OEO, have tried to introduce market-type incentives into public school education. The educational voucher experiment, tried in Alum Rock, California, allowed parents to select from among a set of public schools, with payments going to the parents and then to the schools selected by the parents. The idea was to improve performance by forcing schools to compete for students.[7] The EPC experiment, discussed in more detail below, tried to introduce incentive by hiring private companies to do the teaching, and paying them more the more the students learned.[8]

DIFFERENT TYPES OF EXPERIMENTAL DESIGNS

In all of these types of experiments except type 2, when the subject is a whole market and not the individual, the unit of analysis is an individual subject. However the statistical analysis is to be done, there will be some groups of experimental or treatment subjects and some groups of control subjects. In the usual experiment there will be pre- and postexperiment measurements taken for each group, and the results compared. There are times, however, when it may not be feasible, or may just be very costly, to make all of these comparisons, and other times when it may be desirable to have even more detailed measurements. To analyze the variety of possibilities that exist, it is helpful to have a classification scheme, an example of which is given by Donald Campbell and Julian Stanley.[9] Campbell and Stanley actually give almost 20 experimental designs, of which only an illustrative few are given here. In the notation scheme, an O refers to a measurement point, X to a treatment point, and R: to subjects randomly allocated to the experimental and treatment group.

Just to see the virtues of experimentation, Campbell and Stanley begin with two low-cost nonexperimental designs:

$$\text{Design 2: } O_1 \text{ X } O_2$$

$$\text{Design 3: } \text{X } O_1$$
$$O_2$$

Their design 2, called a one-group pretest–posttest design, involves having no control group at all and just measuring a group before and after treatment. The problem with this design is that there is no way to control for history—if we measured the average height in a fourth-grade class in September and June, we could conclude that fourth grade raised the students' height. We need better information on what would have happened without the treatment. Design 3, again a low-cost nonexperimental design, is called the static group comparison design. Here two groups are chosen, the experimental group in the top line and the control group in the bottom line. One group is subjected to the treatment and one group not, but both are measured afterward. The problem with this design is that there is no controlling for the group: if we measured our fourth graders in June and compared them with fifth graders measured at the same time, we would conclude that fourth grade lowered students' height.

Both of these nonexperimental designs have serious and obvious flaws, which is why we are interested in experiments in the first place. We can then move on to two types of pure experimental designs:

$$\text{Design 4: } \text{R: } O_1 \text{ X } O_2$$
$$\text{R: } O_3 \quad O_4$$

$$\text{Design 6: } \text{R: } \quad \text{X } O_1$$
$$\text{R: } \quad \quad O_2$$

Their design 4 is the classic experimental design, with randomly selected groups and pre- and posttest measures on each. Since the groups are randomly selected, they can be assumed to be alike. In terms of our regression model of Chapter 9, there is no correlation between either the residual, u, or the control variable, Z, and the treatment variable, X. There will, of course, still be problems in knowing whether the treatment was implemented properly and the results measured realistically, but in terms of the design, this is usually the best there is.

Why, then, do we go any farther? Again in Chapter 9 we looked at ways to balance the benefits and costs of additional sampling observation. The idea there was that although for evaluation purposes it would be best to have an infinitely large sample, the agency often cannot afford that and must allocate a limited budget to the evaluation study. Often, the agency cannot afford to spend what is required to implement the classic experiment, and it must find shortcuts. One such shortcut is simply to drop the pretest from the classic design 4, and follow what is called the posttest-only control group design. Again subjects would be randomly allocated to treatment and control group, but now the evaluator is relying more on the randomization. To use our regression model in Chapter 9, with design 4 there would be measurements of all Z variables before the experiment, together with the randomization process, just in case the groups differed in certain ways. In Design 6 there can be no preexperimental measurement of the Z variables, and any differences will be attributed to the treatment. So while design 6 saves on the pretest and is less costly than 4, it is also not nearly as reliable.

There is one more design that is a close cousin of the classic experimental design 4. Design 6 differs from 4 because it drops the pretest; now we differ by dropping the randomization assumption. Sometimes, as in the case of the EPC experiment discussed below, it will be difficult or impossible to select the groups randomly. They still can be made as close together as possible, however, and we could use statistical devices such as measuring their Z variables to try to hold them constant. This design, then, is called the nonequivalent control group design:

$$\text{Design 10:} \quad O_1 \ X \ O_2$$
$$O_3 \quad O_4$$

Even though this design is clearly not as good as design 4, note that it is just as clearly much better than design 2, because we would be comparing the height gain of a sample of children who had been to fourth grade with that of a sample of children who had not. The children could be made the same age, but they would not be randomly selected for the experimental and the control groups—perhaps because their parents wanted to decide whether they went to fourth grade or not.

THE NEGATIVE-INCOME-TAX EXPERIMENTS

The idea for an NIT experiment arose in the early days of the War on Poverty. At that time, conservative economists such as Milton Friedman and liberals such as Robert Lampman and James Tobin were both supporting the NIT as a new concept in income redistribution.[10] They advocated that the existing welfare system—which featured very high effective tax rates on the earnings of many low-income workers, very low levels of support for other low-income families where the male adult was present, and radically different levels of support across different states—be scrapped, in-kind support programs such as food stamps and rent supplements also be scrapped, and a uniform and systematic NIT plan be substituted. Families earning little or nothing would receive a basic guaranteed level of support, with the support gradually phased out, or taxed away, as income rose. Essentially, this sort of proposal was embodied in the Family Assistance Plan first submitted to Congress by President Nixon in 1969, and later modified and revised by both President Ford and President Carter. Although no NIT proposal has ever passed Congress, the institution of an NIT-like supplemental security income program for the elderly, the rapid growth in the food stamp program, and the ease with which it now can be cashed out (see Chapter 10) has made the present welfare system evolve in the direction of an NIT plan over time.[11]

There have been several reservations about the NIT, but even in the early days the big question was its impact on work. For poor families, an NIT would raise incomes—hence perhaps inducing greater consumption of leisure time, or reduced work, by the income effect—and for certain poor families it would also raise the tax rates on wages—hence again lowering the price of leisure time and reducing work effort. Both changes would raise the budget costs of the plan, and just plain be politically unpopular, as taxpayers would be working to pay for the idleness of transfer recipients.[12] Supporters of NIT argued that any work reductions would be small, opponents argued that they would be large, and both sides could marshall evidence from cross-sectional empirical examinations of labor supply to support their case.[13]

Very early in the debate, economists such as Heather Ross and Guy and Alice Orcutt suggested that the matter could be resolved by a controlled social experiment in income maintenance, and by 1968 OEO had decided to go along. They established the first income-maintenance experiment in five sites in New Jersey and Pennsylvania. The first payments to families were made in 1969.

The New Jersey experiment had a relatively small sample in a relatively homogeneous part of the country and was not viewed as totally reliable, so there were later attempts to supplement this experiment with others. OEO initiated another income-maintenance experiment for rural areas in North Carolina and Iowa, and HHS later started yet others in Gary, Indiana, and in Seattle and Denver. Results from the latter, by far the largest experiment and one that is still going on, will be given below.

Diagrammatically, the impact of an NIT can be shown as in Figure 12.2, which essentially reproduces Figure 7.3. On the vertical axis is the family's disposable income, Y, and on the horizontal axis its consumption of leisure time,

FIGURE 12.2 Work Reduction and the Negative Income Tax

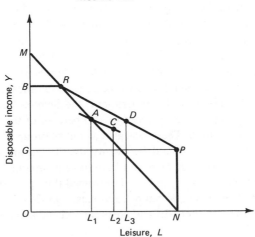

L. The initial (pre-NIT) budget line facing the family is given by *MN*, and the family locates at point *A*. Since the slope of *MN* (*OM* over *ON*) shows the rate at which hours of leisure given up are translated into disposable income, it can be viewed as the pre-NIT average wage rate, *W*, for the family worker.

The negative-income-tax plan is characterized by two magnitudes: the guarantee level, *G*, and the tax rate, *t*. It changes the budget line confronting the family to *MRPN*. If the family would have earned zero disposable income without the plan, with the plan it now gets a disposable income of the guarantee level, *G*. But as its potential earners work more and its income without the plan rises (moving left on the diagram), the difference between the new and old disposable income narrows and finally is eliminated altogether at the break-even level *B*. For the segment *RP*, the rate at which hours can be traded into disposal income is now given by $W(1 - t)$, the average after-NIT wage of the family's worker.

The response of the family to the NIT plan can be decomposed into two components, a substitution effect and an income effect. The substitution effect can be found by drawing a line parallel to *PR* through the initial point *A*, and measuring the impact just of the change in the after-tax wage [from *W* to $W(1 - t)$]. This substitution effect raises consumption of leisure time from L_1 to L_2. Then the income effect is measured by the change in leisure consumed at the new wage rate, $L_2 L_3$ in the diagram. The total change in leisure consumed, $L_1 L_3$, which is the same as the total reduction of hours worked, is the sum of the two effects. This distance $L_1 L_3$ is the key unknown in the experiment: if it is large, the reservations of NIT opponents were well founded; if it is small, they were not. not.

It is obvious from Figure 12.2 that the size of the reduction in work will depend on both the guarantee level and the tax rate. For a given tax rate and type of family, a larger guarantee will raise the distance *PN* and in turn raise the income effect $L_2 L_3$. For a given guarantee level and type of family, a higher tax rate will lower *B*, make the net wage line flatter, and raise the substitution effect $L_1 L_2$. These effects have focused on a particular family. But it is also true that changes in both the guarantee level and the tax rate, in changing *B*, change the composition of NIT recipients. Holding tax rates constant, rises in the guarantee level raise *B* and include more families in the NIT plan; holding guarantee levels constant, rises in tax rates lower *B* and include fewer families in the NIT plan.

In terms of the design of the experiment, the Seattle–Denver project had guarantee levels ranging from 50 percent to 100 percent of the poverty line and tax rates varying from .5 to .8. There was also a control group. It might seem that the total sample of families should be evenly distributed among the different plans, but that flies in the face of sound benefit-cost principles. Recall that in Chapter 9 we presented an analysis that determined the optimal-size sample for an evaluation: here that technique can be, and was, applied even more precisely. In Figure 12.3 we show the benefits and costs for a cheap and an expensive plan.

FIGURE 12.3 Benefits and Costs for a Cheap and an Expensive Plan

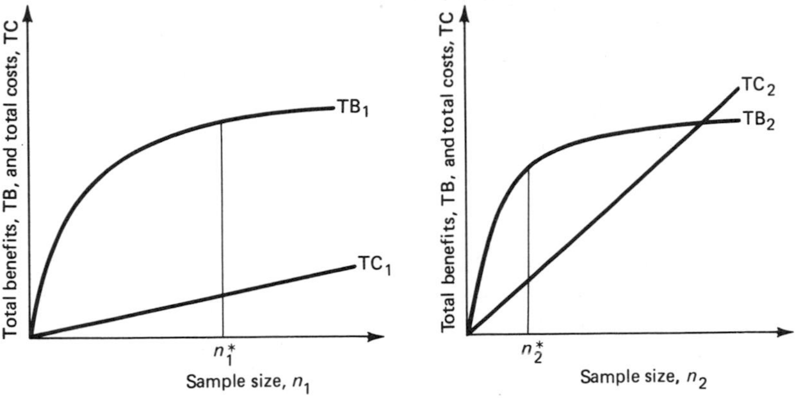

(a) Cheap plan

(b) Expensive plan

In each case the benefits function is the same: as observations are added to each plan, they improve statistical precision but at declining marginal rates. But the marginal costs are not the same. Some plans are very cheap: low-guarantee, high-tax-rate plans; plans with relatively high income poor people; and indeed the control group is the cheapest plan of all. Others, with high guarantee levels and low tax rates, are very expensive. Hence it costs the funding agency more to get a unit of information in the expensive than in the cheap plan, and following our procedures of Chapter 9, it would be optimal to have a larger population of subjects in the cheap than in the expensive plans (note that n_1^* exceeds n_2^*).

The actual procedures used for allocating the sample in the NIT experiments differed from this simple model in a number of ways. For one thing, neither OEO nor HHS allowed the analysts to determine the overall sample size and cost level, only the allocation. Converting Figure 12.4 to marginal costs and benefits, then, the allocation model was as shown there. The MB function is assumed the same in both plans for the sake of simplicity, but the marginal costs and optimal sample sizes differ, as shown in Figure 12.3. But n_1^* and n_2^* are the unconstrained optima: if operating under a total cost constraint, the sample sizes will be n_2 and n_1 (equating MB–MC for each plan). For a second, the results of this allocation process will admit very few extremely poor people into the experiment, particularly in the most generous plans. For political reasons, the allocation of subjects into plans was constrained to admit a minimum number of people of all income levels (among the low-income population) into all plans.[14]

The statistical analysis of the Seattle–Denver results involved fitting regression equations of the form[15]

(1)
$$H = f(H_{-1}, Z, \Delta W, \Delta Y)$$

FIGURE 12.4 **Marginal Benefits and Costs for a Cheap and an Expensive Plan**

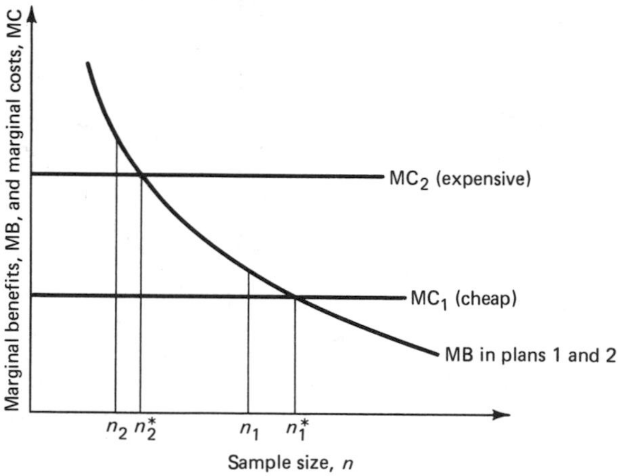

where H is the family's hours of work, H_{-1} their hours of work before the experiment, Z a set of control variables (race, sex, number of workers, etc.), and ΔW and ΔY computations of the impact of the experiment on the family's net wage and disposable income, respectively. For the control families both ΔW and ΔY were zero. For the experimental families they were computed in the way shown in Figure 12.2, with ΔY measuring just the parallel shift in the budget line at point A and ΔW the impact of tax rates on net wages. In contrast to the model we used in Chapter 9, then, the analysts have not just included one variable to say whether families were in the treatment or control group—rather, they have converted the different guarantee levels and tax rates of the plan into wage and income changes in the way that should be done using normal assumptions about what determines labor supply.

There were actually 11 different guarantee/tax rate combinations in the Seattle–Denver experiment, but sample results are given for only six of them. These six are shown in Table 12.1. The guarantee levels are 50, 75, and 100 percent of the poverty level for all families in the group, respectively, and the tax rates are .5 and .7, respectively.[16] These guarantee and tax rates are representative of those most discussed for suggested national plans. For each plan the table shows the change in annual hours, the percentage change in hours, the number of families included in the plan, and program costs before and after the labor supply response, in billions of 1975 dollars.

To see how to read Table 12.1, let us pick the second panel, an NIT with a guarantee level of 75 percent of the poverty line for the family and a tax rate of .5. The top rows in this panel indicate that husband–wife family husbands reduce work effort by 106 hours per year, a reduction of 5.9 percent (apparently husbands in this cell would have worked 1800 hours a year in the absence of the

TABLE 12.1 Labor Supply Response and Program Costs for Six NIT Plans, Seattle–Denver Income Maintenance Experiment Results (costs in billions of 1975 dollars)

PLAN	CHANGES IN ANNUAL HOURS	PERCENTAGE CHANGE	NUMBER OF FAMILIES (MILLIONS)	COSTS, NO LABOR RESPONSE	CHANGES IN COST DUE TO LABOR RESPONSE	COSTS, WITH LABOR RESPONSE
G = 50%, t = .5						
Husbands	−104	−7.0				
Wives	−92	−23.3				
Total H-W	−196	−10.3	2.4	−.1	.3	.2
Total female heads	0	0	2.3	−2.9	−.1	−3.0
G = 75%, t = .5						
Husbands	−106	−5.9				
Wives	−110	−22.8				
Total H-W	−216	−9.5	7.6	5.4	2.2	7.6
Total female heads	−47	−6.7	3.0	.2	.2	.4
G = 100%, t = .5						
Husbands	−119	−6.2				
Wives	−130	−22.7				
Total H-W	−249	−10.0	15.7	19.0	6.5	25.5
Total female heads	−99	−12.0	3.6	4.0	.5	4.5
G = 50%, t = .7						
Husbands	−136	−10.8				
Wives	−111	−29.9				
Total H-W	−247	−15.1	1.3	−.8	.2	−.6
Total female heads	−10	−2.7	2.0	−3.3	0	−3.3
G = 75%, t = .7						
Husbands	−157	−11.2				
Wives	−126	−32.5				
Total H-W	−283	−15.8	2.8	1.6	1.1	2.7
Total female heads	−47	−9.3	2.5	−.6	.1	−.5
G = 100%, t = .7						
Husbands	−164	−10.1				
Wives	−144	−32.0				
Total H-W	−308	−20.6	5.8	6.5	3.1	9.6
Total female heads	−95	−14.9	3.0	2.6	.4	3.0

plan), and wives reduce their work effort by 110 hours. Since wives generally work fewer hours for pay than husbands, this implies a reduction of 22.8 percent. For husband–wife families, then, the total work reduction is 216 hours, or 9.5 percent. Female heads reduce annual work hours by 47, a 6.7 percent reduction. Next, we see from census tabulations that 7.6 million husband–wife families and 3.0 million female-headed families will be included in this plan were it extended throughout the country. Then, had there been no work reduction, this program would have raised total transfer costs by $5.6 billion, with $5.4 going to husband–wife families and only $0.2 billion going to female-headed families. The latter number is small because present public assistance programs are already approximately this generous for female-headed families in most states. But as mentioned above, the labor supply reduction moves families rightward in Figure 12.2 and raises the distance between the pre- and post-NIT budget line, or raises government transfer costs. These amounts are $2.2 and $.2, respectively, leading to a total budget cost of $7.6 for husband–wife families and $.4 for female-headed families—$8 billion in all. Taking into account state and local contributions for public assistance, this would represent about a 30 percent increase in the amount spent on public assistance and food stamps.

Reading the table in this way, we can see that for any tax rate, a rising guarantee level always raises the average work-hour reduction for husbands, wives, and female heads, exactly as Figure 12.2 would have predicted (-104, -106, -119, etc.). Similarly, for any guarantee level, a higher tax rate also raises the average work-hour reduction (the only exception is for female heads in the 100 percent guarantee level plan, where the higher tax rate leads to a slight reduction in the decline in work hours). Similarly, for any tax rate, rising guarantee levels bring more families into the plan, raise preresponse budget costs, and raise labor-supply-change response costs even more. And, for any guarantee level, higher tax rates reduce recipients and budget costs. In fact, both of the 50 percent guarantee level plans actually cost less than the present system, while the 100 percent guarantee level, $t = .5$, plan raises costs by $30 billion.

Broadly, the labor supply results of this and other experiments should perhaps not be terribly disappointing to NIT adherents. The husband's labor supply is never reduced more than 11 percent in any of the plans, and while the wife's often is, that is most significant in the $t = .7$ plan, where it might be expected that wives would not spend so much time in market activity. Presumably, there is a relatively high private and social value placed on this "leisure" time—most commonly the wife will be investing more time in child care. Additions to budget costs through the labor supply reduction are also very modest, only rising above $3.5 billion for the very generous (and politically unrealistic) 100 percent guarantee, $t = .5$, plan.

Although these reductions in labor supply, at least for husbands, are relatively modest, there are three reasons why they may be understated by the NIT experiment. One is the temporary nature of the experiment. It might be expected that there would be a higher incidence of work dropouts if a plan was known to be permanent than in a temporary experiment such as the New Jersey or Seattle–Denver experiments. For this reason, in the Seattle–Denver project the experimental group was segmented, with some subjects to get payments for 3 and some for 5 years. To this point results that compare responses among these groups have not been presented. A second reason is that there may be community effects: one randomly sampled person in an experiment may not drop out of the labor force, but if everybody on the block is getting payments, the social stigma from reducing work may be lessened and all may. A third reason is the well-known Hawthorne effect—people change their behavior if they know they are being studied. At this point there is little way of evaluating these effects—experiments should give much more reliable results than those that can be obtained by analyzing nonexperimental data, but statistical results can never be perfect in any social science research.

Finally, in any project as large and complicated as an NIT experiment, certain unexpected findings will surface. In the New Jersey experiment the main one was the great volatility of income for poor families over time and the difficulties this raised in deciding how to make payments—should support payments be based on averages over a period of time or on month-to-month changes? In Seattle–Denver the unexpected change was even more unexpected: it turns out that experimental families were more inclined to break up than control families.[17] Until these results were reported, it was assumed that the NIT, making payments to families regardless of whether or not the male adult was present (unlike the current public assistance program in many states), would reduce marital dissolution. Hence the Seattle–Denver results going the opposite direction were, to say the least, quite disconcerting to the NIT advocates.

This matter has still not been satisfactorily answered by researchers, but there are at least two puzzling aspects. On a technical level, separation rates were higher in the less-generous plans, and in some cases even when only job training was offered. More fundamentally, even if separations really did increase, it is not clear what to make of the findings: should marriages, or living arrangements, that are so fragile as to be dissolved by a relatively slight infusion of spending power be preserved? Perhaps both partners are better off apart and lived together only to cut down on costs. In such cases, separating may be one of the best uses of the additional income gain. Social scientists will be working on this question for a while yet.

Of course, the ultimate goal of a social experiment is to provide information for policy decisions, and in that sense the final results of 10 years of NIT experimentation might seem disappointing to NIT adherents. Political winds can change quickly, but it does appear to most observers that passage of a full-blown NIT plan is as unlikely politically now as it ever was, even though the present welfare system has evolved in the direction of an NIT over time. The experimental results, which could very easily be interpreted favorably for an NIT, are now being used more as evidence against the plan—both that there is any reduction in work effort at all and the surprising finding on marital dissolution. But surely policy researchers and evaluators should not have expected anything more— whatever the results of an evaluation or experiment, these results will be interpreted in any way that observers choose. What is perhaps a more significant fact is that the results of the NIT experiments, whatever their interpretation, have been regularly discussed in the debate about welfare reform.

EDUCATIONAL PERFORMANCE CONTRACTING

The NIT experiment was a type 1 experiment; now we examine a type 4 experiment. This one is the experience in educational performance contracting (EPC) conducted by OEO from 1970 to 1972.[18]

This experiment took place against a background of generally depressing results of tests of compensatory education programs. These programs have quite consistently failed to improve achievement-type measures of the cognitive skills of students in need of remedial education. Thus great enthusiasm greeted reports in early 1970 that a private firm operating under a ''performance contract'' had succeeded in doubling and even tripling the achievement gains of disadvantaged students in Texarkana, Arkansas. Although the Texarkana project was intended primarily as a dropout-prevention program, the contractual arrangement between the school district and the firm provided that the firm would be paid only to the extent that it improved students scores on standardized reading and math tests by a prespecified amount. If it failed to meet this standard, it was not reimbursed even for costs.

Both educators and policymakers were intrigued by this attempt to introduce principles of market accountability into public school education. EPC offered the short-run promise that the educational technology already accumulated by private firms could be used to improve the cognitive skills of disadvantaged children, and the long-run promise that it would encourage innovative firms responding to market incentives to develop educational technology. It would offer local school boards a chance to make decisions on outputs instead of inputs, to select from competing sources of supply of educational services, and to write incentive contracts that might encourage differential focus on certain disadvantaged students, in certain subject areas, and so forth. As an institution, there was much to be said for it, and there was much initial interest in the Texarkana project on the part of local school boards.

Although it would have been difficult to test the market incentive aspect of EPC in any very scientific way, it was possible to take the first step by testing the short-run hypothesis that private firms, with their already existing technology, could outperform the normal public school system in educating disadvantaged students. Since many school boards were actively considering going into performance contracting on their own at the time, OEO felt that it could perform a valuable public service to these school boards by subjecting the claims of performance contractors to scientific scrutiny before these arrangements were settled. Thus in the spring of 1970 it launched a 1-year controlled experiment in EPC.

Six firms were selected for the experiment, some large and some small, some using very new teaching methods and some quite traditional. There were 18 sites—three for each firm—six grades in each site, 100 experimental and control students in each grade, and each student was given instruction for 1 hour a day in both reading and math, with a pre- and a posttest for all students. In terms of the Campbell–Stanley classification scheme, the closest description of the experiment was the nonequivalent control group design 10. Classrooms were not randomly allocated between experimental and control groups, for the simple reason that the firms thought they could do better with the very worst students, and lobbied for this design. Perhaps OEO should have resisted the pressure, but since good pretest measurements were taken, it was possible later to do a variety of statistical tests to check for biases.

The incentive contracts followed standard models that were beginning to be used at the time. If students did not gain one grade equivalent unit in the year, the firm got no payment at all—an arrangement that the firms themselves suggested, although they were later to lose a lot of money because of it. Beyond this performance guarantee level, firms got a basic payment, plus an additional amount that was proportional to the difference between a student's actual gain and the guarantee level. There was, however, a ceiling amount placed on the overall amount firms could earn. No explicit incentive for firms to concentrate efforts on the most disadvantaged students was built into the experiment, but from the formulas one could discern a very clear incentive to concentrate on those students who seemed able to reach the guarantee level and beyond, and an incentive to forget about students who were hopeless. These were not, then, ideal contracts, either from the standpoint of the firms or the goals of compensatory education, but they did not seem to have much impact on the pattern of gains.

The overall results of the experiment are given in Table 12.2. Although in some cases the enormous sample size turned up evidence of statistically significant gain or loss differences between the experimental and control students, these differences never had any educational significance. The control students in this sample would have typically gained about the .5 or .6 grade equivalent unit per year that they did in the year of the experiment, and so did the experimental students. The educational results of the experiment were about as close to an exact tie as one might ever envision. Hence unlike the NIT experiment, the actual results of the EPC experiment were disappointing to EPC advocates—an educational "innovation" that does no better than to increase students' scores by about .6 of a grade equivalent unit, exactly the rate that occurs anyway in the normal lowly regarded public schools, certainly shows little promise of bringing underachieving students up to par.

Many subsidiary questions were investigated, and almost invariably the

TABLE 12.2 Mean Gains of Experimental and Control Students across All Sites: Grade Equivalent Units

	AVERAGE GAIN OF EXPERIMENTAL STUDENTS	AVERAGE GAIN OF CONTROL STUDENTS	DIFFERENCE
	Reading		
Grade 1	.5	.4	+.1
2	.4	.5	−.1
3	.3	.2	+.1
7	.4	.3	+.1
8	.9	1.0	−.1
9	.8	.8	—
Average	.55	.53	+.02
	Math		
Grade 1	.6	.6	—
2	.5	.5	—
3	.4	.4	—
7	.6	.6	—
8	.8	1.0	−.2
9	.8	.8	—
Average	.62	.65	−.03

results were just as uninteresting. There was no, or very slight, indication that the lower-achievement students within the sample would do any better than average. Of all the large number of grade-site-subject possibilities (18 sites times six grades times two subjects), less than one-fourth showed important gains or losses, and those cases were almost evenly split between gains and losses. There was very weak evidence that the educational firms did better in the South and in rural areas, where perhaps the public schools may have been even more behind the times, but even those differences were not major.

An interesting political drama surrounded the presentation of these lackluster results. The teachers' unions had felt threatened by the experiment all along; they expected the experiment to show large educational gains for the companies, and they were prepared with a list of arguments why the results and analysis should not be believed. The performance contracting companies, on the other hand, expected great successes and they were ready to unleash textbook salespeople by the hundreds to try to capitalize on their successes in the experiment. Both groups received the results of the experiment in stunned silence. It took a month or so before the teachers' unions revised their propaganda sheets to say that they knew EPC would not work all along, although the firms were quicker to begin criticizing OEO.

On a more serious level, one could justifiably criticize the EPC experiment on at least two grounds. First, the experiment lasted for only 1 year. The reason for this was that both OEO and the firms initially felt that this would be a long enough time to test the short-run hypothesis that firms as presently constituted could teach better. The fact that most of the six firms dropped out of the performance contracting business soon after the experiment was completed confirms this feeling, but it remains true that 1 year's time may have been too short a span for the firms to establish their superiority.[19]

A second problem concerns the testing and measurement problem. The ground rules for the EPC experiment, which proved mutually agreeable to both firms and school districts beforehand, were to do all evaluations in terms of achievement tests gains. But it could be that achievement gains are not a good way to measure the impact of educational innovation—either because students gain in noncognitive ways from new techniques such as EPC, because achievement scores may be poor measures of cognitive abilities, because EPC may stimulate desirable institutional change within the school, or because students may simply like EPC-style teaching better. It is impossible to evaluate these claims at this point, but again these types of reservations seem likely always to cloud the results of tests of educational innovations.

Like the NIT, EPC had its unexpected results. The main one was how difficult the contracting provisions were to resolve. OEO had made progress payments to the companies to finance the year's teaching. But since the students did so poorly, in most cases failing to achieve the guarantee level, when the experiment closed OEO was in the position of suing firms to get its money back. After about a year of legal hassling, settlements were reached with three of the six companies, entailing substantial concessions on OEO's part. But the other firms—one of which declared bankruptcy and went out of business—never did negotiate their contract settlements. In the spring of 1973, two years after the actual teaching was completed, negotiations ended because President Nixon put OEO out of business. But the endless and expensive legal skirmishing raised the specter of small, rural school districts being forced to negotiate complex contracts with the legal departments of large teaching firms, surely not a pleasant prospect for most taxpayers.

As an overall evaluation, while EPC did not fare well in the experiment and while the experiment was not nearly as well conceived and executed as the NIT experiments, it might have had a greater policy impact. At the time the experiment began, EPC looked to be a highly promising growth industry. Many school boards across the country were signing performance contracts on their own, and many others were thinking of it. Several factors could have deflated this boom, but the OEO experiment seems clearly to be the most prominent on the list. The educational gains of EPC seemed at best very modest, and there were lots of contractual disadvantages. Although some local districts kept on with EPC for 1 or 2 years after the experiment, most did not and one by one the private companies dropped out of the business. One hears very little about EPC any more.

THE ETHICS OF SOCIAL EXPERIMENTATION

A final problem to be dealt with for social experiments is whether they raise any ethical problems. Normally, government policies are decided upon by democratic political institutions. The process is often imperfect, to be sure, but the decision makers are elected representatives trying to do what is right (somehow interpreted) for the country. Social experiments are fundamentally different in this regard. The decision makers are usually unelected social scientists setting up policies not to do what is right for the country but just to gain information. The welfare of the subjects is secondary, it is only their behavior that is of interest. Does this raise any ethical problems?

The standard that has evolved over the course of many experiments and much discussion is one of voluntary, informed consent.[20] Subjects' welfare is indeed not central to the experiment, but they do not have to participate in it either. Every large-scale social experiment that has been done to this point has allowed the *relevant decision maker* to decide whether to participate or not. For type 1 experiments this decision maker is the individual household—the husband or wife is read a set of provisions of the experiment and either agrees to participate or does not. If agreeable, the household is then randomly assigned either to the treatment or control group. For the other types of experiments, the decision maker must be the experimental unit—a whole town in the case of the housing supply experiment, and school districts for all the educational experiments. It is true that individuals do not have the option of refusing to participate if they live in that housing market or school district, but on the other hand the elected leadership of those bodies routinely makes decisions that influence individuals as much as these types of experiments. Deciding whether or not to join the experiments is a decision no bigger or smaller than those bodies make, and are empowered to make, all the time.[21]

As far as the ethical arrangements go, then, social experiments can be viewed as contracts between the conducting agency and either individual subjects or groups of them (like school districts). Subjects sign these contracts voluntarily, after being as completely informed of their rights as is feasible, must live by its provisions, and get protected by its provisions. This, again, is nothing more or less than subjects do all the time in life. In fact, the only difference is that social experiments, unlike most other contracts, do allow subjects to withdraw without cost at any time.

In this ultimate sense, then, social experiments seem neither illegal nor immoral, but it is well for the experimenting agency to keep in mind that possible problems lurk. For individual-subject type 1 experiments, the policies being experimented with, such as national health insurance programs, may not be well understood by subjects and can have quite uncertain effects on the welfare of the subjects. In this case the experimenters should lean over backward to make sure participants understand what they are getting into, and also design experiments where subjects risk as little as possible. In the health insurance experiment, for example, HHS and the Rand Corporation (the consulting firm actually running the project) decided that when the experiment involved giving people worse health insurance plans than they had already, the people should be compensated by the maximum differential liability they could incur under the experimental plan, even if subjects did not insist on this compensation to participate. This raised the cost of the experiment but was probably worth it in easing fears that the plan might make some subjects financially worse off, even though those subjects had agreed to participate.

A second type of problem involves what economists call a distinction between welfare *ex ante* (beforehand) and *ex post* (afterward). *Ex ante* we can be reasonably sure that subjects are better off participating in the experiment because they agree to it, and except in rare cases (to be dealt with below) we should be willing to let them judge what is good for them. *Ex post*, they may not end up being better off if they are led by the experiment to do something they later regret—say, quit their job with an NIT plan or underconsume health care because now their insurance coverage is incomplete. There is not much an experiment can do about such problems—people decide their own fate all the time, often in ways that later turn out to be foolish, and the experiment is intended to learn about such decisions. But experiments can be designed that do not have much potential for decisions that later prove harmful and, even though there is no moral obligation to do so, there could be a small fund or other provision for helping out those who end up worse off in an *ex post* sense.

A final problem, perhaps the most difficult of all for experiments in general although it has not yet arisen for social experiments, is what to do when subjects for one reason or another are not in position to give voluntary, informed consent. The three standard cases are prisoners, children, and mental patients. In each case there have been small medical experiments that have taken advantage of the lack of decision-making freedom or ability of these groups, a regrettable practice.[22] But to know what to do about the problem is not so easy. One should probably not leave it up to the experimenter to decide what is good for the subjects, because there have been too many instances where past experimenters failed to worry much about subjects' welfare. Perhaps the best that can be done is to force experimenters, whether engaged in large-scale social experiments or small-scale medical experiments, to justify their projects before ethical standards review boards—essentially convincing others empowered to act as decision makers for the prisoners, children, and mental patients that such projects are in the participants' interest.

SUMMARY

This chapter has looked at the recent practice of conducting large-scale social experiments to ascertain better the impact of prospective government policies. Experiments offer many political advantages, since they are easy to close down or modify if the prospective plan does not work out well. They also have many statistical advantages, because subjects can be allocated randomly, there should be no need for any correlation between the treatment received by subjects and the attributes of subjects, programs can be designed to be exactly like the one under investigation, and so forth. The disadvantages of experiments are that they take much time and cost much money, but sometimes—as with welfare reform, health insurance, or educational improvements—the policy questions are of such enduring and important interest that even these drawbacks will not be so great as to question the wisdom of an experiment.

The chapter looked in detail at two examples of present social experiments. One was an NIT experiment, essentially inquiring about the degree to which a transfer plan without a work requirement would reduce subjects' work effort; the other was an experiment with EPC as a means to improve the educational performance of disadvantaged students. The NIT program appeared to work at least moderately well, causing only modest reductions in work effort although perhaps some family splitting—a finding that remains to be interpreted either statistically or substantively. But in later political debates about welfare reform, evidence from the experiments has as often been used against the NIT as for it. EPC, on the other hand, did not pass its experimental test with any of the flying colors expected of it; experimental students increased grade-equivalent achievement levels at just about the rate of control students. In this case the negative evidence about EPC appears to have had a strong political impact. EPC was very popular with local school districts back in 1971 when the experiment began, but has now lost that popularity, and the experiment appears to have had a lot to do with the change.

NOTES

[1]A more extensive and annotated list can be found in Rae W. Archibald and Joseph P. Newhouse, "Social Experimentation: Some Why's and How's," Rand Corporation Working Paper, Santa Monica, Calif., 1979.

[2]An excellent recent analysis of the results of an experiment, presented in a benefit-cost framework, is by Burton A. Weisbrod, "A Guide to Benefit-Cost Analysis as Seen Through a Controlled Experiment in Treating the Mentally Ill," Institute for Research on Poverty, University of Wisconsin, Madison, Wis., 1979. The Weisbrod paper came out too late to be included in the chapter, but it would have been a natural because of the way it combined an analysis of a social experiment with the principles of benefit-cost.

[3]This list and discussion follows that given by Alice M. Rivlin, "How Can Experiments Be More Useful?" *American Economic Review*, May 1974, p. 346.

[4]Several volumes have been written on the negative-income-tax experiments by this time. The first proposal for such an experiment was by Heather Ross, "A Proposal for a Demonstration of New Techniques in Income Maintenance," Mimeo, Data Center Archives, Institute for Research on Poverty, University of Wisconsin, Madison, Wis., 1966. Soon after, Guy Orcutt and Alice Orcutt outlined an experimental design, in "Incentive and Disincentive Experimentation for Income Maintenance Policy Purposes," *American Economic Review*, September 1968, p. 754. A fairly complete summary of the results of and experience with the first negative-income-tax experiment in New Jersey, including contributions by the project directors Harold W. Watts and Albert Rees, is given in Joseph A. Pechman and P. Michael Timpane, eds., *Work Incentives and Income Guarantees: The New Jersey Negative Income Tax Experiment* (Washington, D.C.: Brookings Institution, 1975). A brief summary of the Seattle–Denver experiments is by Michael C. Keeley, Philip K. Robins, Robert G. Spiegelman, and Richard W. West, "The Estimation of Labor Supply Models Using Experimental Data," *American Economic Review*, December 1978. A good writeup of the health insurance experiment can be found in W. G. Manning, C. N. Morris, J. P. Newhouse, L. L. Orr, E. B. Keeler, A. Liebowitz, M. S. Marquis, and C. E. Phelps, "New Evidence on the Insurance Elasticity of the Demand for Medical Care: Preliminary Results from the Experimental Portion of the Health Insurance Study," forthcoming in the *Journal of Econometrics*. For the housing demand experiment, see Abt Associates, *Housing Allowance Demand Experiment*, Cambridge, Mass., 1973.

[5]See, for example, I. Lowry, ed., *Housing Assistance Supply Experiment, General Design Report*, Rand Corporation, Santa Monica, Calif., 1973.

[6]See Alice M. Rivlin and P. Michael Timpane, eds., *Planned Variation in Education: Should We Give Up or Try Harder?* (Washington, D.C.: Brookings Institution, 1975).

[7]See Daniel Weiler et al., *A Public School Voucher Demonstration: The First Year at Alum Rock*, Rand Corporation, Santa Monica, Calif., 1974.

[8]See Edward M. Gramlich and Patricia P. Koshel, *Educational Performance Contracting: An Evaluation of an Experiment* (Washington, D.C.: Brookings Institution, 1975).

[9]Donald T. Campbell and Julian Stanley, *Experimental and Quasi-experimental Designs for Research* (Skokie, Ill.: Rand McNally, 1966).

[10]Milton Friedman, *Capitalism and Freedom* (Chicago: University of Chicago Press, 1962) Chapter 7; Robert J. Lampman, *Ends and Means of Reducing Income Poverty* (Chicago: Markham Press, 1971); James Tobin, "On Improving the Economic Status of the Negro," *Daedalus*, Fall 1965.

[11]See Barry M. Blechman, Edward M. Gramlich, and Robert W. Hartman, *Setting National Priorities: The 1975 Budget* (Washington, D.C.: Brookings Institution, 1974); Chap. 7.

[12]One schooled in Kaldor–Hicks-type evaluation methodology might be mildly surprised at this, for as Chapter 7 points out, the rise in leisure time should also be counted as a national benefit. It is just that contributors do not particularly like to make this form of a transfer.

[13]A collection of studies is given in Glen G. Cain and Harold W. Watts, eds., *Income Maintenance and Labor Supply* (Chicago, Ill., Markham, 1973).

[14]This issue led to a fascinating conflict between the penny-pinching analysts and the do-gooding experimental workers. See Felicity Skidmore, "Operational Design of the Experiment," in Joseph A. Pechman and P. Michael Timpane, eds., *Work Incentives and Income Guarantees.* For an initial writeup of the pathbreaking allocation model that developed this analysis, see John Conlisk and Harold Watts, "A Model for Optimizing Experimental Designs for Estimating Response Surfaces," in American Statistical Association, *Proceedings of the Social Statistics Section,* 1969, reprinted in Dennis J. Aigner and Carl N. Morris, *Experimental Design in Econometrics,* a supplement to the *Journal of Econometrics,* September 1979.

[15]The analysis that follows and results of it are as given by Keeley et al., "The Estimation of Labor Supply Models."

[16]The concept of the poverty line was introduced in Chapter 7. It is the value N in eq. (4), the HHS definition of how much a family of a given size needs for a minimum living standard.

[17]See Michael T. Hannan, Nancy B. Tuma, and Lyle P. Groeneveld, *The Effects of Negative Income Tax Programs on Marital Stability: A Summary and Discussion of Results from the Seattle–Denver Income Maintenance Experiments,* SRI International, Menlo Park, Calif., October 1978; and John H. Bishop, "Jobs, Cash Transfers, and Marital Instability: A Review and Synthesis of the Evidence," *Journal of Human Resources,* Summer 1980.

[18]Most of this summary is based on more detailed information given in Gramlich and Koshel, *Educational Performance Contracting.*

[19]There is evidence from some locally initiated EPC projects not part of this experiment that some firms did very slightly better in their second year. See Polly Carpenter and George R. Hall, "Case Studies in Educational Performance Contracting: Conclusions and Implications," Rand Corporation, Santa Monica, Calif., 1971.

[20]Much of this discussion is contained in Alice M. Rivlin and P. Michael Timpane, eds., *Ethical and Legal Issues of Social Experimentation* (Washington, D.C.: Brookings Institution, 1975).

[21]Sometimes this extension of the consent principle does not have the intended effect. When representatives of HUD took their housing allowance supply proposal before the Green Bay City Council, the HUD representatives carefully explained that this experiment could raise house prices in Green Bay. Instead of being horrified, the council's eager reaction was to calculate the expected rise in property tax revenues. Such is democracy.

[22]See Robert M. Veatch, "Ethical Principles in Medical Experimentation," in Rivlin and Timpane, eds., *Ethical and Legal Issues.*

13 _____

The Evaluator's
Check List

This chapter concludes the book by giving a check list of issues that must be decided before any evaluation can be completed. These issues are the basic ones that have come up at numerous points in the book, each time raising similar logical questions about entirely different substantive matters. They are given here not in order of appearance or even importance, but rather in the order they are liable to arise in an evaluation.

Throughout it all, the fundamental point to keep in mind, as was mentioned in Chapter 1, is that benefit-cost analysis is not an attempt to put everything into formulas or turn everything over to the computer. The book has tried to be quite consistent in stressing the notion that benefit-cost analysis is ultimately a framework for policy decision making, essentially a way to array the pros and cons of a programmatic decision together with a set of rules for weighting the importance of these pros and cons. Most often it will be the case that complicated public policy decisions can be broken into a part that is quantifiable and a part that is not. The goal of a book such as this can only be to help aspiring analysts recognize when a certain problem is amenable to analysis, to help do the analysis, and then hope that the analysis can simplify part of a complex public sector decision. Judgment and political acumen will always remain part of these decisions, and there is here no hope or expectation of eliminating these factors from consideration.

THE TYPE OF EVALUATION

Probably the first question the aspiring evaluator must deal with is the type of evaluation to be made. Is it a summative evaluation, intended to provide a go/no go verdict on a program, or a formative evaluation intended merely to improve the workings of a program? Then, can the benefits of a program, whatever they may be, easily be compared with the costs, making possible the classic type of search for positive net benefits? Or as with income-distribution programs (Chapter 7), endangered species (Chapter 8), and national defense programs (that we have not looked at here), are the benefits of a program simply too difficult to quantify, forcing the evaluator to do a cost-effectiveness comparison of the costs of different ways of meeting the objectives?

THE PERSPECTIVE

A next issue that should be dealt with is that of the perspective of the evaluation. From whose perspective are we assessing this program? Is it an efficiency-type program, in which case we use the Kaldor–Hicks assumption, where all benefits and costs of all groups are just added up? Or is it partly a distribution program, in which event we place an added weight on the gains or losses of those with low incomes or those living in low-income areas? It is also important to keep the jurisdictional question clearly in mind: is the program to be evaluated from the perspective of the national government or a local jurisdiction? Are the gains and losses of people outside the jurisdiction to be included in the evaluation; and as in the Tellico Dam evaluation of Chapter 8, do we add in benefits due to job gains even if we know that these added jobs simply remove workers from other jurisdictions?

THE POLICIES ASSUMED

A third issue is what we assume about other governmental policies. Do we assume that we are doing an evaluation of this small efficiency program, and we will take as given national policies regarding growth, income distribution, unemployment, discrimination, or whatever? Or do we assume that society has not achieved these other important policy goals, and if our program helps even in a small way, that should be included in the benefits of the program? Hence we might want to use the Golden Rule interest rate n as the discount factor, on the grounds that a society investing at the optimal rate would make this public investment, even though a Society that is undersaving would not, or we might want to credit the program for improving the welfare of low-income people by placing a higher social welfare weight on the net benefits of these low-income groups. Or we might want to credit the program for reducing unemployment by placing a below-market cost on any employment gain for otherwise-unemployed workers. In each of these cases it becomes in general very difficult to know how to proceed—just evaluate the program from a narrow efficiency perspective or try to crank in these vague and difficult-to-quantify factors. Perhaps the only sensible advice is for the evaluator to point out these effects whenever they are present, to do sensitivity tests evaluating the program from both the narrow and the broad perspective, and to present the results with a careful explanation of what is involved in making either choice.

HOW DO WE MEASURE BENEFITS AND COSTS ?

Perhaps the most difficult operational question is that of measurement. Just how are we to measure all these benefits and costs?

Usually, measurement of costs is the most straightforward. In expenditure evaluations the costs will be mainly budget costs, and there ought to be solid program estimates, or forecasts, of these. For regulatory evaluations, matters are more complicated, but usually the firms will submit physical cost of compliance estimates. Without these benchmarks, it is hard even to get started on the evaluation. Then, certain adjustments in costs must be made, along the lines pointed out in Chapter 5. If a resource is being supplied monopolistically or is subject to an excise tax not related to any underlying social costs, the budget cost may overstate the true resource cost. The same may be said for resources that are now underemployed or underutilized. If there is some external cost such as an environmental cost that taxpayers are not explicitly "paying for," as in the Tellico Dam, the budget costs could understate the true resource costs. But apart from these types of cases, evaluators should probably stick pretty close to market valuations of resources used, and then budget costs will be a reasonably good proxy for true resource costs.

It is much harder to deal with program benefits because they are so much more diverse. In a wide range of cases the benefits involve consumer surplus gains of one sort or another—the project makes certain goods and services available more cheaply to consumers or saves on resources needed to satisfy consumer demands. In these cases the benefits are simply the consumer surplus gains, requiring an estimate of the relevant demand curve (Chapter 5). In human investment projects, the benefits reflect the fact that citizens are more productive, more valuable in the market, and their income rises. Here human resources have been created, and these define the benefits of the program rather than the saving of resources that supply consumer goods. The measurement technique then becomes the sort of human capital regressions we looked at in Chapter 9. In still other cases the benefits are much more difficult to quantify—the fact that the workplace becomes less noisy, that students have more cultural opportunities as a result of attending college, or that lives are saved. In these cases it may still be possible to use rigorous evaluation techniques, such as some of the quasi-market ways to estimate the value of lives saved, time saved, or pollution costs dealt with in Chapter 5. But if not, the evaluators may just have to content themselves with providing lower bound net benefit figures—assuming the value of these other benefits to be zero in the hopes that a favorable decision can still be made, while recognizing that of course the nonquantifiable benefits are not zero.

TO WHAT EXTENT SHOULD MARKETS BE RELIED ON TO VALUE BENEFITS AND COSTS?

This is a very basic matter that arises in almost all evaluations. Economists have a fondness of and a fascination with markets, and it is perhaps not surprising that they have discovered many ingenious ways to let markets do the valuing of benefits and costs. The whole idea of using budget costs to reflect resource costs builds on the notion that market prices should normally be the expression of the impersonal market of how valuable the resource devoted to this program would have been in some alternative use. The same notion is behind the use of income gains to value human investment benefits, the attempt to value pollution or noise reductions by higher house prices, or safety improvements in wage rate changes. In each case the idea is that central planners cannot know the value of the resources gained or lost, but that producers and consumers in their actions can act it out—a very democratic notion.

At the same time the book has tried to stress that markets do not always work well and that when they do not, market valuations can give very inaccurate results. If coal miners are tied to an area and get relatively low wages, one would not want to say that miners place a negative value on their lives. If workers are unemployed at a high wage, one would not want to say that employing them entails high resource sacrifices. If a construction worker's wages do not rise at all after he completes an adult education course in Shakespeare, one would not want to value the benefits of this program at zero. If a nuclear power plant entails potential safety hazards, one would not want to ignore these costs even though they may not be reflected in electricity rates.

Hence while market valuations have their strengths, they can also be very narrow and misleading. Often they can and should be used, but they must always be *understood*. A reasonable course of action is for the evaluator to try to come up with quasi-market types of ways of valuing human lives, time, safety, or whatever, because often this exercise will lead to insights about values of benefits and costs that could not otherwise be obtained. But the evaluators must also keep firmly in mind all the assumptions they made when doing this, because that will tell whether the market, or "shadow price," values were biased on the low or the high side. This technique then gives basic estimates, and also information about how they may be wrong, and fits neatly into the bracket approach for doing evaluations. Market values should not be believed completely, but they should not be ignored either.

HOW SHOULD ADVICE BE GIVEN?

Perhaps the most basic difficulty of all involves what the report says when the evaluation is all done. In the usual case where the evaluation study has carefully worked out and valued certain benefits and costs of a program but has necessarily omitted a few because of the sheer impossibility of dealing with them, how should such findings be communicated?

There is no easy way to give general advice in a case such as this, but the most useful broad principle to keep in mind is that the evaluation should be honest but informative. It should be honest in stressing what is *not* covered in the evaluation—this factor or that factor is not valued, and decision makers may want to place a subjective weight on it before making any program decisions. There is no point in trying to cover up such gaps, because similar gaps arise all the time in almost any social science study, and they will soon enough be discovered either by the decision makers or outside consultants anyway.

At the same time, it would be a mistake for the analyst having done a careful evaluation to be too humble. The evaluation must also be very clear on what information has been developed—this program leads to net benefits of $700,000 for poor people and net costs of $800,000 for other taxpayers. Just coming up with these sorts of numbers can be enormously difficult and enormously helpful. If they are at all accurate, they focus decisions for political decision makers in a way not ordinarily done for public programs. Moreover, simply having facts like this can give the evaluator enormous leverage in most agency discussions of policies—most other participants in these agency exchanges will not have any facts at all, and the evaluator will often find that she is in the position of being an expert. The evaluation report must be honest in defining the limits of this expertise, but there is no reason why it should not be forthright in presenting the progress that has been made.

Answers
to Problems

CHAPTER 2

2.1 The information is as follows:

PRICE	Q_A	Q_B	Q_C	MARKET DEMAND, Q	ΔQ	η	CS	AFC
5	15	20	12.5	47.5			468.8	9.9
10	10	15	10	35	12.5	−.454	262.5	7.5
15	5	10	7.5	22.5	12.5	−1.086	118.8	5.3
20	0	5	5	10	12.5	−2.692	37.5	3.8

Finding the consumer surplus is tricky because the gain of each consumer must be computed individually to avoid problems that would otherwise be created by negative values of Q or P. Hence for P = 5, the consumer surplus for A is (½)(20− 5)(15), where 20 is the vertical intercept of A's demand curve and 15 is Q_A. Total CS is the sum of the CS for the three consumers, and AFC is CS divided by Q.

2.2 **a.** Using vertical summation, we get:

QUANTITY	MU_A	MU_B	MU_C	PUBLIC GOODS DEMAND, SMU	CS
5	15	20	20	55	50
10	10	15	10	35	200
15	5	10	0	15	450
20	0	5	0	5	625

Here there is one slight catch. We can find the top point on the demand curve by rewriting all individual demand curves to solve for the marginal utility and summing them (examples: $MU_A = 20 - Q$, total marginal utility $= 75 - 4Q$, so 75 is the top point). But because we constrain marginal utilities to be at least zero, the demand curve kinks between $Q = 15$ and $Q = 20$, so the CS for 20 is not the area under the triangle between (0, 75) and (20, 5) but only 450 plus the added trapezoid area between $Q = 15$ and $Q = 20$.

b. The community should buy 10 units, forcing each taxpayer to pay his marginal utility. So A would pay 10, B = 15, and C = 10 per unit to raise the necessary revenue of 35 per unit. Note that the total tax bills of A, B, and C are 100, 150, and 100, respectively. But it is still a good idea to buy the public good, because they all get consumer surpluses equal to:

$$A: \quad (\tfrac{1}{2})(20 - 10)(10) = 50$$

$$B: \quad (\tfrac{1}{2})(25 - 15)(10) = 50$$

$$C: \quad (\tfrac{1}{2})(30 - 10)(10) = 100$$

adding up to the total consumer surplus of 200 computed above.

c. Once individual C learns to falsify his preferences, the apparent community marginal utility for 5 units is 35, so this is what the community buys, charging A 15 per unit, B 20 per unit, and giving C a free ride. The true consumer surpluses are now equal to

$$A: \quad (\tfrac{1}{2})(20 - 15)(5) = 12.5$$

$$B: \quad (\tfrac{1}{2})(25 - 20)(5) = 12.5$$

$$C: \quad (\tfrac{1}{2})(30 + 20)(5) = 125$$

Note that C has raised his consumer surplus by stealing from A and B. But in the process even though prices or tastes have not changed, C's misstatement of preferences has moved the community to a suboptimal point, costing it a consumer surplus of 50. This amount is the dead weight-loss triangle formed by the difference between the true marginal utility at $Q = 5(55)$ and at $Q = 10(35)$, times the quantity difference, or

$$DWL = (½)(55 - 35)(10 - 5) = 50$$

2.3   This problem is solved by reasoning that there is only one equilibrium quantity in the market that makes both demanders and suppliers happy. Hence the equilibrium condition is that

$$Demand \ Q = supply \ Q$$

$$60 - P = .5P$$

$$P = 40$$

$$Q = 20$$

The tax can be found by inverting the supply curve to yield $P = 2Q$. At any Q, the P value gives the marginal return to a supplier. This return is the same whether there is or is not a tax: if a tax with rate .5 is imposed, before-tax P must be $4Q$ to yield an after-tax P actually received by suppliers of $2Q$. So the new supply curve is $P = 4Q$, or $Q = .25P$ and the new equilibrium is

$$60 - P = .25P$$

$$P = 48$$

$$Q = 12$$

The total revenue changing hands in the market is $PQ = 576$, of which the government gets $(.5)(576) = 288$. The loss of consumer surplus is the trapezoid (½) $(48 - 40)(12 + 20) = 128$, and the loss of producer surplus is $(½)(40 - 24)(12 + 20) = 256$, where $24 = (.5)(48)$, or the net price received by producers. The deadweight-loss triangle can be computed directly as ½ $(48 - 24)(20 - 12) = 96$, or indirectly as the total loss of producer and consumer surplus $(128 + 256 = 384)$, less government tax revenue $(384 - 288 = 96)$.

2.4   The equilibria, computed as in the answer to Problem 2.3, are:

	P	Q	MSC AT EQUILIBRIUM Q (= 3Q)
Market equilibrium	40	20	60
Best social equilibrium	45	15	45
With tax equilibrium	48	12	36

In the market equilibrium, the deadweight loss from overproduction is $(\frac{1}{2})(60 - 40)(20 - 15) = 50$. In the tax equilibrium, the deadweight loss from underproduction is $(½)(48 - 36)(15 - 12) = 18$. Here, as it turns out, the tax actually yields an equilibrium closer to the optimum than the no-tax equilibrium, but the best of all worlds would be for a tax rate of one-third, reflecting the true proportion of external costs in total costs (and making the before-tax supply curve $P = 3Q$).

2.5   The income schedule before and after the various redistribution schemes looks as follows (see following table, page 251):

PERSON	INITIAL INCOME	INITIAL DEVIATION FROM MEAN SQUARED	TRANSFER GAIN	TAX LOSS	INCOME AFTER TAX AND TRANSFER	RESULTING DEVIATION SQUARED	WAGE RATE GAIN	INCOME AFTER TRAINING AND TAX PLAN	RESULTING DEVIATION SQUARED
A	2	16	1.5		3.5	6.25	.8	2.8	10.24
B	6			.2	5.8	.04	.4	6.6	.36
C	4	4	.5		4.5	2.25		4.0	4.00
D	10	16		1.0	9.0	9.00		9.0	9.00
E	6			.2	5.8	.04		5.8	.04
F	4	4	.5		4.5	2.25	.8	5.6	.16
G	3	9	1.0		4.0	4.00	.4	3.4	6.76
H	8	4		.6	7.4	1.96		7.4	1.96
I	5	1			5.0	1.00		5.0	1.00
J	12	36		1.4	10.6	21.16		10.6	21.16
Sum	60	90			60.1	47.95		60.2	54.68
Mean, $\bar{Y}$	6				6			6.0	
Variance, V		9				4.80			5.47

Here we see that neither scheme changes the mean level of income, but both schemes redistribute income and lower the variance of income. The transfer and tax scheme is slightly more efficient at doing that, per dollar of tax cost, because it helps all low-income workers, not just the ones that make very low wages. But if hours worked were made a negative function of tax rates or transfer gains, it would also lower the mean (the leaky bucket), whereas if the productivity of training programs were raised, the mean income level would also increase. In these cases the training program would appear to be a better way to redistribute income.

2.6 **a.** This can be found by equating the demand and supply curves:

Demand: $P = 75 - 2Q$
Supply: $P = 25 + .5Q$
Equilibrium Q: $75 - 2Q = 25 + .5Q$, $Q = 20$
$$P = 35$$

b. Now we just equate the new curves:

Demand: $P = 75 - 2Q$
Supply: $P = .5Q$
Equilibrium: $75 - 2Q = .5Q$, $Q = 30$
$$P = 15$$

c. Old consumer surplus: $(\frac{1}{2})(75 - 35)(20) = 400$
New consumer surplus: $(\frac{1}{2})(75 - 15)(30) = 900$
Gain in consumer surplus: $900 - 400 = 500$

This also equals the area of the trapezoid given by $(\frac{1}{2})(35 - 15)(20 + 30) = 500$. Draw the diagram to see why.

d. Producers shift to the lower supply curve with no loss in surplus. Hence we find the change in producer surplus by assuming that we move along the old curve to a higher Q.

Old producer surplus: $(\frac{1}{2})(35 - 25)(20) = 100$
New producer surplus: $(\frac{1}{2})(40 - 25)(30) = 225$
Gain in producer surplus: $225 - 100 = 125$

This also equals the area of the trapezoid given by $(\frac{1}{2})(40 - 35)(20 + 30) = 125$.

e. The budget cost of the subsidy is 30 units times 25 per unit, or 750. The gain to consumers is 500 and to producers is 125, so the net cost, or deadweight loss, of the subsidy, is 125. This also equals the triangle between Q of 20 and 30, or $(\frac{1}{2})(30 - 20)(25) = 125$.

CHAPTER 4

4.1 The information is as follows:

PROJECT	B	C	NET BENEFITS	B/C	OPTIMAL BUDGET	BUDGET = 40	BUDGET = 80	C,D,E,F ALTERNATIVES
A	40	20	20	2.00	×	×	×	×
B	30	10	20	3.00	×	×	×	×
C	30	20	10	1.50	×		×	×
D	10	20	−10	.50				
E	15	10	5	1.50	×	×	×	
F	15	20	−5	.75			×	
Total budget					60	40	80	50
Net benefits					55	45	50	50

The rule that maximizes net benefits for the package always works; maximizing the benefit-cost ratio does not always work.

4.2 **a.** If benefits were estimated at 18, the Corps would not build the dam and the nation would be out the net benefits of 10. In principle, an evaluation study that pinned net benefits down at any positive number would be worth 10.

b. Similar reasoning shows that if benefits are felt to be 22, the Corps will build the dam anyway and the benefits of an evaluation study will be zero.

c. In the mixed case, the Corps has a .5 probability of building the dam, so the benefits of an evaluation that guarantees that they will build it are the net benefits of building (10) times the probability of not building without the knowledge (.5). The value of the evaluation is 5. In Chapter 9 we see how the benefits of an evaluation can be computed from the probability distribution of net benefits and the value of eliminating uncertainty in this manner.

CHAPTER 5

5.1 The expression for the linear demand curve is $P = 15 - Q$, or $Q = 15 - P$ (take your pick). If the price is raised from 10 to 12, Q goes from 5 to 3, and the area of the loss trapezoid is $(\frac{1}{2})(12 - 10)(5 + 3) = 8$. If the price is lowered from 5 to 3, Q goes from 10 to 12, and the area of the loss trapezoid is $(\frac{1}{2})(5 - 3)(10 + 12) = 22$. For a given ΔP, the area is larger at a lower price because Q is larger.

The arc elasticity (formula given in the text and also in Problem 2.1 is

$$\eta = \frac{\Delta Q}{Q} \div \frac{\Delta P}{P} = \frac{-5}{7.5} \div \frac{5}{7.5} = -1$$

If the price is raised from 10 to 12, ΔQ is given by the formula

$$-1 = \frac{\Delta Q}{(1/2)(5+5+\Delta Q)} \div \frac{2}{11}, \Delta Q = -\frac{5}{6}$$

The approximate (because the curve is nonlinear) area of the loss trapezoid is $(\frac{1}{2})(12 - 10)(5 + 4\frac{1}{6}) = 9\frac{1}{6}$, not much different than in the linear case. But if the price is lowered from 5 to 3, ΔQ equals

$$-1 = \frac{\Delta Q}{(1/2)(10+10+\Delta Q)} \div \frac{2}{4}, \Delta Q = 6\frac{2}{3}$$

The approximate area of the loss trapezoid is $(\frac{1}{2})(5 - 3)(10 + 16\frac{2}{3}) = 26\frac{2}{3}$, a larger difference.

5.2 **a.** The easiest way to do this is to find the vertical shift of the intercept that corresponds to an added Q of 50. Note that from the old demand curve $Q = 50$ when $P = 4.00$ (solving it backward). In that case a horizontal shift of 50 equals a vertical shift of 2, so the new demand curve is $P' = 8.00 - .04Q$. Note that when P is 6.00, as before, Q is just the 50 demanded by the government.

b. This can be found by equating the price from the old demand curve with the price from the supply curve—that is the one price that clears the market and is on both curves.

$$P = 6.00 - .04Q = .02Q$$

$$6.00 = .06Q$$

$$Q = 100$$

$$P = 2.00$$

c. Now we just do it with the new demand curve.

$$P = 8.00 - .04Q = .02Q$$

$$8.00 = .06Q$$

$$Q = 133.3$$

$$P = 2.67$$

d. $(50)(2.67) = 133.5$
e. $(\frac{1}{2})(.67)(100 + 83.3) = 61.4$
f. $(100)(.67) = 67.0$

g. $(33.3)[2.67 - (.5)(1.00 + 1.33)] = 50.0$
h. $133.5 + 61.4 - 67.0 - 50.0 = 77.9$
i. $(\frac{1}{2})(2.00 + 2.67) = 2.33$
j. $(\frac{1}{2})(1.00 + 1.33) = 1.17$
k. $33.3/50 = .67$
l. $16.7/50 = .33$
m. $SC = (50)(.33 \times 2.33 + .67 \times 1.17) = 77.6$ (differences are due to rounding)

5.3 **a.** Since this market does not clear, we do not compute the clearing wage rate but simply set $W = \$2.00$ in both demand and supply curves. For demand, $W = 2$ implies that $L_d = 90$. For supply, $W = 2$ implies that $L_s = 100$. Unemployment is $100 - 90 = 10$.
b. If the government hires 5 units of labor, the budget cost is obviously $(5)(2) = 10$ per hour. The social cost using the supply curve depends on the valuation of leisure time of the soon-to-be employed workers. Since the supply curve is a ray from the origin to the point (100, 2), any of these 100 workers might be unemployed when the wage is $2, and any might get employed if the government hires at random from the pool of workers. The only sensible technique is to use the average supply price over the interval, $1, yielding a cost of $(5)(1) = 5$ per hour. Finally, if there were no social value to idleness, or cost of working, the social cost is zero and the entire $10 is simply a transfer payment.
c. All of these conclusions are not changed in the least by unemployment insurance—that merely transfers the cost of idleness, or the surplus gains when work begins, between various groups in the population.

5.4 If $(\Delta P/P)^e = 0$, $\Delta P/P = 0$ when $U = 5$ percent. When $U = 4$ percent, $\Delta P/P = .5$ percent. When $U = 6$ percent, $\Delta P/P = -.3$ percent. If U were held at 4 percent, in the first year the inflation rate would be .5 percent. In the second year (or soon thereafter), $(\Delta P/P)^e$ would become .5 percent and the inflation rate would become 1 percent. Then 1 percent inflation becomes expected, and actual inflation rates move to 1.5 percent. So it goes, and there is no end to the process in this complete adaptation model.

Under this model of the inflation process, any unemployment rate below 5 percent cannot be sustained. If this project did make such a reduction, it would be contributing a small bit to inflation and forcing an equal-sized offset somewhere else. The social cost of labor is then *not* overstated by using budget costs—it is $10 per hour.

5.5 Nobody is sure how good the numbers are, but if you give economists some information, they can make the calculations. In the case at hand, we know that a typical worker insists on a compensation of $100 to accept a 1:1000 death probability in that year. Extrapolating to the 1:1 probability (an unbelievably heroic assumption) yields the compensation to accept a certain death as $100,000 (there would surely be a nonlinearity in this function). All of the criticisms in the text can be made of this estimate, but at least it is a lower bound.

5.6 The expected income with the project is just 100, equal to the family's actual income, so by this way of reckoning the net benefits of the project to the family are zero. But this is not a very good way to do the calculation because the utility function says that the family gains less from a positive outcome than it loses from a negative outcome. To see this, if there is a positive outcome, $Y = 144$ and $U = \sqrt{144} = 12$. If there is a negative outcome, $Y = 56$ and $U\sqrt{56} = 7.5$. The expected value of utility is 9.7, exactly the value that would be yielded by a certain income of 94. Hence the utility change for the family is $94 - 100 = -6$, and -6 is the measure of net benefits of the project.

CHAPTER 6

6.1   **a.** B is the best ($PV_B = \$111.63$) but do both ($PV_A = \$107.55$).
      b. A is the best ($PV_A = \$102.70$) but do both ($PV_B = \$101.78$).
      c. A is the best ($PV_A = \$99.13$) but do neither.
Note that as r increases, all projects look worse, but B, with more deferred gratification, gets worse faster.

6.2   **a.** If the stream starts 1 year from now, we have exactly the formula of note 1, yielding a present value of 100/r. This is $1000 when $r = .1$ and $2000 when $r = .05$.

      b. When there is inflation, if the stream is in real dollars, it must be discounted by the real discount rate of 5 percent, yielding a present value of $2000.

If the stream starts this year, we must modify note 1 slightly.

$$PV = 100 + \frac{100}{1 + r} + \frac{100}{(1 + r)^2} + \cdots$$

$$PV\left(\frac{1}{1 + r}\right) = \frac{100}{1 + r} + \frac{100}{(1 + r)^2} + \cdots$$

$$PV\left(1 - \frac{1}{1 + r}\right) = 100$$

$$PV\left(\frac{r}{1 + r}\right) = 100$$

$$PV = \left(\frac{1 + r}{r}\right) \times 100$$

When $r = .1$, PV $= 1100$ (just $100 more than before). When $r = .05$, PV $= 2100$ (again, $100 more than before). In this way you can modify this formula to take account of a variety of situations.

6.3   The internal rates of return are 13 percent for 2 years on the first investment and 10.5 percent for 4 years on the second. Which is the most desirable cannot be told from this information—essentially it depends on the interest rate in the remaining 2 years of the first investment. If this rate is high, above 10 percent or so, the first will be better because the $60 returns could be reinvested at a high rate. If low, the second will be better. The only way out is to specify a discount rate and compute the present value of each stream of returns.

6.4 **a.** It is easiest to do the calculation in real terms, in which case real benefits are $.1 million in perpetuity, the real interest rate is 5 percent, and the discounted present value of benefits is $.1/.05 = $2 million. Build the bridge. The logic is that private investment is also discounted by the same rule, and use of the same discount rate assures that only the best-paying investments are made.

b. Following the Golden Rule reasoning, we could use that interest rate. The logic is that we might expand the investment proportion until the discount rate, or marginal product of capital investment, equals n, which in the example is 2.5 percent. Using that rate, the present value of benefits comes to $4 million, clearly yielding positive net benefits. Although there is uncertainty about what discount rate to use between n and r, here it does not affect the verdict at all.

6.5 **a.** The equilibrium condition is $sy = nk$. Inserting values, we have $(.2)(\sqrt{k}) = .05k$, yielding $k = 16$ and $y = 4$. Both k and y will stay here as long as n and s are fixed. But the gross level of capital and output will grow at the rate of .05 per year, just the rate of growth of the labor force. To find the private-sector discount rate, we need to know the marginal product of capital, or dy/dk. Differentiating the production function, which you need calculus to know how to do, yields $dy/dk = 1/8 = .125$.

b. The easiest way to do the problem is to note that the optimal saving rate is just the share of capital in total output—see note 19. This is

$$\frac{rk}{y} = \frac{dy}{dk}\frac{k}{y} = \left(\frac{1}{2}\right)\left(\frac{y}{k}\right)\left(\frac{k}{y}\right) = .5$$

A less elegant, but no less effective way is to reason that in this Golden Rule equilibrium, $r = n = .05 = dy/dk$. Since $dy/dk = (\frac{1}{2})(y/k)$, the condition that $sy = nk$ becomes $sy = (\frac{1}{2})(y/k)k$, implying that $s = .5$. At this s,

$$\frac{dy}{dk} = \left(\frac{1}{2}\right)\frac{\sqrt{k}}{k} = .05$$

implying that $k = 100$ and $y = 10$.

CHAPTER 7

7.1 **a.** Taking up flood damage first, the total value of real property owned by the community is $(50)($30,000) = $1.5 million. The probability of a washout now is .01, so the expected annual losses from floods are $.015 million. The present value of these losses is $.015/.03 = \$.5$ million, which is also one of the benefits of high-income groups. On power, high-income families save $150 each, times 50 families, for a total of $7500 per year, or $.25 million in present-value terms. The net benefits for high-income families are $.75 million. Low-income families save $75 each, $11,250 in total, or $.375 million in present-value terms. The Corps adds them all up, gets total project benefits of $1.125 million, net benefits of $.125 million, and builds the dam.

b. Clearly yes and clearly no, respectively.

c. The net value of benefits to low-income people must be $1.2 - .75 = .45$ to make the project worthwhile. If the $.375 in actual benefits received gets a utility weight of 1.2, the project is worthwhile. If, however, some of the taxes were paid by low-income groups, the distributionally weighted costs would also be larger than $1.2 million and the calculation must be redone.

7.2 Under the Kaldor–Hicks standard, compensation is not paid, and the question is only whether it could be. Translated, this means that all gains are just summed, in which case project A, with net benefits of 1.6, is the best. If the tax system is used and the rates are .2 and .15, a .2 sacrifice is $(.2/.15)$ times as painful for the poor—hence the relative distributional weight is 1.33. Project A has distributionally weighted net benefits of $(1.33)(.5) + 1.1 = 1.77$, exceeding those of project B. If the rates are .6 and .2, the relative weight is $.6/.2 = 3$ and project B has distributionally weighted net benefits of $(3)(1.0) + .2 = 3.2$, exceeding those of A. Finally, if we want to find the weights (w) that make society indifferent, we simply solve the equation

$$(.5)(w) + 1.1 = (1.0)(w) + .2$$

$$w = 1.8$$

7.3 Initially, she works 1500 hours at $3 per hour and makes $4500. At this level of YD she gains $250 under the NIT, which is also her transfer payment had she not changed her hours worked. Since the tax rate is .5, her net wage is lowered by 1.5. Plugging these values into the hours equation, we get $H = 1500 + (50)(-1.5) - (.1)(250) = 1400$ as her new hours worked. Here her market earnings are $(1400)(3) = 4200$ and her transfer gain is 400, yielding a new disposable income of $4600.

7.4 **a.** Initially, the equilibrium comes at the market-clearing wage, found in the usual way by equating demand to supply:

$$W = 7 - .05L = .02L$$

$$L = 100$$

$$W = 2$$

b. Under the public employment plan, $2.50 = .02L_t$, $L_t = 125$ is total employment in the community. Of this, private employment (L_p) is found from the private demand curve at $2.50 = 7 - .05L_p$, $L_p = 90$. The public employment plan then employs 35 workers at a cost of $(35)(2.50) =$

$87.50 per hour. But total costs paid by contributors are even larger, because the higher private wage entails a surplus loss to employers equaling $(\frac{1}{2})(2.50 - 2.00)(100 + 90) = \$47.50$.

CHAPTER 8

8.1 When consumer surplus does not decay at all, the present value of net benefits is $(200/.05) - 1000 = 3000$. When the decay rate is .05, the present value is $[200/(.05 + .05)] - 1000 = 1000$. When the decay rate is .10, the present value is $[200/(.05 + .10)] - 1000 = 333$. In each case the dam is profitable, but obviously its profitability declines as the decay rate increases.

Without environmental costs the net present value of the dam is $200/(.05 + .05) - 1000 = 1000$. With them decaying at 5 percent per year, we have

$$\frac{200}{.05 + .05} - \frac{20}{.05 + .05} - 1000 = 800$$

not much change. With them stable at 20, we have

$$\frac{200}{.05 + .05} - \frac{20}{.05} - 1000 = 600$$

still not a terribly great change. When they grow by .025 per year, we have

$$\frac{200}{.05 + .05} - \frac{20}{.05 - .025} - 1000 = 200$$

But if they grow by .05 per year, the environmental cost term goes to infinity and the dam's net benefits are negative infinity.

8.2 If the maintenance cost of using the area is $5 and the commuting cost is $2, the effective price to hunters is $7 and the number of users is 93. The loss of this area rubs out their consumer surplus given by the area under the demand curve and above $7. The P intercept of the demand curve is 100, and the area of the triangle is $(\frac{1}{2})(100 - 7)(93) = \$4325$ per day. This is substantially more than the total revenue on the area of $(95)(\$5) = \$475$, showing the fallacy of using that means of calculating the loss.

CHAPTER 9

9.1 The program would not pass the Kaldor–Hicks test. Net discounted benefits of students are $10,000 and the net discounted losses of others are $12,000. Adding up yields an overall net benefits figure of −$2,000. But that may not be the right test. If we are concerned with education as a distributional program, we may want to put an extra distributional weight on the individual benefits column, in which case the program may be a success even if the losses of others exceed the gains to participants.

9.2 **a.** Incorrect and you are confident of it. The required return for the program can be found by inverting the present-value formula as $(.05 + .05)(100) = \$10$. The actual return is $14. Hence you know the marginal benefits of the program are greater than the marginal costs. Indeed, you can even be very confident of that verdict, because the standard deviation of $2 means that actual benefits of $14 are more than two standard deviations above the required return of $10. In layman's terms, this means that 95 percent of the times those data are sampled, the net benefits of the program will be positive.

b. The variance of X is computed from the formula

$$S_X^2 = \sum_{i=1}^{10} \frac{(X_i - \bar{X})^2}{n-1}$$

If 5 out of 10 are in the program, $\bar{X} = .5$ and each $(X_i - \bar{X})^2 = .25$, so the variance would be .28. If 8 out of 10 are in the program, $\bar{X} = .8$ and $S_X^2 = .18$. If 10 out of 10 are in, $\bar{X} = 1.0$ and $S_X^2 = 0$. Assuming that variations in S_Y^2 as a result of these changes in S_X^2 are small,

$$\phi_X = a_1^2 \frac{S_X^2}{S_Y^2} = .10 \quad \text{when } S_X^2 = .28$$
$$.064 \quad \text{when } S_X^2 = .18$$
$$.0 \quad \text{when } S_X^2 = 0$$

We have, in other words, not changed the marginal benefits of the program at all, but simply broadened its availability, and we find that the ϕ_X is affected. This is why you want to look at a_1.

c. Yes. If interest rates are higher, society has enough high-yielding alternative investments that this one no longer passes the benefit-cost test. In fact, if 10 percent is a good interest rate to use for poor people (some argue that they have higher rates of time preferences than others), the poor people themselves would rather have $100 to invest (earning $10 in perpetuity) than $14 which declines by 5 percent every year.

9.3 **a.** Total benefits are given by $4020N - 2N^2$ and total costs by $3,000,000 + 20N$. The optimal sample size is that where marginal benefits (the slope of the total benefits curve) equal marginal costs. The most concise way to do this is by differentiating each curve:

$$\text{MB} = \frac{d\text{TB}}{dN} = 4020 - 4N$$

$$\text{MC} = \frac{d\text{TC}}{dN} = 20$$

and then equating them and solving for N:

$$4020 - 4N = 20$$

$$N = 1000$$

If you do not know calculus, you can reason that what you are doing is maximizing TB − TC, or $4000N - 2N^2 - 3,000,000$, with respect to N. When $N = 1000$, this difference is slightly larger than for any other value of N.

We can then find the amount spent on the evaluation just by plugging $N = 1000$ into the cost equation:

$$\text{TC} = 3,000,000 + 20(1000) = 3,020,000$$

b. But you would not do the evaluation unless it were mandated. The reason is that even at the optimum sample-size point,

$$\text{TB} = (4020)(1000) - 2(1000)^2 = 2,020,000$$

a number less than the cost of the evaluation. The net benefits of doing the evaluation are negative.

9.4 **a.** Yes and yes. Elementary statistics books give the formula for the standard error of a difference as

$$\text{SE}_d = \sqrt{\frac{\text{SE}_1^2}{N_1} + \frac{\text{SE}_2^2}{N_2}}$$

where SE_d is the standard error of the difference, SE_1 and SE_2 the standard errors in the open- and closed-book tests, and N_1 and N_2 the respective sample sizes. This equation can be filled out as follows:

$$\text{SE}_d = \sqrt{\frac{9}{20} + \frac{9}{20}} = .95$$

The 10-point difference in scores easily is statistically significant.

b. The fatal defect is self-selection bias. The better students may well have chosen the closed-book exam. In the terminology of the chapter, if X

is correlated with u, the observed differences in test scores will be biased in favor of the closed-book exam. The true difference may well be much less than 10—indeed, it may even be negative if the u values are large enough (say that all the good students do 15 points better).

c. Next year he randomly picks 20 students to take the closed-book and 20 the open-book exam. He intentionally breaks self-selection bias. Now, using the formula in part **a**, the difference in scores is only one standard deviation—not enough to be significant. Then the instructor either decides that there is no way he can answer this question unless he gets a bigger class, or he gives up teaching.

CHAPTER 10

10.1 The poor community has average expenditure benefits of $1000 - (.02)(5000) = 900$ and needs a proportional tax rate of $900/5000 = .18$ to finance its public services. The rich community has benefits of $1000 - (.02)(10000) = 800$ and needs a proportional tax rate of only $800/10000 = .08$ to yield benefits along the same schedule.

The benefits and taxes are given by the following table:

FAMILY INCOME	POOR COMMUNITY			RICH COMMUNITY		
	BENEFITS	TAXES	RESIDUAL ($T-B$)	BENEFITS	TAXES	RESIDUAL
$ 6,000	$880	$1,080	$ 200	$880	$ 480	$-400
12,000	760	2,160	1,400	760	960	200
18,000	640	3,240	2,600	640	1,440	800

Notice that the rich person pays $1800 more a year for the same bundle of services in the poor community. In actual fact, the differences in taxes are probably less, but the service bundle is probably also worse in the poor community.

The answers are mostly obvious. All persons will try to go to the rich community, but only the wealthy ones will be able to afford it, spreading out incomes and fiscal residuals even more.

Since the communities are equally large, average expenditure benefits in both communities together are $850, and average income is $7500. We need an overall tax rate of $850/7500 = .1133$ on all income. In the poor community this raises $(.1133)(5000) = \$567$ of revenue, requiring a grant of $900 - 567 = \$333$. In the rich community it raises $1133 of revenue, yielding a surplus available for transfer of $1133 - 800 = \$333$. Magically, both amounts are the same and we do not have anything left for your commission.

10.2 **a.** The subsidy rate is computed to be .2. Using arc elasticities the relative price change is .2/.9 and the consumption of food increases by $(900)(^2/_9) = 200$ to 1000. (If you are rusty on computing arc elasticities, go back to Problem 5.1.) The family takes all the stamps and spends the entire grant, or bonus value, on food. Here the program is working exactly as intended.

b. The increase is $.5(600 + 750)(^2/_9) = 150$ using arc elasticities, to a level of food consumption of 750. If the program worked like a true A grant, the family would like to take a bonus value of 150 and spend it all on food. As it happens, this family would have been forced to take the entire amount of stamps or nothing in the old days, hence either not participating (if they could not bear the extra reduction in consumption), or going to the same point as the family in part **a** and actually spending more than 750 on food. Since food stamp participation rates were low for families at this income level, most probably did not participate.

c. It might seem that we should apply the price elasticity again, but in fact we should not, because this family gets no more price subsidy after spending $1000. They can get $200 free dollars on the food expenditures made already, however, and since their income elasticity of food consumption is 1, their consumption rises by $200/2500 = .08$, to 1083. This family is spending only $83/200 = .41$ of the stamps on food, exactly the proportion of free income they spend on food. Here the grant is cashed out and is not working as intended.

d. They do not like the fact that fat people can cash out the subsidy. This lowers the benefits of the program in their eyes. The obvious way to correct this feature is to increase the maximum amount of stamps families can buy so that even fat people will not cash out the program.

e. They do not like the fact that middle-sized and thin people *cannot* cash out the subsidy. This reduces the increment in utility per dollar of budget cost, in effect throwing away some of the dollars spent on the program for thin and middle-sized people. The obvious way to correct this feature is just to cash out the whole program.

f. Now at least for these families only $200 is paid in stamps, and all families can happily cash out the program. HHS won.

10.3 Your program just got folded into special revenue sharing. The localities will probably drop the manpower program, use the money to hire people they would have anyway, and either reduce taxes or raise normal expenditures. The net benefits for the poor are likely to plummet. Possible compromises are to say that local governments have to spend money on manpower training or if used for hiring, it has to be used for hiring poor people. But dropping all categorical restrictions is a good way to kill the program.

10.4 **a.** In the first year the grant reduces prices by .25 and raises spending by $(.5)(.25)(2)$, to $2.25 billion. Grant levels are $(.25)(2.25) = $.5625$ billion, and it is a case A grant. Were the same money given out with no strings attached, it would raise income in the community by $.5624 billion, and since the income elasticity is 1, preserve average spending propensities. If the counties spent one-tenth of income on education before, they would do so now. Spending becomes $2.056 billion and we see that the A grant stimulates more spending than the B grant by virtue of the price reduction.

b. Were there no funds limit, spending would be $2.8125 billion and the grant $.703 billion. But that cannot happen because the limit is $.6 billion. Counties would spend $2.5 billion with no grant at all, implying that the grant does not reduce prices at "the margin." Hence counties just take the $.6 billion, add it to income, spend one-tenth on education, and end up with spending of $2.56 billion. The funds limit has become so tight that the grant has been converted to a B grant.

c. If the benefit-cost calculation is based on the benefits of education, the BCR goes down. Before, for a state expenditure of $.5625 billion, education spending rose by .25 billion—slightly less than half of the grant. Now for expenditure of $.6 billion, education spending rises by a mere $.06 billion. The price substitution effect has been emasculated by the tight funds limit. If the benefit-cost calculation is based on local utility, of course, the BCR has gone up, but now the grant is just the same as a simple transfer of funds.

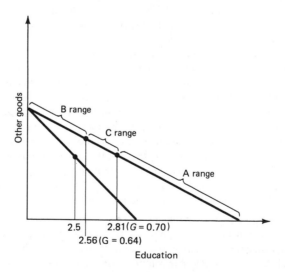

d. Refer to the accompanying diagram. If the grant were open-ended, the community would spend $2.81 billion with a grant of $(.25)(2.8) = $.7 billion. If we simply move along the income-consumption line to the new price ratio, expenditures are $2.56 with a grant of $(.25)(2.56) = $.64 billion. Hence a 25 percent price-reduction grant with a funds limit greater than $.7 is case A, less than $.64 is case B, between is case C.

CHAPTER 11

11.1   **a.** The straightforward way to do this is to minimize FWSC total accident-oriented costs, the sum of prevention costs and consequences costs. For the π values shown, the minimum comes at $\pi = .2$, where $W_1 = 9800/.96 = \$10,208$, $W_1 L_1 = \$510,400$, total consequences costs $= \$510,400 - (9800)(50) = \$20,400$, and total accident-oriented costs $= \$40,400$. OSHA regulations will cost the company \$39,600.

b. Consequences costs fall to zero, so the firm will naturally spend nothing on prevention either, π will rise to .5, and OSHA regulations would cost the firm \$80,000.

c. The example should make clear some of the problems. The market valuation of safety is affected by the number of daredevils (the valuation is zero in the second example), their average wages, the nature of the loss, and other costs. Only in special circumstances will market valuations provide a good measure of social valuations. But they should provide a lower bound measure. It may also be possible for enterprising evaluators to use the example's probability of accident, multiply by a more precise measure of the gross cost of the accident to the city, and multiply again by numbers of riders to generate the gross cost of accepting the consequences of skateboarding accidents for the city. You do not want to ignore the market, but you want to think before accepting its results uncritically.

Index

A

ABC program, 190–92
Agriculture, Department of, 7
Allocation programs:
  actual data on:
    federal, 36–37
    local, 38
    state, 38
  defined, 13
  normative objectives of (*see* Economic
    efficiency)
Arrow, Kenneth, 107
Asset value changes, 74–75
Average concept, 46–47

B

Baker, Howard, 148
Before-tax rate of return on private investment, 95–98
Benefit-cost analysis, 1–10
  checklist, 243–47
  defined, 2–3
  government programs and, 4–5
  history of, 7–10
  information for (*see* Social experimentation)
  misconceptions about, 5–6
  types of evaluations, 6–7

valuation (*see* Governmental decision
  making; Government regulatory activities; Physical investments; Valuation of benefits and costs at different times; Valuation of benefits at time of occurrence; Weighting gains and losses of different groups)
Benefit-cost ratio, 44–45
Benefit spillovers, 181–83
Bolt, Beranek, and Newman (BBN),
  215–16
Bracketing weights, 121–22
Bradford, David, 107
Budget Bureau, 7, 8, 9
Budgeting, evaluation and, 49–50

C

Campbell, Donald, 224–25
Capital intensity, rate of, 101–6
Capital/labor ratio, 101–6
Carter, Jimmy, 9, 148, 226
Case A grants, 182–83, 187, 189
Case B grants, 185, 187–88, 189
Case C grants, 186, 188, 189, 194
Cash assistance:
  actual data on:
    local, 39
    state, 38
  defined, 36

"Check-writing" programs (*see* Cash assistance; Grants, intergovernmental)
Civilian Conservation Corps, 195
Clement, Frank, 147
Coleman Report, 167–68
Communication of findings, 247
"Compensating variation" demand curves, 30, 31
Competitive price, 16
Comprehensive Employment and Training Act (CETA), 195
Consumer Product Safety Commission, 202
Consumer surplus, 29–31, 55–57
Cost-effectiveness procedure, 7, 12, 46
  income redistribution programs, 123–33
    programs, 126–31
    results, 131–33
Council on Wage and Price Stability, 202

D

Deadweight loss, 24, 25–26
"Defective telescopic faculty" of market interest rates, 96–97
Demand:
  consumer surplus and, 22, 29–31
  environmental costs and, 142–43
  for foreign currency, 68
  for labor, 62–66, 130
  natural monopolies and, 21, 22, 55, 57–60
  for new saving, 98–100
  physical investments and, 140–42
  for private goods, 17–18
  for public goods, 18, 19
  secondary markets and, 83–85
  taxed activities and, 23, 24
Discounted future earnings (DFE) approach, 69, 71
Discount rates, 89–109
  before-tax rate of return on private investment, 95–98
  defined, 89
  discounting approach, 107–8
  inflation and, 94–95
  relationship between present value and, 90–92

Discount rates (cont.)
  social discount rate, 101–7
  weighted-average rate of return, 98–100
Displaying gains and losses, 120
Distribution programs:
  actual data on:
    federal, 37
    local, 38
    state, 38
  defined, 13
  grants and, 183–85
  human investment (*see* Human investment programs)
  normative objectives of, 13, 16–17, 24–26
  transfer programs (*see* Transfer programs)
  (*see also* Weighting gains and losses of different groups)
Distributive equity, 13, 16–17, 24–26
  -economic efficiency interrelationship, 41–43
Douglas, William O., 147
"Drop in the bucket" problem, 189, 190, 194
Dupluit, Jules, 7

E

Econometric analysis, 74
Economic efficiency, 13, 15–24
  -equity interrelationship, 41–43
  externalities and, 19–20
  market system and, 13–15
  natural monopolies and, 20–22
  paying for the public sector and, 22–24
  prices and, 15–16
  public goods and, 17–20
Economic growth, 17
Educational performance contracting, 234–38
Elementary and Secondary Education Act of 1965, 167
Environmental benefits, 74–75
Environmental costs, 142–54
Endangered Species Act (ESA) of 1966, 147, 148
Endangered Species Committee, 148–54
Environmental Protection Agency (EPA), 202

Equal Employment Opportunity Commission, 202
"Equivalent variation" demand curve, 30, 31
Ethnier, David, 148
Externalities, 19–20, 96

F

Federal government expenditures, actual, 36–37
Federal road-building programs, 190–92
Feldstein, Martin, 107
Flood Control Act of 1939, 7
Food stamps, 192–94
Foreign exchange, 67–68
Formative evaluations, 17, 244
Franklin, Benjamin, 2
Friedman, Milton, 65–66, 76
Fundamental principle of evaluation, 43–45

G

Garms, Walter, 162
Golden Rule of capital accumulation, 106
Government activities, actual data on, 35–40
   federal, 36–37
   local, 39
   state, 38
Governmental decision making, 41–51
   complete information, 45
   economic efficiency-equity problem, 41–43
   evaluation-budgeting connection, 49–50
   evaluation-politics connection, 50
   fundamental principle of evaluation, 43–45
   inadequate information, 45–47
   physical constraints, 47
   political constraints, 48–49
Government intervention objectives, 12–27
   distributive equity, 13, 16–17, 24–26
   economic efficiency, 13, 15–24
      externalities and, 19–20
      market system and, 13–15
      natural monopolies and, 20–22

Government intervention objectives (cont.)
      paying for the public sector and, 22–24
      prices and, 15–16
      public goods and, 17–20
   functions of government, 13–17
   stabilization, 13, 17
Government programs, benefit-cost analysis and, 4–5
Government regulatory activities, 201–18
   OSHA noise standard example, 214–17
   subtopics in regulation, 211–14
   theory of, 202–11
Grants, intergovernmental, 180–96
   actual data on:
      federal, 37
      state, 38
   defined, 36
   evaluation of, 189–95
      federal road building, 190–92
      food stamps, 192–94
      public service employment, 195
      special revenue sharing, 194–95
   impact on spending, 186–89
   rationale for, 181–86
Great Society legislation, 36
Green Book, 7
Greenleigh Associates, 162
Gross rate of return on private investment, 95–98

H

Handout programs (*see* Cash assistance; In-kind assistance)
Haveman, Robert, 162
Harberger, Arnold, 119–20
Health and Human Services (HHS), Department of, 124, 222–24
Helping-hand programs (*see* Human investment programs)
Hicks, Sir John, 7, 43
Housing and Urban Development (HUD), Department of, 223
Housekeeping functions:
   defined, 36
   federal, 37
   local, 39
   state, 38

Human investment programs, 26, 158–76
   actual data on:
      federal, 37
      local, 39
      state, 38
   defined, 36
   evaluation of:
      benefits and costs, 159–62
      example, 162–65
      implementation problem, 169
      interpretation of results, 167–68
      measurement problems, 169–70
      methodology, 165–67
      scale of, 172–75
      selection problems, 170–71
      social experimentation and, 171–72
Human life, valuation of, 69–71

I

Income distribution (*see* Distribution pro-
      grams)
Income effect, 30, 31
Income-maintenance experiments, 223
Income tax, 23–24
   negative, 126–29, 131–33, 222, 226–34
Indifference curves, 14–15, 16, 17,
      187–88
Individual response experiments, 223
Inferring weights, 121
Inflation:
   present value and, 94–95
   unemployment and, 65–66
Information:
   complete, 45
   inadequate, 45–47
   (*see also* Social experimentation)
In-kind assistance:
   actual data on:
      federal, 37
      state, 38
   defined, 36
Inter-Agency Committee on Water Re-
      sources, 7
Intergovernmental grants (*see* Grants,
      intergovernmental)
Internal rate of return, 93
Internal weights, 122
Interstate Highway Program of 1956, 36
Interstate Highway System, 190–91

J

Johnson, Lyndon, 36

K

Kaldor, Nicholas, 7, 43
Kaldor-Hicks principle, 43–45
   (*see also* Governmental decision mak-
      ing)

L

Labor market programs, 129–31
"Leaky bucket" problem, 26
Local government expenditures, actual, 39
Loss of life, valuation of, 69–71

M

McNamara, Robert, 8
Marginal concept, 46–47
Marginal cost, 14–16
   of accident prevention, 206–7
   natural monopolies and, 21–22, 59–61
   taxed activities and, 24
   unemployed labor and, 63–64
Marginal utility, 15–16
   consumer surplus and, 22
   of income, 76–77
   natural monopolies and, 22
Marglin, Stephen, 101
Market imperfection, 16
Market response experiments, 223–24
Markets, valuation of benefits and costs
      and, 246–47
Measurement of benefits and costs,
      245–46
Minimum wages, 129–33
Monopolistic sellers, 16
Monopsonistic buyers, 16
Musgrave, Richard, 13

N

National defense, actual expenditures on,
      37

National Environmental Policy Act (NEPA) of 1969, 147
National Highway Transportation Board, 202
National Institute of Occupational Safety and Health (NIOSH), 214–15
Natural monopolies, 20–22
  benefit-cost analysis examples, 54–61
Negative income tax, 126–29, 131–33, 222, 226–34
Net benefits, 44, 45
  social, 43–45
Nixon, Richard M., 36, 194, 226
Normal demand curve, 30, 31
Normative social science, 6

O

Occupational safety (*see* Government regulatory activities)
Occupational Safety and Health Administration (OSHA), 202, 211
  noise standard of, 214–17
Office of Economic Opportunity (OEO), 222, 234–38
Office of Management and Budget (OMB), 9, 10
Okun, Arthur, 26
Orcutt, Alice, 227
Orcutt, Guy, 227

P

Pareto, Vilfredo, 7, 42
Perspective of evaluation, 244
Phelps, Edmund, 65–66, 101
Phillips, A. W., 65–66
Physical constraints, 47
Physical investments, 138–54
  actual data on, 37
  evaluation of:
    including environmental costs, 142–54
    without environmental costs, 139–42
Pigou, A. C., 96
Planning, Programming, and Budgeting System (PPBS), 2, 8–9
Political constraints, 48–49
Politics, evaluation and, 50

Positive social science, 6
Poverty standard, 124
Present value, 89–109
  appropriate discount rates, 95–107
    before-tax rate of return on private investment, 95–98
    social discount rate, 101–7
    weighted-average rate of return, 98–100
  defined, 89
  discounting approach, 107–8
  inflation and, 94–95
  vs. internal rate of return rule, 92–93
  relationship between discount rates and, 90–92
President's Council of Economic Advisers, 202
Prices:
  as accurate social valuations of benefits and costs, 54–58
  consumer surplus and, 22, 29–31
  impact of grants on, 186–89
  as inaccurate social valuations of benefits and costs, 56–68
    scarce foreign exchange, 67–68
    unemployed labor, 61–67
  inflation (*see* Inflation)
  natural monopolies and, 21–22
  role in market economy, 15–16
Private investment, before-tax rate of return on, 95–97
Production function, 101–6
  experiments, 224
Production incentive experiments, 224
Production-possibilities curve, 14–15
Properties of weights, specification of, 122–23
Public employment programs, 130–33, 195
Public goods problem, 17–20
Public sector, paying for, 22–24

R

Rate of capital intensity, 101–6
Recreational benefits, 74–75
Required compensation (RC) approach, 69–71
Revenue-sharing programs, 36
  special, 194–95

Road building programs, federal, 190–92
Ross, Heather, 227

S

Sacred cows, 48–49
Savage, L. J., 76
Scarce foreign exchange, 67–68
Secondary markets, 83–85
Shadow price, 60
Side payments, 42–43
Social discount rate, 101–7
Social experimentation, 171–72, 221–40
    educational performance contracting,
        234–38
    ethics of, 238–39
    innate advantages of, 172
    negative-income tax experiments, 222,
        226–34
    types of, 222–24
    types of experimental designs, 224–26
Special revenue sharing, 194–95
Stabilization programs, 13, 17
Stanley, Julian, 224–25
State government expenditures, actual, 38
Stiles, Robert, 148
Stokey, Edith, 43
Summative evaluations, 6–7, 244
Supply:
    of foreign currency, 68
    of labor, 62–66
    natural monopolies and, 59–61
    for new saving, 98–100
    physical investments and, 140–42
    of private goods, 17–18
    of public goods, 18, 19
    secondary markets and, 83–85
    taxed activities and, 23–24

T

Taxes:
    economic efficiency and, 23–24
    income (*see* Income tax)
    vs. regulation, 211–13
    (*see also* Distribution programs)
Tellico Dam, 146–54
Tennessee Valley Authority (TVA), 7,
    147–54

Time saving, 72–74
Trade Readjustment Assistance Act,
    42–43
Transfer programs, 25–26
    cost effectiveness study of, 126–29,
        131–33
    (*see also* Cash assistance; In-kind assis-
        tance)
Travel cost method, 75

U

Uncertainty, 75–77
Unemployed labor, valuation of, 61–67
Upward Bound, 162–65

V

Valuation of benefits and costs at different
        times, 88–109
    appropriate discount rates, 95–107
        before-tax rate of return on private in-
            vestment, 95–98
        social discount rate, 101–7
        weighted-average rate of return,
            98–100
    definitions, 89
    discounting approach, 107–8
    inflation and, 94–95
    present value rule vs. internal rate of re-
        turn rule, 92–93
    relationship between present values and
        discount rates, 90–92
Valuation of benefits and costs at time of
        occurrence, 53–78
    market prices exist and accurately repre-
        sent social values, 54–58
    market prices exist but do not represent
        social values, 58–68
        scarce foreign exchange, 67–68
        unemployed labor, 61–67
    markets do not exist, 68–75
        environmental and recreational bene-
            fits, 74–75
        loss of life, 69–71
        time saving, 72–74
    secondary markets, 83–85
    uncertainty, 75–77

W

Weighted-average rate of return, 98–100
Weighting gains and losses of different
      groups, 116–33
   cost-effectiveness study of alternative
      income redistribution programs,
      123–33
     programs, 126–31
     results, 131–33
     standards for redistribution, 124–26
   estimation of weights, 120–23

Welfare economists, 42
Welfare *ex ante* and *ex post,* 239
Welfare ratio, 124–26
Works Progress Administration, 195

Z

Zero-Based Budgeting (ZBB), 9–10
Zeckhauser, Richard, 43